# THE
# BATTLE
# OF BRITAIN
## MEMORIAL FLIGHT

## 50 Years of Flying

*The BBMF badge features the silhouettes of a Lancaster, Hurricane and Spitfire, symbolising the Flight's three principal types. (© Crown Copyright)*

# THE
# BATTLE
# OF BRITAIN
## MEMORIAL FLIGHT

## 50 Years of Flying

Jarrod Cotter

Pen & Sword
**AVIATION**

First published in Great Britain in 2007 by
Pen & Sword Aviation
An imprint of
Pen & Sword Books Ltd
47 Church Street
Barnsley
South Yorkshire
S70 2AS

ISBN 978 1 84415 566 8

A CIP catalogue record for this book is
available from the British Library

Printed and bound in Singapore
By Kyodo Printing Co (Singapore) Pte Ltd

Pen & Sword Books Ltd incorporates the Imprints of Pen & Sword Aviation, Pen &
Sword Maritime, Pen & Sword Military, Wharncliffe Local History, Pen & Sword
Select, Pen & Sword Military Classics and Leo Cooper.

For a complete list of Pen & Sword titles please contact
PEN & SWORD BOOKS LIMITED
47 Church Street, Barnsley, South Yorkshire, S70 2AS, England
E-mail: enquiries@pen-and-sword.co.uk
Website: www.pen-and-sword.co.uk

# Dedications

Dedicated to Group Captain Peter Thompson DFC AE MBIM RAF, founding father of the Battle of Britain Memorial Flight, and to all the many RAF airmen who have lost their lives in the service of our country from World War One to the present day.

> *When you go home,*
> *Tell them of us, and say,*
> *For your tomorrow,*
> *We gave our today.*

John Maxwell Edmonds

*A poppy collected from in front of Buckingham Palace after being dropped by Lancaster I PA474 on National Commemoration Day in July 2005. (Author)*

*Group Captain Bob Judson graces an atmospheric skyscape over Coningsby in Hurricane PZ865 during his last sortie with the BBMF. (Author)*

# Acknowledgements

As is always the case with a project of this kind, to name everyone who helped in the preparation of this book just isn't possible. But I would like to pay particular thanks to the following who were instrumental in making it possible in so many ways.

OC BBMF Squadron Leader Al Pinner MBE, former OCs BBMF Squadron Leader Paul Day OBE AFC and Squadron Leader Clive Rowley MBE. Clive has contributed greatly to the content of this book with superbly researched histories of the paint schemes of both Hurricanes and the history of Spitfire Vb AB910, as well as with first-hand accounts of flying BBMF fighters.

Flight Lieutenant Ed Straw, who was the inspiration behind this book!

Coningsby's Station Commander Group Captain Stuart Atha DSO ADC MA BSc former Coningsby Station Commanders Group Captain Bob Judson and Wing Commander Paul Willis, BBMF 'Bomber Leader' Squadron Leader Stuart Reid,

*The inspiration behind this book was Flight Lieutenant Ed Straw, seen after a sortie in the aircraft he had always wanted to fly - Lancaster I PA474. (Author)*

Squadron Leader Jeff Hesketh, Flight Lieutenant Garry Simm, Flight Lieutenant Jack Hawkins, Flight Lieutenant Scott Greig, Flight Lieutenant Dave Chadderton, Warrant Officer Dick Harman, Chief Technician Keith Brenchley, Chief Technician Paul Blackah, Sergeant Steve Duncan, Corporal Andy Bale, Corporal Norman Pringle and Junior Technician Chris Elcock. I'd also like to give a special mention to Public Relations Officer Jeanette O'Connell, Jim Stewart and Di Holland at the BBMF HQ for all their hospitality and help during my visits. Thanks for all the coffees Jim, and thanks Di for continually calling me to say 'Jarrod, I've found some more pictures you might be interested in'.

Outside the BBMF I had much co-operation from Mrs Mimi Thompson and her son David, who generously allowed me access to Group Captain Peter Thompson's logbook and archive material.

Also Ann Ringrose, the daughter of the Flight's first Engineering Officer, Squadron Leader E H Sowden, who again generously provided archive material.

Similarly to Mrs Nancy Griffiths, for access to view Air Vice-Marshal Arthur Griffiths' logbooks and for photographs of PA474's first air test at Waddington.

Others who have contributed include John Dibbs, former OC BBMF Squadron Leader Scott Anderson, Ken Ellis at *FlyPast* (www.flypast.co.uk), Pete West, Martyn Chorlton, Peter Green, Michael Turner of Studio 88 (www.studio88.com), Sean Whyte (www.swafineart.com), Nicola James at the Royal Air Force Benevolent Fund and PR and Marketing Manager at the Imperial War Museum Duxford Tracey Woods. Battle of Britain historical information and the procedure used in the 11 Group Operations Room at Uxbridge was compiled using information kindly supplied by Chris Wren, former Curator for twenty years, and Hazel Crozier.

Finally my wife Clare for putting up with my many nights sat at the computer – and prompting me to get to it on the nights when I wasn't! My sons Jamie and Matthew for their constant interest, which acted as a source of inspiration to me. And to my mum and dad, Margaret and George Cotter for their constant encouragement.

I simply could not have produced this book without all their various contributions of both material and support.

# Contents

# Foreword

The year 2007 is not a particularly auspicious year when it comes to RAF anniversaries. In 2005 we celebrated the sixtieth anniversary of VE/VJ Day, when the BBMF led the flypast over London, but in 2007 we are not commemorating any specific national events. However, we are celebrating our own golden anniversary. But what makes this special? As you read on through this deeply researched and well-written book you will learn how the Flight came about, why it was formed and what it was intended to commemorate. You will follow the changes of name, the fortunes of the aircraft we have flown and the various moves that the Flight has been subjected to, but you will see that the core values and the underlying purpose of the Flight have remained the same.

Having taken over as OC BBMF in January 2006, one of my hopes was that a book on the history of the Flight would be written and I was delighted when Jarrod proposed to do just that. Having already published a tremendous book called *Living Lancasters*, Jarrod's credentials were impeccable and we were confident that he was the man to chart our history. Since its formation the BBMF has been run on a shoestring, manned at minimal levels and flown by volunteers. While the archives are voluminous, they are also completely disorganised and Jarrod has had a monumental task to sift through all that information. But it is not only from our archives that Jarrod has crafted this book, he has unearthed a myriad of information from many sources that would have been lost for ever.

As I prepared to write this Foreword, I read those in previous BBMF annual brochures and I realised what a privilege and an honour it was to be invited to pen a few words, yet how unqualified I was to undertake the task. The

*Al Pinner in front of Battle of Britain veteran Spitfire IIa P7350 at Coningsby. (Author)*

Foreword to the 1999 brochure by the founder of the Flight, Peter Thompson, is included later in this book and to my mind typifies the intelligence, the humour and the self-effacing modesty of 'The Few'. As you read his words you will appreciate that when he wrote them, the 'Bottom of the Barrel' was nowhere in sight, yet, as I write, it has finally been reached.

Born in 1965, the son of Ken, an RAF fighter pilot who flew Meteors in the 1950s, I was brought up on a diet of flying stories covering aviation from both world wars. The likes of Johnnie Johnson, Douglas Bader, Bob Stanford-Tuck, Laddie Lucas, Ira Jones to name but a few, were my heroes, guiding lights and mentors as I stumbled my way through school. By the age of ten I had already decided that a career as a fighter pilot was for me and in common with most schoolboys it was the Spitfire of which I dreamed. Having spent my formative years in Lincolnshire, it was the frequent sight of the BBMF flying overhead that cemented my desire to fly. Joining the RAF in 1983, I wanted to fly the Harrier and ultimately the Typhoon. But, throughout my flying training and beyond, I harboured a desire to fly the Spitfire.

The Flight has evolved significantly since its inception on 11 July 1957, but I hope that this year you have enjoyed seeing the original four aircraft, our two Mk.XIX Spitfires, the Rolls-Royce Mk.XIX along with Hurricane IIc LF363, flying together fifty years on; testament to the skills, devotion and dedication of the backbone of the Flight, our engineers. I am incredulous at how much is achieved by such a small team of engineers, maintaining the fleet of eleven aircraft to such a high standard. In the early days, the Flight made fewer than fifty public appearances each year. The 2006 season saw an incredible 761 planned individual appearances at 410 separate events.

These events can be split into three separate categories – the commemorative, the promotional and the inspirational. Commemorative sorties are the Flight's *'raison d'être'*; we were formed as a result of leading the annual London flypasts to remember 'The Few', and these still comprise the most important aspect of BBMF – 'Lest We Forget'. The promotional sorties are the display flying we perform each year, both at home and abroad, demonstrating that we can maintain these venerable aircraft in perfect flying condition and show them off, sympathetically, with the same panache, professionalism and skill as they were flown in yesteryear. Finally, we fly numerous flypasts all around the country, from village fetes to the opening of major public events, and it is through these sorties that we, undoubtedly, still inspire the younger generation to wish to fly and to serve their country in the RAF. There are few sights and sounds more evocative than that of the Lancaster, Spitfire and Hurricane flying overhead.

In these politically correct days it is vital to remember the debt we owe, not only to those who fought in Fighter and Bomber Command in World War Two, but to the ingenuity and inventiveness of British engineers, the likes of Royce, Mitchell, Camm and Wallis, without whom we would not have won the war. Similarly, we should remember that it is through their legacy that this country can still produce aircraft and weapons systems that are truly competitive on a global scale. But, we must also remember that the descendants of this era, the modern RAF, have been engaged constantly in operations around the globe since the first Gulf War in 1991 and currently are fighting over both Iraq and Afghanistan.

One of the beauties of my job, in essence the curator of a living, breathing, flying museum of priceless pieces of national heritage, is that I frequently get the opportunity to meet men and women who previously fought for this great nation of ours during World War Two. But, this generation is rapidly approaching the edge of living history, and 'The Few' in particular are becoming fewer.

I am often asked how long the BBMF will continue and I respond that while there is a public will to maintain this national icon it will continue. Yes, the Flight has changed shape over the years, from commemorating initially 'The Few', to becoming a tribute to all those who fought in the air during World War Two. However, nowadays I believe that we should be seen as a national tribute to all who have served, and continue to serve, this country in the air since the inception of air warfare to the current day.

Ladies and Gentlemen, I give you fifty years of commemorative service of the Battle of Britain Memorial Flight. I am sure that you will derive a great deal of pleasure from this definitive book and we on the BBMF would like to thank Jarrod for his tireless energy, his enthusiasm and for producing such a wonderful and informative work.

Sqn Ldr Al Pinner MBE RAF
Officer Commanding
Battle of Britain Memorial Flight

*A Squadron Leader's flag flies outside the BBMF Headquarters denoting the rank of the Officer Commanding. (Author)*

There can be a no more fitting tribute to the gallant aviators who became known as 'The Few' than genuine Battle of Britain veteran Spitfire IIa P7350 gracing the skies over our wonderful land – and still on the books of the RAF after nearly seventy years since 'enlisting'! (© 2006 John M. Dibbs/Plane Picture Company)

# Introduction

To have such classic British aircraft as the Hurricane, Spitfire and Lancaster still flying with the Royal Air Force is something this country can be incredibly proud of. The men who flew these famous types helped save our nation in a desperate time of need, and that such aircraft still take to the air to pay tribute to the brave airmen who gave their all is simply wonderful.

Nowadays the Battle of Britain Memorial Flight is a household name and a national institution, and whether the spectator is an avid aviation enthusiast or not, just about all of them will stop in their tracks as the familiar three-ship formation arrives at any venue providing an emotive and inspirational sight and sound. But it wasn't always so…

The modern BBMF has been built from somewhat more humble beginnings, which paid exactly the same noble tribute though under fairly considerable constraints. From being tucked away in the corner of the Station Flight hangar at Biggin Hill, who at the time would have thought that fifty years later the BBMF would have become renowned as the custodians of so many priceless assets of British aviation heritage and a major link

between the RAF and the great British public – seen by in the region of six million people each year. So as we reach the fiftieth anniversary of the formation of what was originally named the Historic Aircraft Flight, it is the most

*Atmospheric sunset scene of Spitfire Vb AB910 over Rutland Water as it makes its way home to Lincolnshire. (RAF Coningsby Photographic Section/© Crown Copyright/MOD)*

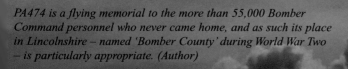

*PA474 is a flying memorial to the more than 55,000 Bomber Command personnel who never came home, and as such its place in Lincolnshire – named 'Bomber County' during World War Two – is particularly appropriate. (Author)*

opportune time to tell the story of how it all began, some of what has happened along the way, and how these precious aircraft are operated today.

For me, to be given the opportunity to compile a book on the BBMF to help celebrate its fiftieth anniversary season is an honour. I have admired and studied the Flight closely for many years, ranging from watching the aircraft at air shows as a young lad in the early 1980s to being generously invited to observe closely their operations and even most fortunate enough to fly with them in recent years.

But while I thought I knew a reasonable amount about the BBMF and its history, on beginning to carry out the research for this book I quickly realised just how relatively little I did actually know! And while I also thought that the task of getting the information I needed should be relatively straightforward, it soon struck me that very little material on the formation of the Flight, and the background about why it came into being, was readily available.

On investigating the formation of the Historic Aircraft Flight, I was more than a little taken aback once I discovered the material that was available. What predominantly caught my interest was to find out that one man, Group Captain Peter Thompson DFC (who was at the time a Wing Commander), was primarily responsible for its inception.

As I investigated further, I wondered if it would be possible to make contact with Group Captain Thompson to ask him about it all, but former OC BBMF Squadron Leader Paul Day OBE AFC informed me that he had passed away some years previously – though he was still in touch with his wife. On tentatively contacting Mimi Thompson to ask if she might be willing to talk to me about her husband and the formation of the Flight, I was most grateful when she generously offered to allow me to visit and listen to her recollections of the time, and look through her husband's logbook and the photographs he had kept and no doubt treasured.

This I found quite humbling, especially when Mimi told me about the reasons that had given Peter the idea to form the 'BoB Flight', as he always referred to it. That his innovative wish largely lies behind what we see today, and that to date Peter Thompson has received virtually no due recognition, was in my opinion something that needed to be addressed.

But Peter Thompson was obviously a very modest man. He wrote a Foreword in the 1999 BBMF brochure, and if I may repeat a quote from that as it appears in Chapter 1 of this book, the first paragraph read:

> I can think of only two reasons why I have been asked to write the Foreword to this year's brochure. Firstly, the number of people who more properly might be asked to do so is now woefully, sadly and rapidly decreasing; I suppose the bottom of all barrels has to be reached at some point in time; and secondly, I did have a hand in collecting together the aircraft that in due time formed the nucleus of what is now the Battle of Britain Memorial Flight.

It is rare that I would disagree strongly with the words of such a distinguished airman, but in this case I will make an exception. I cannot think of anyone more appropriate to have been asked to write it!

After gaining his wings in the summer of 1940, Peter Thompson was soon flying Hurricanes during the Battle of Britain. His next tour of duty saw him at the forefront of the Battle of Malta, where, as well as the arduous difficulties of daily aerial combat and

*Often overshadowed by its more glamorous fighter cousin, it should always be remembered that the Hurricane formed the backbone of fighter operations during the Battle of Britain and largely outnumbered Spitfires at that time. The 'Hurri' served operationally on every day throughout hostilities, from the British Expeditionary Force days during the Battle of France to the front line in the Far East at war's end. Hurricanes were responsible for more victories than any other Allied fighter. (Author)*

being heavily bombed while on the ground, there was also the severe lack of food and other essential supplies to cope with. To then go on and be awarded the Distinguished Flying Cross and become the inspiration for the RAF's Memorial Flight, and years later to consider himself as being at the 'bottom of the barrel', demonstrates this pilot's immense modesty. I'm certain most of the rest of us are in awe of Group Captain Thompson's credentials and I hope if nothing else that this book puts the record straight and gives Peter Thompson his long overdue credit.

Similarly, the story of how the late Air Vice-Marshal Arthur Griffiths AFC became a driving force behind getting PA474 flying on a regular basis makes fascinating reading. While I appreciate that this was several years before the 'Lanc' joined the BBMF, it is such a fundamental part of the Flight nowadays – and indeed considered by many to be the flagship – that it deserves to be told as part of this book. And again, tracking down a transcript written by Arthur Griffiths telling this story in his own words was a significant achievement during my research.

As I spent many long hours poring through memoirs, documents and photographs, the story that unfolded was full of surprises and not as I would have expected it to be. Where I have included extracts from memoirs and wording from historic documents, I have left the style as the original to give a flavour of the time. A good example of this is aircraft serial numbers, which by some were written as L.F. 363, with full stops after the letters and a space between them and the numbers. Nowadays serial numbers are generally written as LF363.

Throughout the 2006 flying season I switched between researching the Flight's early years and looking at how the BBMF is operated nowadays. For me this will always be a special memory, as I found the contrasts so fascinating – and it is my sincere hope that as you read this book you too will find the story absorbing.

The information that lies within is by no means comprehensive. I have selected what I thought to be particularly notable events and occasions that stand out in the Flight's history. Aircraft histories vary in depth too, depending on the amount of information I found on their record cards and other information that came to light along the way. Also, the stories of the current paint schemes worn by the two Hurricanes are particularly interesting as ways of telling the kind of heritage that lies behind the airmen to whom the Flight's aircraft pay tribute; and researched by former OC BBMF Squadron Leader Clive Rowley MBE, I have included these with his permission for this reason. Of course the schemes change regularly and by the time this book is published P7350, AB910 and PA474 will be wearing new identities that will bring to the forefront more stories of brave airmen fighting in hostile environments.

And it is the way that the BBMF pays such tributes that leads me to feel that, after having travelled the world to see many of the best known aircraft museum collections and warbird operators, and having seen many wonderful aircraft operated in magnificent ways, I honestly believe there is something truly magical about what goes on in the BBMF hangar at Coningsby that can't be compared with anywhere else on this planet. The provenance of these still military operated aircraft is certainly beyond compare, none of them are static exhibits, the hangar is open to the public so that it may all be seen, and the aircraft can be viewed starting up and returning home at close quarters from the 'other side of the fence' throughout the flying season. Long may this continue, as to see the RAF devoting these priceless assets to the memories of the airmen to whom we owe such a great debt just goes to demonstrate the Battle of Britain Memorial Flight's motto: 'Lest We Forget'.

Jarrod Cotter
Lincolnshire
February 2007

*Nowadays the aircraft of the BBMF are housed in a dedicated facility at RAF Coningsby – a far cry from their early days being 'tucked away' in the corner of the Station Flight hangar at Biggin Hill. (JT Rachel Warnes/© Crown Copyright/MOD)*

*Fine studio portrait of Wing Commander Peter Thompson DFC. (Courtesy Mimi Thompson)*

# CHAPTER 1

# Group Captain
# Peter Thompson

Peter Douglas Thompson was born in East Ham, London, on 7 September 1920. His father had served with the Royal Flying Corps during World War One flying the Royal Aircraft Factory FE.2b, and so, at the time of the 1938 Munich crisis, Peter joined the Royal Air Force Volunteer Reserve to start an illustrious career in military aviation.

He was asked to write a Foreword for the 1999 BBMF brochure by the then Officer Commanding of the Flight, Squadron Leader Paul Day OBE RAF. By necessity of space his original script was not included in full in the brochure, but with the permission of Mrs Mimi Thompson it is presented here in its complete form. This was one of the few times when the modest Peter Thompson publicly recorded in any way his wartime experiences, so it is most worthwhile of inclusion in this book.

A sentence from a covering letter written later by Peter that accompanied the original draft helps to explain why he finally opened up about his experiences: 'I wrote the Foreword not as "my" story but as the story of all those men who volunteered for aircrew during World War Two.'

What follows contains not only the truly fascinating story of a wartime fighter pilot, but also the only documented information known to the Author of this book on the formation of the Flight by its founder.

I can think of only two reasons why I have been asked to write the Foreword to this year's brochure. Firstly, the number of people who more properly might be asked to do so is now woefully, sadly and rapidly decreasing; I suppose the bottom of all barrels have to be reached at some point in time; and secondly, I did have a hand in collecting together the aircraft that in due time formed the nucleus of what is now the Battle of Britain Memorial Flight.

Memories become blurred with the passage of time, but with the aid of my logbooks, retrieved from the attic, I will try to recall past events of a career in the Royal Air Force, which I think fairly represents the careers of hundreds of other young men who had the good fortune to be born at the right time, i.e. circa 1920.

September 1938. The month of my eighteenth birthday and the month of the Munich crisis and Neville Chamberlain's infamous piece of paper.

At this time I was Articled to a well known firm of Chartered Accountants with offices in the City of London. I had plans to qualify as a Chartered Accountant on reaching the age of twenty-five or thereabouts but these plans, as were the plans of countless other young men, were soon to be frustrated.

Before the year was out all the young men in the office had volunteered to join the reserve forces of one Service or another. Most opted for the Territorial Army and others the Royal Navy Volunteer Reserve but, with an aversion to mud and not a strong swimmer, plus the fact that my father had flown the FE.2b in the Royal Flying Corps, I had no hesitation in applying to join the Royal Air Force Volunteer Reserve.

After various interviews, a Selection Board and a medical examination, I was accepted (I don't think they were very choosey in those days) and I became a Sergeant U/T Pilot thereby temporarily outranking the other chaps from the office who had chosen one or other of the more senior Services.

I was required to attend two nights each week at the London Town Centre in Store Street (off the Tottenham Court Road) for ground instruction and at the weekends I learned to fly the Tiger Moth at the Elementary & Reserve Flying Training School at Gravesend in Kent.

*Wonderful pose of Biggin Hill's Station Commander in 1950s jet flying gear. (Courtesy Mimi Thompson)*

1939 was a wonderful year weatherwise and flying hours increased at a satisfactory rate. My first brush with authority came when on my first solo flight I completed more circuits and bumps than the statutory one. My reason for so doing, that it was great fun, was not well received.

However, all these good things came to an end on August 30th when orders arrived to report to Store Street to be 'kitted out'. Wearing the rough blue serge uniform was no hardship and the three stripes on each arm gave one a certain standing – or so we thought until a few weeks at an Initial Training Wing convinced

*Later to become a founding member of the BBMF, all over silver Hurricane IIc LF363 is seen in formation with Hunter F.5 'PT' on a sortie out of Biggin Hill. Note the Hunter has Peter Thompson's initials on its tail as this was the Station Commander's personal aircraft. (Courtesy Mimi Thompson)*

us that we were probably the lowest form of animal life ever to be permitted to wear the King's uniform.

In October, a short time at Hanworth Aerodrome (now Heathrow) to keep our hands-in flying the Miles Magister then into the real world at No.2 Flying Training School at South Cerney to fly those wonderful biplanes, the Hawker Hart and Audax.

In the early days of the war, during the so called 'Phoney War', the casualty rates forecast by the planners were not reached and our training proceeded at a leisurely pace. It was not until May 1940 when the balloon went up in France that a sense of urgency seized the training system.

In July, wings were sewn on to uniforms and life became a more serious affair. Along with the wings came a commission in the RAFVR as an Acting Pilot Officer on Probation.

My first posting was to Old Sarum to fly Hectors and Lysanders, but this was short lived because by this time, in what was later to be called the Battle of Britain, things were beginning to warm up and with mounting casualties someone in a high place decided to my great delight that I would be more useful flying Hurricanes instead of Lysanders and off I went to the Operational Training Unit at Sutton Bridge.

*Page from Peter Thompson's logbook showing the sortie in PS915 from Duxford to Biggin Hill on 11 July 1957 along with 'Johnnie J' and 'Jamie R' – and thus was formed the Historic Aircraft Flight! Other entries include flypasts of Dunkirk in LF363 on 27 and 29 June, a refamiliarisation trip in PS915, a local flight in PS853 and four sorties in Peter's personal Hunter F.5 'PT'. (Courtesy Mimi Thompson)*

After completing a short conversion course on to the Hurricane I was posted to No.32 Squadron, then 'resting' at Acklinton near Newcastle after a rather torrid time down south. Thus it was that I started my operational career in a reasonably quiet sector and with a fair number of flying hours under my belt, albeit not many on Hurricanes. A far cry from the 14-18 go-around when new pilots joined squadrons in France with only a handful of flying hours in their logbooks.

With hardly time to settle down, however, orders came for two pilots to be posted to 11 Group Squadrons. It was only fair that as the newest arrival I should be one of them and so off I went, this time to No.605 (County of Warwick) Squadron, Royal Auxiliary Air Force, then flying from Croydon, the pre-war London Airport.

The RAuxAF was not a 'reserve' for the Royal Air Force but a separate air force, formed squadron by squadron over the years 1924-1936 on a regional basis. All 22 Squadrons were declared operational shortly after September 1939. The dedication of these 'part time' flyers was such that they were able to compete with, and match, the regular professional squadrons in most respects except in the level of experience. Not surprising then that they suffered considerable losses. When I joined 605 shortly after my twentieth birthday I found that most of the pre-war squadron had left for one reason or another and replacements had come from regular and other auxiliary squadrons and now from the Volunteer Reserve.

The CO was Squadron Leader Archie McKellar DSO DFC*. A wee Scot and the leading ace in Fighter Command at that time, Archie survived the Battle of Britain by one day. On the 1st of November 1940, he was killed when he failed to return from combat over Kent with some Me 109s.

Archie was renowned for his welcoming remarks to new pilots. He warned them that clean underwear should be worn at all times. This in no way implied that one's personal hygiene was at fault, but to bring home in a dramatic way that from now on there was a good chance of being shot at with possibly unfortunate results.

Some memories from my Croydon days. On one occasion, when I was busy shooting at an Me 109, another Me 109 was busy shooting at me. I claimed a 'damaged' and I hope the German pilot did so too, because he removed one of my propeller blades close to the spinner, which led to a marked loss in performance and a fair amount of vibration. However, I managed to clatter back to Croydon and land safely.

Another memory is far more painful. It was after the Battle had been 'officially' declared over and we had more time on our hands and I arranged to take a delightful young lady for a joyride in the squadron Magister. All went well until the motor stopped. I was over the airfield and to force land was no problem. However, I was met by a very irate Flight Commander, Christopher 'Bunny' Currant DSO DFC who awarded me seven days extra Orderly Officer duties, which effectively confined me to camp. On the termination of this punishment I was chagrined to discover that my pretty lady had transferred her interest to another officer, none other than my revered Flight Commander who was obviously living up to the old adage that 'It's all fair in love and war!'

Early in 1941 the Squadron moved to Martlesham Heath to form a Wing with 242 Squadron, then commanded by Douglas Bader. We mostly flew patrols over the North Sea convoys and life entered a less hectic phase.

As my first tour on operations was coming to an end word came that pilots were wanted to ferry Hurricanes to Malta. I forgot the basic rule of military survival and put my name down. And so in April 1941 I found myself with twenty-three other pilots on HMS *Ark Royal* steaming due east from Gibraltar. Our twenty-four Hurricanes were ranged on the flight deck and this left precious little deck for the leading Hurricane.

Now the flaps on the Hurricane can be selected either up or down. To get more lift for take-off we lowered the flaps, inserted a wooden wedge then raised the flaps to hold the wedge in place and thus give us 20° of flaps, a great help for a short take-off. Once airborne, we were to lower the flaps again and the pieces of wood would

fall away. They did.

Twenty-three of us arrived safely in Malta. We never did find out what happened to Number 24. Rumour had it that with engine trouble he had headed west and finally caught up with the *Ark Royal* and landed back on!

On the way out to Gibraltar I had noted that not all the pilots were tour expired and some had come straight from OTU. I thought there was skulduggery afoot and how right I was.

A few of us were ushered into the presence of the Air Officer Commanding Malta. Air Vice Marshal Keith Park had commanded 11 Group during the Battle of Britain and was well known to us as we were to him. After a big Hello, he said he was delighted to inform us that he had the authority to keep us in Malta and that he had decided to let us form No.185 Squadron. Goodbye Alexandria! Goodbye Cape Town! Hurrah! Hurrah!

For the first three months the *Luftwaffe*, flying from Sicily in their Me 109Fs, made life very uncomfortable for everybody. I note from my logbook that during the first two weeks of May we lost ten Hurricanes, four pilots killed and four hospitalised. Escalating events in Russia caused the *Luftwaffe* to be withdrawn for several months leaving us to contend with the *Regia Aeronautica*, a very different kettle of fish, but the 109s returned in December and had things very much their own way until the Spitfires arrived in 1942.

My turn came in January and that was a close run thing. I was forced to part company with my poor old Hurricane at a very low altitude and in fact we landed in the same field.

Not much later I was posted to the Middle East and arrived in Khartoum and became an instructor at the OTU at a romantically named airfield, Gordon's Tree. Not for long, however, because I suffered a series of attacks of malaria which so puzzled the local medics that I was sent to Ismailia on the Suez Canal to be under

*Peter and Mimi Thompson's 1957 Royal Tournament programme – the event at which they saw some Spitfire XVIs to add to the Historic Aircraft Flight! (Courtesy Mimi Thompson)*

the watchful gaze of the RAF Hospital at Heliopolis.

At Ismailia I flew as a test pilot for an Aircraft Repair Unit and this was not without its exciting moments... Some months passed before I was declared fully fit and then I was sent to join 601 Squadron as a Flight Commander and here I met the Spitfire for the first time. The Squadron was equipped with the Spitfire Vb and what a lovely thing she was.

We moved up behind the 8th Army along the coast of North Africa and into Tunisia ending up at an ex-*Luftwaffe* airfield at La Fauconnerie. With the final defeat of Rommel in North Africa there was much to celebrate, but in the Aircrew Mess there lacked the wherewithal to do so. Now the Spitfire with its guns and ammunition pans removed could carry a fair load and I volunteered to fly to Tripoli where I knew my friends from Ismailia, now stationed there, would be happy to provide the necessary goods [whisky! - JC].

All went as planned. I flew to Mellaha, loaded up and prepared to take off for the return flight but then things went sadly awry. The Italians, for reasons known only to themselves, had erected a windsock plumb in the middle of the airfield and then removed the windsock sleeve. Practically airborne, I was suddenly faced with a large metal mast. Too late to avoid it, my lovely Spitfire was a complete write-off and I was sent to renew my acquaintance with the RAF Hospital at Heliopolis.

The only message from the Squadron bemoaned the fact that I had failed in my mission and referred me to a (mis)quote from Shakespeare's Tempest. 'Where the wind socks there sock I'. I rejoined the Squadron at Lentini in Sicily and with them followed the 8th Army up into Italy until in early 1944 I was posted back to England to become an instructor at the Fighter Leader School.

June 1944 and to my great surprise I was given a squadron of my own to play with. No.129 (Mysore) Squadron was equipped with the Mustang Mk.III and with a Merlin engine was an improved version of the American P-51.

At first with 84 Group operating over France, then with four of the six guns removed we chased 'Doodlebugs' (the V-1) until the launching sites in the Pas de Calais were overrun. Finally, with very large long range tanks we provided fighter escort for Bomber Command during the closing stages of the war.

The war over and a Permanent Commission offered and gratefully accepted (the thought of going back to accountancy appalled me) and to find that life in a peace time Air Force was as much of a challenge as in wartime and certainly not lacking in exciting moments. I well remember during an Air Defence exercise having the tail of my Meteor knocked off by an American F-86 Sabre. This time I landed in Guildford High Street.

In 1955 I was posted to RAF Biggin Hill as the Wing Commander Flying and then in 1956 as the Station Commander when it became a Wing Commander Station, and this brings me to the beginning of the BBMF story.

Hurricane LF363 had been kicking around in Fighter Command for some time but had not been treated with the tender loving care that venerable aircraft deserve and needed a complete overhaul – this was provided gratis by Hawkers and Rolls-Royce. On the 28th of June 1956 I went to Hawkers Aerodrome at Langley and flew LF363 back to Biggin Hill. One year later the lonely Hurricane was joined by the three Spitfire XIXs from Woodvale and by the Spitfire XVIs from the static display

*Strapping into a Spitfire XIX in 1957. (Courtesy Mimi Thompson)*

at the Royal Tournament.

At this time there was no question of forming a separate Flight. Part of the deal was that the aircraft would be serviced and maintained from Station resources, but there was never a lack of volunteers from the ground staff who happily worked at weekends and in after duty hours to keep the aircraft flying.

Early in 1958 I left Biggin Hill to go to America and lost all direct contact with the aircraft, but heard from time to time of their travels, rather like the wandering tribes of Israel before finally reaching the promised land of Coningsby.

In September 1998 I accepted an invitation to visit the BBMF. A very warm welcome in a cosy office outside the hangar and an escort to meet my old friends.

No longer tucked away in a cluttered corner of the Station Flight hangar at Biggin Hill but in a proud display in immaculate surroundings. Thoroughbreds – every one, even Spitfire XIX PS915 which I flew into Biggin Hill more than forty years ago and it, as well as all the others, in splendid condition.

In times of peace the Fighting Services have ever been the target of the Treasury moneymen and I am astounded that the BBMF has survived. I can well imagine the battles fought over the years not only to keep the aircraft flying but also to have the Flight established with its own real estate and its own personnel.

The Battle of Britain was a much closer run thing than either the battles of Trafalgar or Waterloo and had the outcome been not in our favour we would today be living in a very different British Isles. Pull down Nelson's Column? Change the name of Waterloo Station? But keep the BBMF intact for as long as possible to commemorate a vital victory and in memory of the 3,080 aircrew (2,543 from the British Isles) who fought in the Battle and of the 537 who lost their lives.

Peter Thompson's final RAF appointment was as Air Attaché at the British Embassy in

Lima, Peru. Having learned Spanish for this assignment, he settled with his family in Menorca on retirement. Peter died on 2 March 2003, aged 82.

I think it appropriate to include in this chapter dedicated to Peter Thompson some words taken from a letter written to his son David by Squadron Leader Paul Day after the BBMF's founding father had died:

> As I have previously said to your mother there are many people today and there will be many more in times to come who will know an unknown debt of gratitude to your late father every time a Spitfire or Hurricane graces events across the whole country over many summers to come. Without the foresight and determination of men like him we would all be poorer.

*Peter Thompson proudly posing in a Spitfire XVI, probably TE330. (Courtesy Mimi Thompson)*

As I learned more of Peter Thompson being the driving force behind the formation of the 'BoB Flight', I developed a determination that this book should make that 'unknown debt of gratitude' known. Mimi and her son and two daughters have much to be proud of.

Peter was a much revered father to his son David, who wrote the following after I had visited him and his mother during the preparation of this book:

> My father, Peter, was a modest man. He was driven by principles of loyalty and service to King and country and to his family
>
> His motivation in forming the Battle of Britain Flight was solely to commemorate his peers who had sacrificed their lives in the war.
>
> To proclaim any particular kudos in originating the Battle of Britain Flight would have been in direct conflict with his purpose. By any standard, and in particular by today's standards, my father was a very moral man.

*Superb painting by Philip E West depicting a typical aerial combat scene during the Battle of Britain as Flight Lieutenant Geoffrey Wellum DFC enters combat head-on with a Dornier in his Spitfire I. He was part of a small group of ten Spitfires from 92 Squadron at Biggin Hill facing 150-plus enemy bombers and fighters. Other friendly fighters joined battle but the defenders were still vastly outnumbered, a scene repeated on many occasions during the summer of 1940. On this particular day Flight Lieutenant Wellum scored a Heinkel destroyed, together with a Dornier as a probable. (Courtesy SWA Fine Art Publishers)*

# CHAPTER 2

# From the Battle to the Flight

At the very height of the Battle of Britain on 15 September 1940, Prime Minister Sir Winston Churchill turned to Air Vice-Marshal Sir Keith Park in the 11 (Fighter) Group Operations Room at Uxbridge, Middlesex, and asked: 'How many reserves do we have?' Air Vice-Marshal Park replied: 'There are none.'

When Fighter Command was formed in 1936, it had in the region of just thirteen squadrons for home defence, all equipped with ageing biplane fighters: Bristol Bulldogs, Hawker Demons and Gloster Gauntlets. As the early rumbles of war were being heard throughout Europe, Nazi Germany was creating an air force second to none.

This was the position faced by Air Chief Marshal Sir Hugh Dowding, the Air Officer Commanding-in-Chief of the newly formed Fighter Command. Dowding immediately set about organising his Command into an effective force that would be capable of carrying out its principal role; the defence of Great Britain against air attack.

He set up a headquarters at Bentley Priory, Middlesex, and then divided the country into regional Fighter Groups. These were then sub-divided into Sectors, and operational control was to be exercised through Operations Rooms at Command, Group and Sector Stations.

The first of the regional Groups to be established was No. 11, with its headquarters at Uxbridge, Middlesex. Its area of responsibility ran from the bulge of the Suffolk coast, inland to the North of London, down the Hampshire/Dorset border and along the South East coast.

Initially the Operations Room was above ground and housed in a former Sergeants' Mess. With the feared onset of hostilities fast becoming a reality, a decision was made to construct an underground complex 60 ft below the surface – excavation began in late 1938.

The Operations Room, which is actually a series of rooms on two levels, is surrounded by a protective layer of concrete (4 ft below, 2 ft around and 30 ft of concrete/earth above) and could not be penetrated by any bomb available at the time; it was also gas-proof. The complex became operational ten days before the outbreak of war, its purpose being to serve as a nerve centre through which information was received, evaluated and acted upon.

In June 1940, Britain faced the threat of being invaded by the German Army massing across the Channel. Over 338,000 British and Allied troops had been rescued from the shores at Dunkirk, but they had been forced to abandon all their artillery, tanks and heavy equipment. During the Battle of France, which had lasted six weeks, the RAF lost nearly 1000 aircraft, including 450 Hurricanes and Spitfires – and 300 pilots.

*The three Spitfire PR.XIXs of the THUM Flight lined up at Woodvale ready for their intended delivery to Duxford and a return to the RAF to form the Historic Aircraft Flight. From left to right, PS915 went unserviceable and failed to start, PS853 had an engine failure on take-off and crashed, while PM631 got airborne but returned to base when its pilot noticed that PS853 had 'failed to get off'. (BBMF Archives)*

On 18 June Prime Minister Sir Winston Churchill exclaimed: 'The Battle of France is over, I expect that the Battle of Britain is about to begin.' Operation *Sealion* (*Unternehmen* Seelöwe), the planned invasion of the UK, depended on the *Luftwaffe* gaining air superiority over the RAF.

Prior to mounting their offensive, the *Luftwaffe* could call on 2500 bombers and fighters. Fighter Command had approximately 700 fighters to defend the country. No. 11 Group, under the command of Air Vice-Marshal Keith Park, would bear the brunt of the Battle of Britain.

On 10 July the *Luftwaffe* began its operations against Britain by attacking shipping in the Channel. On 12 August it targeted the RDF (Radio Direction Finding) stations and then switched its offensive to the fighter airfields on 15 August. Throughout August and into September the *Luftwaffe* concentrated on destroying the RAF both in the air and on the ground.

On 16 August, Winston Churchill made one of several visits to the Operations Room at Uxbridge to witness the progress of the Battle. On leaving, he said to General Ismay: 'Never in the field of human conflict was so much owed by so many to so few.' He repeated those famous words in an address to Parliament on 20 August.

The situation for Fighter Command was becoming grave. The losses of Hurricanes and Spitfires gave obvious cause for concern, but the main worry for Dowding was the attrition rate being suffered by his fighter pilots. During the last week of August and the first week of September, Fighter Command casualties amounted to 105 pilots killed and 126 seriously injured.

On the afternoon of 7 September, a force of 300 German bombers escorted by 600 fighters crossed the Channel and struck at London – the Blitz had begun. On Sunday 15 September, Winston Churchill, accompanied by his wife Clementine, was again present in the Uxbridge Operations Room. The *Luftwaffe*, believing that the RAF was on the verge of defeat, launched two major raids against London. The *Luftwaffe* lost nearly sixty aircraft that day – and two days later Hitler postponed Operation *Sealion*.

On 31 October the intensive daylight raids ceased. Although the night blitz on London and other cities continued, the Battle of Britain was effectively over. The RAF had held out against overwhelming odds, and Great Britain remained undefeated. Despite a desperate shortage of pilots and with its aircraft outnumbered, RAF Fighter Command's victory over the *Luftwaffe* during the Battle marked a significant turning point in World War Two.

Even though the Battle occurred quite early on in the war and is, of course, principally thought of as a vital victory at that point in time, it also had longer-term significance too. This can be judged by some words written by the *Luftwaffe*'s General Werner Kreipc after the war:

> Though the air battles over England were perhaps a triumph of skill and bravery so far as the German air crews were concerned, from the strategic point of view it was a failure and contributed to our ultimate defeat. The decision to fight it marks a

*Following engine trouble on take-off at Woodvale on 12 June 1957 with the intention of flying to Duxford, PS853 'pranged' and ended up on its nose. The pilot, John Formby, who only two days before had flown PS853 on its last operational flight, stepped out shaken though unhurt. Fire tenders raced to the scene and soon had their 'emergency sprays trained on the aircraft', but fortunately it didn't catch fire.*
*(Southport Visitor/BBMF Archives)*

# The Plotting Room

During 2005 a group of BBMF pilots visited the 11 Group Operations Room at Uxbridge to gain a further understanding of how the Battle was controlled from this underground complex. A great many people were needed to staff the facility. There were four watches in total, with seventy personnel on each - around 85 per cent of them female. The watches were eight hours long, thus three watches would cover a 24-hour period. The Group Controller and his immediate staff sat in a glass-fronted cabin overlooking the plotting room. The glass was curved and tinted to stop reflections, and also helped to reduce the sound from the noisy environment on the other side. Adjacent cabins were occupied by Naval, Army Anti-Aircraft Command and Observer Corps personnel. In the plotting room was a large table map featuring a Kassini military grid reference system. The map was divided up into Group, Sector and Observer Corps areas of responsibility. The room also contained a large illuminated tote board showing the readiness states and deployment of the mainly Hurricane and Spitfire squadrons.

Displayed on the board at the top and bottom were the names of the seven Sector airfields in the South East: Tangmere, North Weald, Hornchurch, Kenley, Biggin Hill, Debden and Northolt. These Sector airfields then controlled the twenty-one Satellite airfields, such as Manston, Hawkinge and Hendon. Underneath each of the Sector airfields was listed the squadrons that flew from them and their relevant Satellites: 602, 23, 213, 607; 46, 25, 249; 41, 603, 222; 605, 253, 501, 600; 92, 72, 66, 141; 257, 17, 73; 1(Can), 303, 229, 264 and 504. At the time, seven of these squadrons were flying Spitfires, while fourteen had Hurricanes on strength. The balance, predominantly comprising night-fighter squadrons, operating Boulton Paul Defiants and Bristol Blenheims.

Below each squadron was a series of readiness states, each with four coloured lights. As the readiness state changed, the lights would be illuminated accordingly. They represented the two flights, which were further split into two sections, of the fighter squadrons; 'A' and 'B' Flight, Red/Yellow and Blue/Green sections.

The availability states were: Released (stood down from 'ops'); Available 30 Minutes (ready but not by aircraft); Available; Ordered to Readiness; At Readiness (fifteen minutes to go, by aircraft); Ordered to Standby; At Standby (two minutes to go, pilots in aircraft with engines running); Ordered on 'I' Patrol ('I' for Independent); Left Ground; In Position (the position to which the aircraft had been vectored to meet the enemy by the Sector Controller); Detailed to Raid (approaching enemy, told by Sector Controller where the enemy formation is); Enemy Sighted (in combat); Ordered to Land (training patrols etc not in combat, ordered to land when enemy sighted); Landed and Refuelling. In the heat of battle the lights would be frantically jumping around between the various

availability states. Beneath the tote board another display showed the pilot and aircraft states ('P' and 'A'), barrage balloon heights and airfield weather states.

Around the table would be about twenty WAAFs working in pairs, one as a plotter and the other a 'teller'. They would be busily updating the progress of the action in the skies. Symbols were placed on the map showing the position of the defending squadrons once they had been 'scrambled' by the Controller. Information was received through their headsets from the Radio Direction Finding (RDF) stations, later known as radar, via HQ Fighter Command. Once the enemy aircraft had crossed the coast, the information on their numbers, height and course was received from the Observer Corps. As the information of a raid was received, the plotters would make a hostile plot – marked with an 'H', code number and number of aircraft in the formation. This would then be slid into position on the table and the enemy plots would be tracked across the Channel. Coloured tracking arrows – red, yellow or blue – were placed along the path of the plot. The colours corresponded to the triangular red, yellow and blue segments on the Sector clock, each representing a five-minute interval. Each enemy plot was colour-coded to indicate the time it was first reported – the relevant colour being assigned depending on where the minute hand was at the time of the report. However, only two colours of tracking arrows would ever appear for a plot, as information more than ten minutes old was considered unnecessary in this frenetic environment.

The colour-coding and the elaborate communications network that provided the necessary information produced a very effective and efficient system. It resulted in fighters getting airborne and being on their way to an intercept within five minutes of the initial contact. Generally speaking, at that time it took thirteen to fifteen minutes for a Spitfire squadron to scramble and reach 15,000 ft, and sixteen minutes for Hurricanes. With radar giving around twenty minutes' warning, this only gave a few minutes for the Controller at Group to make a decision. Fighter Command's coloured time coding procedure was the world's first fully integrated air defence system.

If the RAF had lost the Battle of Britain, World War Two would have taken a very different course after the summer of 1940. The 11 Group Operations Room at Uxbridge undoubtedly played a vital role in the UK's future survival. Preserved exactly as it was at 11:00 on 15 September 1940, it can be viewed by the public by prior arrangement only – and as visitors enter the map room it truly feels as though time has stood still. (Author)

*On 11 July 1957, the three ex-THUM Flight Spitfire XIXs are pictured* en route *from Duxford to Biggin Hill joined by a Hunter and Javelin. Note that following its repairs PS853 is seen leading the formation with a replacement black spinner. (Courtesy Mimi Thompson)*

turning point in the history of the Second World War. The German Air Force was bled almost to death, and suffered losses which could never again be made good throughout the course of the war.

The height of the Battle of Britain was 15 September, and so with the war over, on that date in 1945 many thankful people of England gathered in London to gaze skywards as masses of RAF fighters led by the legendary Group Captain Douglas Bader CBE DSO DFC in a Spitfire took part in the first of what was to become an annual flypast over the capital. The RAF was proud to commemorate the occasion with such a tribute to this highly significant achievement, and so in the years immediately following World War Two it became traditional for a Hurricane and Spitfire to lead the flypast over London.

As the years went by though, the aircraft that were once the mainstay of RAF fighter operations decreased in numbers as the jet age took its grip and made the familiar and fondly loved piston-engined types rapidly obsolete from front-line service. By the mid-1950s Hurricane IIc LF363 was the only airworthy representative of its type with the RAF. When the Spitfire was phased out of RAF service in 1957, the only three airworthy examples were being flown by the civilian-operated Temperature and Humidity (THUM) Flight, which was by then based at Woodvale, Lancashire. So the number of available aircraft had become critical.

This brought to fruition action to uphold the belief of some members of the RAF that the service's greatest Battle Honour should continue to be commemorated in a fitting fashion with the familiar sight and sound of the legendary fighters in the air. One man in

*The aircraft of the Historic Aircraft Flight on the ground at Biggin Hill on 11 July 1957. Seen far left is Hurricane LF363, which had by then lost its all-over silver paintwork in favour of a camouflage scheme. The three Spitfire XIXs are next, with three Hunters then three Javelins completing the ceremonious line-up. (Courtesy Mimi Thompson)*

*The three wartime pilots discuss the sortie to Biggin Hill: Wing Commander Peter Thompson and Group Captains James Rankin and 'Johnnie' Johnson. (Courtesy Mimi Thompson)*

particular was the driving force behind forming the Flight – Wing Commander Peter Thompson DFC, a Hurricane pilot during the Battle of Britain itself and who was by then Station Commander of the former Sector airfield at Biggin Hill in Kent.

The inspiration to form the Flight first came to Wing Commander Thompson during early 1956. Mimi Thompson recalls:

> We held a showcase for the commemoration of the Battle of Britain every year and we would put on a huge display. It was very well attended, an enormous amount of people would turn up. It was a pageantry day as well as a memorial day. And I think really that was the beginning when my husband realised how many people were deeply interested in that period of our history. Having these aeroplanes available at the time he thought 'well let's get this thing together'. I think what was in his mind was to try and preserve some of the history of our great nation, particularly as it was the Royal Air Force that was very responsible in the end, 'The Few', for the way the world has turned out today. Perhaps it would have all been so very different without them.
>
> Whatever occasion required one he would make sure the aeroplanes were available and he would fly them himself, as he did over Dunkirk when the Queen

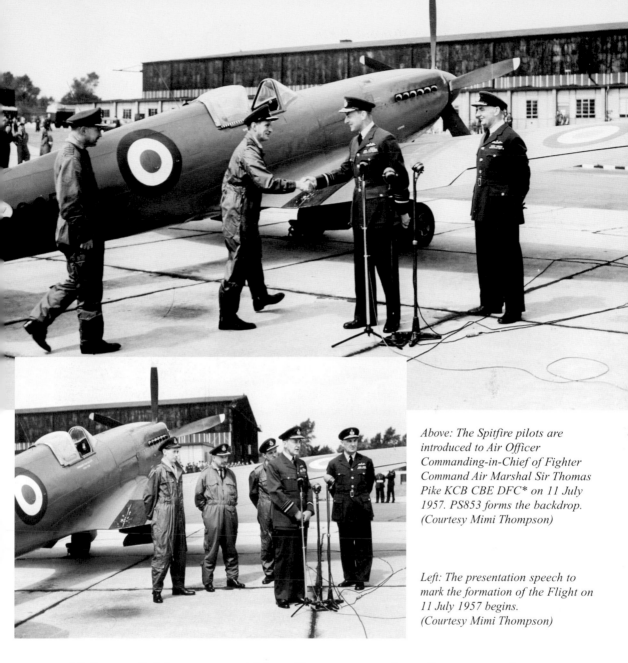

*Above: The Spitfire pilots are introduced to Air Officer Commanding-in-Chief of Fighter Command Air Marshal Sir Thomas Pike KCB CBE DFC\* on 11 July 1957. PS853 forms the backdrop. (Courtesy Mimi Thompson)*

*Left: The presentation speech to mark the formation of the Flight on 11 July 1957 begins. (Courtesy Mimi Thompson)*

Mother unveiled the new memorial there. He was very proud actually, a very proud man of what others had done during that period of time. His friends he had lost; he felt he owed something to them after all those years.

I can't remember, and I probably didn't even know, how it went from there. I knew that it was a strong feeling that he had to do this thing, to get the aircraft together as a Memorial Flight. He always used to refer to it as the Battle of Britain Flight. To him I think it was a very deep feeling. He never liked to discuss too much the war years, I think he lost too many wonderful people, good friends. Particularly in Malta. This was part of his legacy of the war I suppose, that he was never able to really come out and talk about his experiences. It was very difficult for him. But he was very proud of the aeroplanes he flew, the Hurricane and the Spitfire.

The idea of the Flight was conceived by my husband as a way of keeping alive the memories of so many young men who gave their lives to save us all.

Obviously the logistics required to form such a unit were not without many complications. Topping the list was where to obtain sufficient numbers of airworthy aircraft of an obsolete design!

Wing Commander Thompson already had Hurricane IIc LF363 at Biggin Hill, so this fighter, which still serves on the BBMF, became the founder member of the Flight. LF363 had gone to Hawker at Langley on 30 September 1955 for a rebuild. It was designated as an 'Exhibition Aircraft' on its record card and was allocated and moved to the Station Flight at Biggin Hill on 28 June 1956 painted in an all-over silver scheme. That September it took part in the Battle of Britain flypast. Therefore, being recently refurbished, LF363 was an ideal starting point for the intentions in mind.

While Wing Commander Thompson had gained the necessary authority to form the Flight, it was pointed out to him that no public funding for maintenance or fuel would be forthcoming. It was also made clear that all the manpower required to establish and maintain the Flight would have to be purely on a voluntary basis.

It was at this point that Wing Commander Peter Thompson called Squadron Leader E H Sowden, who was OC Engineering at Biggin Hill, to one side. Wing Commander Peter Thompson knew he had an ideal candidate in Squadron Leader Sowden, as prior to being commissioned he had been an aircraft engineer with the British Expeditionary Force during the Battle of France, and as soon as he returned from the Continent in 1940 he was put to work repairing Spitfires and Hurricanes on the airfields of Kent during the Battle of Britain. Having this much experience getting his hands dirty to keep the fighters in the air during such a crucial stage of the war, he knew inside-out how the aircraft worked.

As Squadron Leader Sowden recalled forty years later: 'The first news of the idea to form a Battle of Britain Flight at Biggin Hill was told to me in July 1957 by Peter Thompson – the Station Commander. He was an ex-Spitfire pilot and he was very keen on the idea – but there were difficulties to overcome, and that was where I came in.'

There was still the obstacle of obtaining a Spitfire. The only examples of the type left in flying service at this time were three PR.XIXs, which had been used by the THUM Flight for meteorological work. These aircraft were used to ascend to around 30,000 ft on a regular basis, and once at their specified altitude would record the required meteorological conditions of any one day. The PR.XIXs were ideally suited to this work, as they had a long endurance and their pressurised cockpits were necessary for the high altitudes at which they were required to fly. However, spares were becoming a real problem so it was decided to phase them out. The type's last sortie with the THUM Flight took place on 10 June 1957, and was carried out with PS853.

With their useful operational careers over, the three remaining Spitfire PR.XIXs of the THUM Flight (PM631, PS853 and PS915) were authorised for allocation to the newly forming unit. They were scheduled to be delivered to Duxford on 12 June, however PS915 went unserviceable with engine trouble, PS853 had an engine failure on take-off and crashed, while PM631 got airborne but returned to base when its pilot noticed that PS853 had 'failed to get off'. Net result – 'trip abandoned'.

Part of a story in the *Liverpool Daily Post* of the following day, 13 June 1957, reported PS853's incident as follows:

A veteran Spitfire – one of the last three aircraft of its type left in the country – crashed at 150 m.p.h. as it took off from Woodvale, near Southport, last evening. With engine roaring, the Battle of Britain fighter raced along the runway in a vain attempt to take to the air. It overshot the runway, and took a header into the ground.

An official spokesman at the time was later reported to say: 'The damage is to the propeller shaft. It can be made airborne again. The Spitfires were getting to the end of their days and they had been giving trouble for the past three weeks.'

After the unserviceabily of PS915 and the damage caused by PS853's mishap had been remedied, during the remainder of June the three aircraft gradually made their way to Duxford, Cambridgeshire. From there, a three-ship Spitfire formation made its way to Biggin Hill on 11 July flown by legendary wartime ace Group Captain J E 'Johnnie' Johnson DSO DFC (PS853), Group Captain James Rankin DSO (PM631) and Wing Commander Peter Thompson (PS915). While Peter Thompson spoke very little about his service career, his wife Mimi laughingly told me that one thing he did speak much of was the 'allocation' of the Spitfire PR.XIXs for this flight – which he found very amusing. Apparently, PS915 was not in great shape at the time, and as Wing Commander Peter Thompson was outranked by 'Johnnie' Johnson and James Rankin, he often told of how he was left to fly that aircraft from Duxford to Biggin Hill!

*En route* they were joined by jet escorts as Hawker Hunters of 41 Squadron from Biggin Hill and Gloster Javelins from 46 Squadron based at RAF Odiham, Hampshire, formed up with them. So much was thought of the event that on arrival at Biggin Hill, the classics were greeted by the Air Officer Commanding-in-Chief of Fighter Command, Air Marshal Sir Thomas Pike KCB CBE DFC*. Officially called the Historic Aircraft Flight, it was on 11 July 1957 that the new memorial unit was formed at Biggin Hill.

The following entry was later placed into the RAF Biggin Hill Form 540:

At 11:00 hours on the 11th of July 1957, three Spitfire aircraft were flown into Biggin Hill as the first move towards the formation of a 'Battle of Britain' Flight. The event, which was treated with some ceremony, was given much publicity and aroused considerable public interest. Sir Thomas Pike, K.C.B., C.B.E., D.F.C., Air Officer Commanding-in-Chief, Fighter Command, was present to receive the flight on arrival.

The pilots selected to fly the aircraft in were,

Group Captain J. Rankin, D.S.O., Group Captain J. E. Johnson, D.S.O., D.F.C., and Wing Commander P. D. Thompson, D.F.C. They were escorted on the flight by Hunters and Javelins.

In the attached photograph [as appears on page 37 - JC], the aircraft are seen lined up on the A.S.P. after landing together with Hurricane LF363, which was already on the strength of the Station. It is the last airworthy Hurricane left in the Service, and will also be allocated to the 'Battle of Britain' Flight.

The arrival and fly-past of the Spitfires and escorts was covered by the B.B.C. and I.T.A. television and sound broadcasts, and by representatives of the National and local press.

The formation of the 'Battle of Britain' Flight is still in the initial stages. It is the intention that it should comprise two or three Spitfires and the Hurricane, but to ensure that the Spitfires can be maintained in a serviceable condition some exchanges and/or cannibalisation of the present Spitfire 19s will be necessary. Spares are available for the Mk.16, but not for the Mk.19.

While Peter Thompson was surely delighted that his concept had come to fruition, there was a general consensus that it was not right to form a tribute to the Battle of Britain with a variant of the Spitfire that was not designed for offensive operations.

Squadron Leader Sowden again:

The only flying Spitfires left in the RAF were three elderly Spitfire Mark 19s – the P.R. version which had been in use for meteorological reconnaissance work and had now come to the end of their days. These aircraft were to be transferred to Biggin Hill. Nobody liked the idea of trying to form the Battle of Britain Flight with aircraft that were not made to fire guns, but what alternative was there? The alternative came in the form of three Spitfire Mark 16 Fighters which had been stored for years in a Maintenance Unit and which had recently been brought into ground use at the Royal Tournament Display 1957, to depict the defence of Malta during the war.

Exactly how Wing Commander Thompson persuaded the appropriate authorities to acquire these aircraft for the Flight may remain a mystery, but Mimi Thompson remembers what happened at the Royal Tournament:

We went to the 1957 Royal Tournament because Peter had been in Malta and we were very interested in the wonderful display on the period in Malta when he was there. In fact in many ways that was a more frightening part of one's life than the Battle of Britain even. It was a terrifying experience and a very hard time.

During the display we spotted the Spitfires that were being used to portray the feeling of Malta and the atmosphere of the time. I said to my husband, 'Darling, look, more Spitfires to add to your collection.' And he replied 'Ah yes, good, I'll look into that'. And that was basically the beginning of getting another three aeroplanes.

Most reports seem to suggest that the Spitfires had been static exhibits at the Royal Tournament, but some extracts from *Air Clues* of November 1958 give a different description of how at least TE330 was used:

In 1957, after a period in store, it [TE330 - JC] was selected for stardom at the Royal Tournament, an annual London pageant staged by the three Services. The Spitfire appeared in a dramatic episode reconstructing the siege of Malta. For a fortnight it taxied twice daily into the arena, thrilling thousands as its engine was run up before 'taking off' to meet enemy bombers attacking the Mediterranean strong-point.

At about this time the famous R.A.F. Fighter Command station at Biggin Hill, Kent, was given the task of maintaining a small 'Battle of Britain Flight', composed of a Hurricane and several Spitfires which could be flown on ceremonial and historic occasions. The first Spitfires available were of the photographic

R.A.F. BIGGIN HILL

| Year 1957 | | AIRCRAFT | | Pilot, or 1st Pilot | 2nd Pilot, Pupil or Passenger | DUTY (Including Results and Remarks) |
|---|---|---|---|---|---|---|
| Month | Date | Type | No. | | | |
| — | — | — | — | — | — | — Totals Brought Forward |
| SEPT | 3 | SPITFIRE 19 | 853 | SELF | AIR TEST | AIR TEST |
| | 5 | HUNTER 5 | 41-C | SELF | - | EXERCISE |
| | 10 | SPITFIRE 16 | 330 | SELF | - | AIR TEST |
| | 10 | SPITFIRE 16 | 330 | SELF | - | AIR TEST |
| | 11 | SPITFIRE 16 | 330 | SELF | - | AIR TEST - B of B REHEARSAL |
| | 12 | SPITFIRE 16 | 330 | SELF | - | B of B REHEARSAL |
| | 12 | SPITFIRE 16 | 330 | SELF | - | — " — — " — |
| | 15 | SPITFIRE 16 | 330 | SELF | - | B of B FLYPAST. |
| | 19 | HUNTER 5 | PT | SELF | - | AEROBATICS. |
| | 23 | HUNTER 5 | P.T | SELF | - | I.F. GCAs. |
| | 25 | HUNTER 5 | 41-K | SELF | - | I.F. FLAME OUTS. |
| | 30 | METEOR 8 | 481 | SELF | - | ASSY. LANDINGS. |
| | 30 | HUNTER 5 | PT | SELF | - | AEROS. IF. |
| OCT | 1 | SPITFIRE 16 | 330 | SELF | - | AIR TEST |
| | 2 | SPITFIRE 19 | 853 | SELF | - | AIR TEST |
| | 3 | SPITFIRE 19 | 853 | SELF | - | A-A PHOTOGRAPHY |
| | 3 | SPITFIRE 19 | 853 | SELF | - | A-A PHOTOGRAPHY |
| | 10 | SPITFIRE 16 | 330 | SELF | - | AIR TEST |
| | 13 | VAMPIRE T11 | 432 | SELF | F/O REID | DOAL. AEROS - IF. |
| | 13 | SPITFIRE 16 | 330 | SELF | - | PHOTOGRAPHY — HOOD OFF!! |
| | 17 | SPITFIRE 16 | 330 | SELF | - | To BENSON |
| | 17 | SPITFIRE 16 | 330 | SELF | - | FROM BENSON |
| | 25 | VAMPIRE T11 | 432 | SELF | MR. WILCOX | LOCAL |
| | | | | GRAND TOTAL [Cols. (1) to (10)] | 2636 Hrs. 20 Mins | Totals Carried Forward |

*A page from Wing Commander Peter Thompson's logbook from September and October 1957 showing numerous sorties in Spitfire Mk.XIX PS853 and Mk.XVI TE330. Of particular note are two 'B of B' rehearsals on 12 September, and the first official 'BoB Flight' Battle of Britain flypast on 15 September. (Courtesy Mimi Thompson)*

reconnaissance PR.XIX version, which had flown many hours on daily meteorological sorties to provide data for the weather forecasters.

After the 1957 Royal Tournament the Biggin Hill Station Commander made a formal application for the Spitfire XVIs. He felt that although these aircraft were now regarded as purely ground demonstration models and no longer airworthy, enthusiastic work by the Biggin Hill ground staff could soon get them flying once more. They were, too, more appropriate representatives of one of the world's most famous fighter aircraft than the unarmed PR.XIXs.

*Made airworthy at Biggin Hill after ground display duties at the Royal Tournament of 1957, Spitfire Mk.XVI TE330 is seen being put through it paces by Biggin Hill's Station Commander Wing Commander Peter Thompson. (Courtesy Mimi Thompson)*

The PR.XIXs would appear to have been the safest and easiest bet – they were in airworthy condition and had been suitably maintained for the past several years. The three Mk.XVIs had been allocated a ground category. However, their participation in the Royal Tournament had of course seen them brought up to better condition, and as mentioned above at least TE330 could be ground run.

It was eventually agreed that, as the task of servicing and flying these aircraft would be the responsibility of Biggin Hill, the OC Engineering at the base would take delivery of all six Spitfires. He was then to inspect them and submit a recommendation stating the unit preference, whether LF.XVI or PR.XIX. In what can perhaps, on one hand, best be described as a case of 'heart over mind', after much deliberation Squadron Leader Sowden recommended that priority be given to bringing the Mk.XVIs up to flying condition. There was also a more practical reason though, as spares for the Mk.XVIs were more readily available.

Following the Royal Tournament the Spitfire XVIs were dismantled and moved to Hendon where they were placed into storage pending a final decision on their disposal. TE330 was allocated for display at West Malling in Kent, though this was subsequently cancelled in August and it was instead allocated to the 11 Group Communications Flight – at Biggin Hill. Once allocated to the unit, the Mk.XVIs were moved by road to Biggin Hill and placed in a corner of the Base's Aircraft Servicing Hangar.

Squadron Leader Sowden takes up the story:

On the face of it the P.R. Mark 19s looked the safest bet – at least they had been serviced as flying aircraft, whereas the three F. Mk. 16s had been given a ground category and had been allowed to deteriorate accordingly. Discussions were held but no definite decision resulted. It was finally agreed that, as the task of servicing and flying these aircraft would be the responsibility of Biggin Hill, the Senior Technical Officer of Biggin Hill would take delivery of the three P.R. Mk. 19 and

*Spitfire Mk.XIX PS853 on take-off. It had quickly been given a coat of camouflage paintwork after being put on the strength of the Historic Aircraft Flight. (Courtesy Mimi Thompson)*

the three F. Mk. 16 Spitfires. He would then inspect these aircraft and submit a recommendation stating the Unit preference, P.R. Mk. 19 or F. Mk. 16.

I recommended that the F. Mk. 16 aircraft be brought up to flying condition for the Battle of Britain Flight and then the real work started. After the Royal Tournament the three Spitfire Mk. 16 aircraft used had been dismantled and then carted away to Hendon for storage pending final disposal. They had been transferred by road to Biggin Hill and dumped in the corner of the Aircraft Servicing Hangar. I knew that with limited personnel and equipment available, the Unit was only capable of tackling one aircraft at a time. So I selected T.E. 330, which appeared to be in better condition than the other two, and set my team of eight to work. About half the team had previous Spitfire experience, with Sergeant Mateer in charge of the Airframe tradesmen and Chief Technician Pucaynski in charge of the engine men. [TE330 had been refurbished at St Athan, South Glamorgan, for ground instructional duties just before the Royal Tournament. It was allocated the Maintenance number 7449M and the intention was for it to go to West Malling. Its record card shows that this was all cancelled in August 1957 and the same month it was allocated to 'RAF Biggin Hill, 11 Group Comms Flight' (with which it would continue to be until being transferred to the RAF Biggin Hill Station Flight in March 1958).]

I thoroughly briefed these men to ensure that the task would be approached with thoroughness and care and that the work proceeded along the following lines:

(a) The removal of sub-standard and incorrect components, installed for use during the Royal Tournament display, and the restoration of the aircraft structure to its original condition.

(b) The inspection, assembly and checking of all functional systems, electrics, joints, attachments, tanks, pipe lines and controls. Special care had to be taken to ensure that any damage resulting from storage or previous mishandling was remedied.

(c) Final assembly, engine installation and aircraft major inspection before recategorisation as an airworthy aircraft and air test.

Spitfire F. Mk. 16 T.E. 330 was air tested at Biggin Hill on Sunday 8th September 1957 by the Station Commander Peter Thompson, who assessed it as a very satisfactory aircraft. The Spitfire was taxied across to the Station Flight hangar where it joined up with our sole flying Hurricane L.F. 363, which had been in our custody since June 1956. The Battle of Britain Memorial Flight had been born and later that month made their first fly past over Westminster Abbey on Battle of Britain Day 1957.

Peter Thompson first recorded TE330 as being taken on an air test on 10 September 1957. He immediately pronounced it airworthy and assessed it as 'a very satisfactory aircraft'. The Spitfire was given another air test later that day.

The following day TE330 carried out another sortie, which was partly a third air test and partly a Battle of Britain flypast rehearsal. On 12 September two more separate 'B of B rehearsal' sorties in TE330 were recorded in Peter Thompson's logbook. Three days later, on 15 September, the Historic Aircraft Flight carried out its first commemorative flight over Westminster Abbey for Battle of Britain Day 1957. TE330 and LF363 took to the skies over London representing their respective types and the role they played in safeguarding England – what would later become the Battle of Britain Memorial Flight and a national institution had been born!

Offering her personal recollections of this time is Ann Ringrose, who is the daughter of Squadron Leader Sowden:

> My father, Wing Commander Sowden [as he was later promoted], was at Biggin Hill at the same time as Peter Thompson who was the Station Commander. They already had a Hurricane in June 1956, but no Spitfire, and Peter Thompson had the idea of forming the BBMF and basically asked my father to help him in July 1957. They got six Spitfires, three Mk.XIXs and three Mk.XVIs. Basically they cannibalised them and took spare parts from other Spitfires including the one outside the chapel at Biggin Hill [Mk.XVIe SL674 - JC] and one that had crashed in the marshes near Southend. My father's 'day job' was organising the servicing of two squadrons of Hunters, but he got a team of enthusiasts together to work on the Spitfire [TE330].
>
> I lived in married quarters at the time and was 14-years-old, roughly the same age as Peter Thompson's daughter Julie. Julie and I used to go to chapel together on Sunday mornings.
>
> I do remember the Sunday morning when the first Spitfire was air tested. It was Sunday September 8th 1957 and my father was on edge. It was done on Sunday because officially this plane did not exist. I have a sort of Under Milk Wood vision of Biggin Hill that Sunday morning; Julie and I in chapel, my mother cooking the Sunday roast, Peter Thompson flying the Spitfire, and my father watching him praying that it wouldn't crash and land both of them in a Court Martial. Peter Thompson took it up, flew around a bit, landed, pronounced it airworthy and taxied it into the hangar where it joined Hurricane LF363.

[Please note: Squadron Leader Sowden and his daughter Ann Ringrose definitely state that TE330's first air test was out carried on Sunday 8 September 1957, in the latter's case for the reasons given above. However, there is no entry in Peter Thompson's logbook for this aircraft until 10 September, so whether this is a mistake of memory or for some reason the sortie was not recorded in Peter's logbook may remain a mystery. But is has been stated to me that Peter Thompson was meticulous in keeping his logbook accurate. JC]

*PS853 flown by Wing Commander Peter Thompson in formation with 41 Squadron Hunter F.5 WN983 piloted by Flight Lieutenant R Irish on a sortie out of Biggin Hill on 11 October 1957. (Courtesy Mimi Thompson)*

# CHAPTER 3

# Testing Times

By the time the Flight's first Battle of Britain flypast had been carried out in September 1957, it had already lost one of its PR.XIXs. As mentioned in Chapter 2, the condition of PS915 was not best when it was flown to Biggin Hill on 11 July. It was retired from flying fairly promptly, and as early as 2 August 1957 was allocated to RAF West Malling in Kent for display to take up static duties that were originally intended for TE330 to have carried out. Wing Commander Peter Thompson flew PS915 to West Malling on 8 August. (It later moved to Leuchars in Scotland and then Brawdy in Wales for gate guard duties.) The Flight was then down to five Spitfires.

Squadron Leader Sowden describes the situation as it was shortly after TE330 had been made airworthy and carried out the flypast:

> Our task had only just begun, however, because a decision was made that Spitfire Mk. 16 T.E. 330 would be presented to the United States Air Force Academy. In order that the Battle of Britain Memorial Flight could survive, it was therefore necessary to produce two more flying Spitfires. This task was tackled by the same men at Biggin Hill and on Tuesday 10th December, 1957, Spitfire Mk. 16 T.E. 476 was air tested by Peter Thompson.
>
> By this time the team was determined to complete the task and nothing seemed impossible any more. The big difficulty – as always – was the lack of spare parts

*PS915 on display at West Malling. Having been lost from the Flight, it was flown there by Wing Commander Peter Thompson on 8 August 1957. (BBMF Archives)*

*PS853 pictured over the white cliffs circa 1958. It was to be lost from the Flight in April that year. (Courtesy Mimi Thompson)*

and serviceable components. The search for Spitfire parts led us along a variety of paths and nothing was sacred once the required part had been located.

Our Station Commander – Peter Thompson – had been posted away, but the work on the third Spitfire Mk. 16 went on steadily. On Sunday 23rd February, 1958, Spitfire Mk. 16 S.L. 574 was air tested by Peter Chambers, the O.C. Flying at Biggin Hill, and the task was completed. It had taken us a long time, but don't forget that it was only a side line – our main job was servicing Hunter fighter aircraft.

On the subject of obtaining spare parts, another extract from *Air Clues* of November 1958 makes fascinating and amusing reading:

Under the direction of the Station Technical Officer, teams of airmen scoured R.A.F. scrap dumps for spare parts to make the Spitfire XVIs serviceable. Encouraged by his comrades, one airman went to Station Stores and, wearing a 'dead-pan' expression, presented the Equipment Officer with a formal demand note for certain Spitfire spares. The Officer's reply is not on record.

In February 1958 it was announced that RAF Biggin Hill was to close. Promoted to Group Captain, Peter Thompson was posted away from Biggin Hill in February 1958, and on the 21st of that same month the Historic Aircraft Flight was officially renamed the Battle of Britain Flight. The Flight was informed it would have to move to North Weald in Essex by March 1958, and of course would have to do so without its 'founding father'.

The Station Commander at North Weald at the time was a Group Captain Sutton, who piloted LF363 in the flypast over Buckingham Palace for the Queen's birthday that April. The Flight's stay at North Weald was brief, and there are few records of its participation in other flypasts while based there.

That April the Flight was to lose a second Spitfire PR.XIX, as PS853 was allocated to RAF West Raynham, Norfolk, on the 14th. The airworthy Spitfire was then for some reason struck off charge as Cat 5 (c) – 'Beyond economical repair or surplus, but is recoverable for breakdown to components, spare or scrap' – on 1 May 1958. However, it was instead placed on display at the gate. (In later years PS853 was made serviceable again and placed on the charge of the Central Fighter Establishment on 31 October 1962. Then in April 1964 it was returned to the Flight.)

By now down to four Spitfires, another major setback was to fall upon the Flight very quickly. With many non-airworthy examples of the Spitfire around the UK, news was given that the Flight's principal 'flyer', TE330, was to be presented to the United States Air Force Academy at Colorado Springs for museum display. In what must have caused immense frustration to the Flight's personnel, the best of the Flight's Spitfire XVIs was to become a museum exhibit!

In an article on the presentation of TE330 to the USAF after it had made the flypast over Westminster Abbey on Battle of Britain Sunday in 1957, *Air Clues* of November 1958 reported the situation as follows:

> Meanwhile the suggestion had been made that the Royal Air Force should present a Spitfire to the U.S.A.F. Academy, and TE.330 was chosen as the best aircraft available. Up to this time the main emphasis had been on making the Spitfires airworthy, and restoration of the interior equipment – armament, gun sight and other instruments – had been a secondary consideration. But it was felt to be essential that the presentation aircraft should be complete in every detail, and the task of final restoration was given to R.A.F. Maintenance Command. No.32 Maintenance Unit at St Athan, South Wales, was chosen to do the work, which was again tackled with enthusiasm and ingenuity far beyond the calls of normal duty.
>
> The restoration of the armament installation alone required the provision of 51 distinct items, 30 of which had long been obsolete and out of stock. Authorised

*Also to be taken away from the Flight was its favoured fighter, TE330. Following a handover to the USAF Academy at RAF Odiham in July 1958, the Spitfire XVI is seen on static display in the USA. Note the scripts and badge painted on its forward fuselage. (Peter Green Collection)*

raiding parties – officially termed Spares Recovery Teams – collected many of the required items from exhibition Spitfires parked by the gates of R.A.F. Stations in various parts of the United Kingdom. Parts which could not be found were made at the Maintenance Unit. A more modern gun sight was adapted to become a replica of the original type fitted and the appropriate camera gun was obtained from the manufacturers. A protracted search covering many R.A.F. Stations eventually produced the correct I.F.F. set (I.F.F. - Identification, Friend from Foe, was the device fitted to all Allied aircraft during the war to give an indication of identity to ground radar controllers).

When the restoration was complete consideration was given to external finish. Various camouflage schemes were employed during the war and the colours used on fighters were changed when the heavy enemy raids on Britain diminished and Fighter Command went over to the offensive which called for much flying over the sea. The Spitfire remained in front-line service throughout the war and thus spent much time in the offensive role, but there is little doubt that it will be best remembered for its part in the Battle of Britain. For this reason Spitfire TE.330 has been finished in the earlier colour scheme.

TE330's paintwork also featured a script in three layers with the words 'This Spitfire is representative of the aircraft flown by the pilots of Fighter Command during the Second World War' painted within. A fourth curve of the script had the Fighter Command badge painted over it.

On 14 May 1958 TE330 was transferred from North Weald to Odiham in Hampshire. On 2 July a formal presentation to the USAF was made. Present was Air Chief Marshal Sir Thomas Pike who handed the Spitfire over to Colonel Benjamin B Cassidy, Deputy Commandant of the USAF Academy. The first Spitfire to carry out a Battle of Britain flypast for the Flight had gone.

With things going from bad to worse, in May 1958 RAF North Weald closed, and the

*Biggin Hill during early 1958, shortly before the Flight was to leave the station for North Weald. (BBMF Archives)*

*Servicing and refuelling a Spitfire Mk.XVI, circa 1959. (BBMF Archives)*

*Strapping into a Spitfire XVI, 1959. (BBMF Archives)*

*Spitfire XVIs TE476 and SL574 prior to a sortie in 1958. (BBMF Archives)*

*An extremely rare colour picture of TE476 in Flight service taken at Baginton Airport, Coventry, in September 1959. (John Withers)*

BoB Flight needed to be found yet another new home. It next moved to Martlesham Heath in Suffolk where it was to stay for three years.

It was while at Martlesham Heath that the Flight lost its favoured Spitfire Mk.XVIs, and indeed also its principal event participation. The catalyst for this was a series of accidents and reliability problems with this mark during 1959.

On 28 May 1959, SL574 suffered a flying accident at Martlesham Heath and was given a Cat 5 designation. It was sent to 71 Maintenance Unit at Bicester, Oxfordshire, for repair on 4 June and returned on 1 July.

Then on 10 September TE476 was involved in a flying accident. Reports have it that the pilot landed back at Martlesham Heath after his radio failed and forgot to lower his undercarriage.

It was consequently decided that 20 September 1959 would be the last time that the fighters, including the Hurricane, would participate in the Battle of Britain flypast over London. That decision was perhaps vindicated when SL574 suffered a complete engine failure during that very sortie.

It crash-landed on the OXO cricket ground while being flown by Air Vice-Marshal Maguire. Air Vice-Marshal Maguire commented that prior to the flypast over London SL574 had been suffering from carburettor problems, and that the engine had not been running smoothly at all, though repairs were carried out to rectify the faults.

It was 4:30 pm and Harold Macmillan, who had just left Westminster Abbey after the service of remembrance for 'The Few', was on the dais. SL574 and LF363 soared over

*Left: Servicing Spitfires inside a hangar at Martlesham Heath during 1959. (BBMF Archives)*

*Below: Squadron Leader Sowden (centre) and his team of engineers, circa 1959. (BBMF Archives)*

Horse Guards Parade leading the annual Battle of Britain flypast, and shortly after its initial pass the Spitfire's engine failed totally and Air Vice-Marshal Maguire was forced to look for somewhere to put the Spitfire down in quick time.

His best option appeared to be an 'empty' sports field in Bromley – fortunately the OXO cricket team and their opponents had just retired for tea. Skimming the sight screen, the Spitfire went in with its flaps down and wheels up. It had 200 yards to stop, and after hitting the grass one of the Spitfire's wingtips took one set of stumps off (having embedded themselves in the wing, folklore has it they still exist somewhere), before it skidded 60 yards into the outfield and stopped, with the raised dust gently settling over it.

The groundsman and one of the umpires helped Air Vice-Marshal Maguire out. He then waved to LF363, which was circling above to check he made it down OK. The pilot then went into the pavilion, made a phone call to explain what had happened, then had tea with the players and apologised for damaging the wicket. SL574 was pushed over the boundary and play resumed soon after! (For those who are interested, OXO were taking on the Old Hollingtonians in their last game of the season, and just before the Spitfire pancaked on the ground they were 120 for 9.) Apparently, by this time several hundred more 'spectators' had also arrived at the ground.

Newspaper reports of the time made a great deal of this, with headlines such as 'The Last Spitfire Prangs'. SL574 was also dubbed 'Sugar Love' in the papers, and the reporting was somewhat sensationalistic. Writing went along the lines of: 'The old

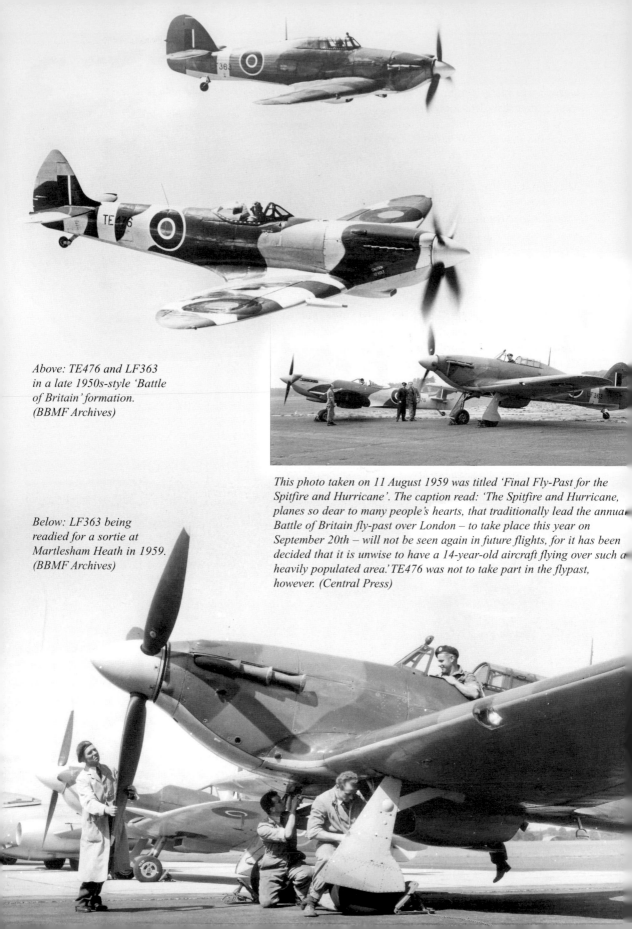

*Above: TE476 and LF363 in a late 1950s-style 'Battle of Britain' formation. (BBMF Archives)*

*Below: LF363 being readied for a sortie at Martlesham Heath in 1959. (BBMF Archives)*

*This photo taken on 11 August 1959 was titled 'Final Fly-Past for the Spitfire and Hurricane'. The caption read: 'The Spitfire and Hurricane, planes so dear to many people's hearts, that traditionally lead the annual Battle of Britain fly-past over London – to take place this year on September 20th – will not be seen again in future flights, for it has been decided that it is unwise to have a 14-year-old aircraft flying over such a heavily populated area.' TE476 was not to take part in the flypast, however. (Central Press)*

warrior was really getting past it now, and this must definitely be its last appearance in the London sky.' Sensationalistic maybe, but also true.

SL574 was sent for repair at 71 Maintenance Unit again – the engineers perhaps frustrated that all their earlier work had been undone – but was eventually relegated to gate guard duties, which it took up at HQ Fighter Command, Bentley Priory, Middlesex, in November 1961. (Nowadays SL574 is on display at the San Diego Air & Space Museum, California, USA.)

TE476 was also transferred for similar duties. This aircraft went on the gate at Neatishead, Norfolk, in January 1960. (TE476 now forms part of the collection at Kermit Weeks' incredible Fantasy of Flight aviation complex at Polk City, Florida, where it was airworthy for several years named *Winston Churchill*.)

In November 1961 the Flight was forced to move again, and this time went to RAF Horsham St Faith in Norfolk (now Norwich Airport). The Flight was still under the care of its resident unit's Station Flight. By this time the Flight just comprised Hurricane LF363 and Spitfire Mk.XIX PM631, and would stay so until 1964.

Continuing the series of set-backs for the Flight, Horsham too was to close while it was stationed there. On 1 April 1963 the remaining brace of fighters made their way to nearby Coltishall in Norfolk – surely the Flight was due some better fortune?

*Right: SL574 looking somewhat forlorn after force-landing on the OXO cricket pitch at Bromley on 20 September 1959. It did attract a lot of attention from the local lads though, and note that play has resumed! (BBMF Archives)*

*Below: TE476 after its landing accident at Martlesham Heath on 10 September 1959. That was the end of its Flight service. (BBMF Archives)*

*All the Flight's four Spitfires seen at some point between 1969 and 1971 positioned for a picture from a high-level vantage point at Coltishall. Nearest is PM631, then AB910, P7350 and PS853. (via Martyn Chorlton)*

# CHAPTER 4

# Changing Fortunes at Coltishall

After a succession of knock-backs, it was while at Coltishall that fortunes would improve significantly for the Flight. In April 1964 PS853 was returned to the Flight from the Central Fighter Establishment, which was by then based at Binbrook in Lincolnshire.

In September 1965 another Spitfire was presented to the Flight as Vickers-Armstrong parted with Mk.Vb AB910. This aircraft was flown to Coltishall by Jeffrey Quill, a famous test pilot who will always be remembered for his work during the development of the Spitfire. (Jeffrey died in 1996. He is buried with his wife Claire in the grounds of the church at Andreas on the Isle of Man, close to the former wartime airfield of the same name. The top of the gravestone includes a picture of a Spitfire.)

The new fighter carried the QJ-J code of 92 Squadron, and at the time was the only

*A Flight pre-sortie briefing at Coltishall in 1969 – a wonderful comparison with how things are carried out nowadays. (BBMF Archives)*

*For a number of years the Flight only had Hurricane LF363 and Spitfire XIX PM631 on strength. The aircraft are seen flying along the south coast of England in July 1973, by which time the ranks of the Flight had swelled considerably while being based at Coltishall. (BBMF Archives)*

aircraft of the Flight to wear unit markings. This now brought the Flight's inventory back up to four aircraft; however spares were few, which resulted in a reduction of the number of appearances by the fighters. This was rectified as a more structured system of logistical support was put in place.

In 1968 the Flight's aircraft were used for the filming of the following year's aviation classic *Battle of Britain*. This film utilised a large number of historic aircraft of various types, and was very much a turning point in the warbird movement generally. The Flight's aircraft were used for filming from Monday to Friday, and then carried out their display duties at weekends. They were of course still wearing their film markings while doing so, thus giving many air show visitors the opportunity to get photographs of them in 'distressed' combat liveries.

After the film work, there was to be a major coup for the Flight when it was presented with Spitfire IIa P7350, the world's oldest airworthy example of its breed and a genuine combat veteran of the Battle of Britain. With burgeoning ranks of aircraft, in 1969 the Flight was notably established on a more formal basis.

In a letter (AMSO/517) dated 1 April 1969, Air Marshal Sir Thomas Prickett KCB DSO DFC at the Ministry of Defence Main Building, Whitehall, London, wrote to Air Chief Marshal Sir Dennis Spotswood KCB CBE DSO DFC, Air Officer Commanding-in-Chief, Headquarters Strike Command, announcing that he had obtained the agreement of the Air Force Board Standing Committee that the Flight should be established on a formal basis. It was agreed that the Flight should be added to the policy statement for RAF Coltishall, that the necessary servicing personnel should be established, and that the Flight should continue in existence as a charge to Air Votes until circumstances warranted a review. The Standing Committee agreed that the Flight should consist of one Hurricane and four Spitfires, i.e. the original inventory plus P7350. It was also floated that the possibility of adding a fifth Spitfire was under examination.

The letter additionally stated that the Standing Committee had agreed that 'The Waddington Lancaster' – as PA474 was termed at the time – was to be kept in flying condition at RAF Waddington until the end of 1969, in accordance with the same conditions as agreed in 1968. These were:

a) that the aircraft should be flown only by selected aircrew from Waddington,

b) that all servicing should be undertaken on a voluntary basis by qualified tradesmen and officers at Waddington, and

c) that all personnel should be regarded as being on duty while working on or flying in the aircraft.

The letter concluded by requesting that the future of PA474 should be reviewed at the end of 1969 and asking if a report detailing its utilisation with a further recommendation of its continued operation could be put forward at that time.

In his reply to AMSO/517, Air Chief Marshal Sir Dennis Spotswood wrote:

I am delighted to learn that the Memorial Flight is to be formally established at Coltishall. I am sure that this is the only practical solution to the problem of our continuing to keep our few flyable World War Two aircraft well maintained and properly prepared for display.

I was also relieved by the 'stay of execution' on Waddington's Lancaster. Subject to the conditions you enumerate it will, I am sure, continue to give us valuable, if only occasional, service.

*The Flight's first boost at Coltishall came in April 1964, when Spitfire PR.XIX PS853 was returned to it from the Central Fighter Establishment. From 1972, 74 Squadron ZP-A code letters were applied to it. (BBMF Archives)*

An engineering Policy Directive was drafted as follows.

# BATTLE OF BRITAIN MEMORIAL FLIGHT ENGINEERING POLICY DIRECTIVE

## INTRODUCTION

1. The Battle of Britain Memorial Flight (BBMF) is established at Coltishall with Hurricane and Spitfire aircraft. Its duties are to mount flypasts and flying displays on suitable formal occasions.

## AIMS OF THE DIRECTIVE

2. Most engineering aspects of these aircraft can be covered most effectively by HQSTC under delegated responsibility from MOD (Air). The Aims of this Directive are, therefore, as follows:

a. To define the Engineering and Servicing Policy.

b. To outline the degree of delegation of engineering staff functions to HQSTC.

## ENGINEERING POLICY

### Servicing Standards

3. The BBMF aircraft are to be serviced to normal RAF standards by the tradesmen specially established at Coltishall for this task. Local familiarisation training on Hurricane and Spitfire is to be given. Servicing documents are to be signed in accordance with AP3158 Volume 2, Leaflet C10.

*In 1968 the Flight's fighters became involved in the filming of the renowned aviation classic released the following year, Battle of Britain. The aircraft carried many different fictitious serial numbers and squadron code combinations during the film work. This is PS853 marked as N3319 EI-K. With their long noses and five-bladed propellers, the Griffon-engined Spitfire PR.XIXs were generally flown to the rear of formations so they didn't stand out as being obviously inaccurate models for a story set in 1940! (Tony Overill)*

*The Flight's Hurricane IIc LF363 and Spitfire Vb AB910 (wearing the 92 Squadron QJ-J code) await start-up at Waddington in readiness for a practice formation with Lancaster I PA474 on 5 March 1968. The three-ship formation was being arranged to mark the stand-down of Fighter Command and Bomber Command, and the formation of Strike Command on 30 April that year. While the Lancaster was not yet part of the Flight, this really was very much the shape of things to come of what is nowadays the Flight's 'trademark' formation. (BBMF Archives)*

### Servicing Policy (Mechanical)

4. First and Second Line Servicing. Hurricane and Spitfire aircraft are to be serviced to the periodic servicing pattern laid down in APs 1564 and 1565 respectively.

5. Third Line Servicing. Work which is beyond Unit second line capacity because of man hour content, special skill requirements or necessity for special equipment will be undertaken by Maintenance Command.

6. Modifications. The only modifications undertaken will be Command Modifications and SRIMS, and these are to be kept to a minimum.

7. STI/SI/AFEN/PW. The only STI/SI/AFEN/PW will be Command issues, as required.

8. Fatigue. Spitfire and Hurricane aircraft have an indefinite fatigue life, if flown within the limits set out in Pilot's Notes. There is no requirement for fatigue data recording.

9. Servicing of Mechanical Components. Mechanical components are to be serviced, and repaired on defect to the maximum extent practicable within the established facilities available in STC and subject to the availability of Bay Servicing Schedules or Manufacturer's Instruction Books.

10. Aircraft Weighing. Aircraft are to be weighed and the weight or alterations are to be recorded in accordance with AP3158 Volume 2, Leaflet A12. HQSTC is responsible for deciding on the frequency of weighing.

11. Flight Testing. Flight testing is to be done as laid down in AP3158, Volume 2, Leaflet B26. HQSTC is responsible for publishing the appropriate Flight Test Schedule.

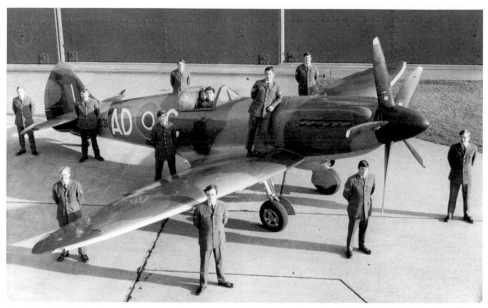

*At Coltishall the Flight's fortunes improved considerably, even to the extent that a team of full-time engineers became part of its establishment for the first time. This is the team as at 1975 posed around, and inside, PM631. (BBMF Archives)*

### SERVICING POLICY (AVIONICS)
### (to be completed by D Elect Eng branch)

### Management Organisation

12. Servicing Documentation. Normal RAF documentation is to be used for all aspects of servicing of Hurricane and Spitfire aircraft. The records and documents are to be maintained in accordance with AP3158 Volume 2, Leaflet C2.

13. Defect Recording and Reporting. There are no defect recording and reporting requirements, other than normal servicing documentation on F700.

14. Cat 3/4/5 Reporting Action. Hurricane and Spitfire aircraft requiring salvage and/or repairs beyond the capacity of RAF Coltishall are to be reported under the standard categorisation procedure.

### DELEGATION OF RESPONSIBILITY FOR IMPLEMENTATION OF POLICY

15. In addition to the normal day-to-day management of the engineering activities of the BBMF, the following overall responsibilities are delegated to HQSTC. These delegated responsibilities are to be implemented within the policy guidelines set out in the previous sections.

a. General

(1) Deciding servicing cycles, depth, frequency of inspection etc. and taking local amendment action to servicing schedules as necessary.

(2) Providing detailed engineering advice, as required, to MOD(AFD) Finance and provisioning Branches.

(3) Referring engineering problems to DG Eng (RAF) staff in all cases where STC Air or Supply Staff consider it necessary similarly to notify or consult with MOD(AFD) Air or Provisioning Staffs, e.g. when flying commitments or limitations are involved or provisioning of common-user items is affected.

b. Mechanical Engineering

(1) Referring all matters concerning fatigue, stress corrosion and any other structural or aerodynamic factors which might significantly affect airworthiness to DG Eng (RAF) staff.

(2) Full investigation of all defects and accidents/incidents due to technical causes, and taking all remedial action required. Technical advice may be obtained direct from the relevant manufacturer. Any action involving the use of resources outside the capacity of STC (engineering or financial) is to be referred to MOD for approval and authorisation.

c. Avionic Engineering (to be completed by D Elect Eng branch)

*Another newcomer to the Flight while at Coltishall was Hurricane IIc PZ865, which is seen being inspected in May 1972 shortly after its arrival and still carrying its G-AMAU civilian registration. (BBMF Archives)*

*By the time this picture was taken in 1973, the Flight could muster four Spitfires and two Hurricanes into the air – how times had changed since 1959! (Harry Martin/BBMF Archives)*

Wing Commander C King at Headquarters Strike Command, High Wycombe, wrote the following letter for the Air Officer Commanding in Chief on 19 February 1969. It outlines a wish to formally establish P7350 and also gives the identity of the fifth Spitfire, which was considered for addition to the Flight:

> Reference A detailed the refinishing of one Hurricane and three Spitfire aircraft, by HQMC. It is highly desirable that the fourth Spitfire held by RAF Coltishall (P7350) be included in this HQMC programme of work. Accordingly, it is requested that arrangements be made with HQMC to add Spitfire P7350 to their programme, but extra to the financial arrangements mentioned in Reference A.
>
> The advantages of such a resort are considerable. It relieves Coltishall of a task for which they are inadequately equipped and established, ensures that the Memorial Flight aircraft are brought to a common (high) standard of appearance and exploits the facilities and expertise that will be set up by HQMC while they are refinishing the other aircraft.
>
> It is further requested that arrangements be made with HQMC for Spitfire MK 16 SM 411 to be brought to a satisfactory flying condition, should it be decided by MOD to include this aircraft as part of the Coltishall Flight. Initial survey of SM 411 indicates that the aircraft can be made airworthy provided a large amount of work, acquisition of some replacement parts, detailed survey, an element of reconditioning and a major servicing, is carried out.

Summarised below are the outstanding requirements of the aircraft at the time together with some dates when they were to be available for feed-in to Maintenance Command.

> Hurricane LF 363 – All fabric surfaces need renewal and subsequent repainting (metal surfaces previously finished in polyurethane), available now but serviceable for flight to MU only.

*All three of the flying Hurricanes used during the Battle of Britain wearing Polish red and white 'chessboards'. PZ865, which would join the Flight a few years later, is nearest the camera and was wearing the markings H3424 MI-G. Next in line is the Flight's LF363, painted up as H3421 MI-D. The third Hurricane is Mk.XII S377 wearing the serial number H3426 and code MI-C. Many years later in February 1993 this aircraft was sadly destroyed in a hangar fire at the Canadian Warplane Heritage Museum, Hamilton, Ontario. (Tony Overill)*

Spitfire Mk 5b AB 910 – Elevators and rudder require recovering, remainder of external surfaces need stripping and repainting, available now.

Spitfire Mk 19 PM 631 – Elevators and rudder require recovering, remainder requires repainting (was previously finished in polyurethane), available now.

Spitfire Mk 19 PS 853 – Undergoing extensive rectifications, requires repainting (was previously finished in polyurethanc). Estimated available by 3rd March.

Spitfire Mk 2 P 7350 - Presently on Minor Servicing for Acceptance Check, VHF radio fit and propeller inspection by Dowty Rotol, requires repainting, estimated available by mid March.

The drawings showing the appropriate camouflage paint schemes for each aircraft are held by RAF Coltishall, and will of course be made available to Maintenance Command immediately upon request.

Also at this time came another change of name. Even though it was already widely known as the Battle of Britain Memorial Flight as we are familiar with today, it was not until 1 June 1969 that this name is officially recorded as coming into force.

Another major milestone in the Flight's history came in March 1972 when Hurricane IIc PZ865 was presented to the BBMF after refurbishment by Hawker. This aircraft was the last Hurricane off the production line and hence had the legend *'Last of the Many'* painted on its sides.

However, Hurricane IIc LF363 was nearly lost to the RAF Museum later that year and was indeed flown to RAF Wattisham in Suffolk on delivery in company with PZ865. At the last minute, however, after a number of comments from higher authority, it was decided to use another airframe and LF363 was returned to Coltishall.

During 1973 the fighters had performed at eighty displays throughout the country. November 1973 saw the arrival of a new and significant type on the Flight's books. On

*Start-up at Coltishall in 1973.*
*(Harry Martin/BBMF Archives)*

*This evocative silhouette shot could almost pass as a mixed formation of Hurricanes and Spitfires during the Battle of Britain. (Harry Martin/BBMF Archives)*

the 20th of that month Lancaster I PA474 was officially transferred from RAF Waddington where it had been refurbished and looked after by station personnel. Its popularity was growing at a rapid pace, and maintained by station resources only, this was proving difficult with an increased demand for appearances. The obvious answer was to place the Lancaster under the care of the BBMF, which was by then better equipped with the necessary expertise and infrastructure to maintain it. However, there was an outcry from many residents of Lincolnshire, who had come to think of the bomber almost as part of the county's 'folklore'. The move went ahead, although it was agreed that the bomber would be adopted by the City of Lincoln and wear its Coat of Arms to reflect this – PA474 still proudly wears it.

With that controversy over, less than two years later the people of Norfolk were to raise their disagreement with a similar, and perhaps even more controversial, decision. It was decided that the BBMF was to move to Coningsby in Lincolnshire. At first it was thought by some that this was to appease Lincolnshire by returning the Lancaster to 'Bomber County', however that was not the case and the reasons were of an operational nature with regards to the future of Coltishall. But the proposition caused much outcry and generated a series of meetings between Norfolk MPs and the Under Secretary of State (RAF).

Air Commodore C E Ness, Director of Organisation and Administrative Plans (RAF) at Headquarters Strike Command, wrote the following on 18 June 1975:

I am directed to state that it has been decided to deploy the Battle of Britain Memorial Flight (B of B MF) from RAF Coltishall to RAF Coningsby.

Executive authority is given for the B of B MF to move from RAF Coltishall to RAF Coningsby during the first quarter of 1976, the precise timing to be at the discretion of the Air Officer Commanding-in-Chief Strike Command.

A public announcement is not required.

You are invited to implement the above decision and to notify MOD DDO(RAF) on completion so that SD155 action may be taken.

Other documents raised concerning the move included the following:

## BATTLE OF BRITAIN MEMORIAL FLIGHT MOVE FROM RAF COLTISHALL TO RAF CONINGSBY

**Reference: AF/4464/Part VI/S9B(Air) dated 30 September 1975.**

You asked for comments and additional material for the brief attached to Reference.

You may wish to add the following details to:

Para 2. Although the accommodation for the Flight at Coningsby will be similar to that at Coltishall there will be more space at the new location, which will allow the historic aircraft to be displayed as a permanent static show (i.e. a miniature museum).

Para 3. The engine hours of the historic aircraft must be conserved as far as possible. The move will have the advantage of being nearer to the centre of the concentration of effort for displays, which is in the East Midlands and South East. Thus it should save some transit flying time.

The move will also serve to return control of the Flight to HQ No 11 Group, the traditional home of the Spitfire and Hurricane.

Para 5. All requests, including those for the Memorial Flight, for RAF participation in air displays are referred to the Participation Committee. In considering requests, it is essential to keep the Royal Air Force in the public eye and to seize every opportunity to display to the public every aspect of Service life. This, coupled with the prestige and recruiting value, is the major reason for participation in public events. Therefore, it is indefensible to allocate priority to any particular geographical area. However, there is still no reason to suppose that the move of the flight would diminish the number of appearances in Norfolk.

*Hurricanes LF363 and PZ865 lead a BBMF formation in 1973. (Harry Martin/BBMF Archives)*

## THE BATTLE OF BRITAIN MEMORIAL FLIGHT – MOVE FROM RAF COLTISHALL TO RAF CONINGSBY

To preserve the historic aircraft of the Flight in flying condition for as long as possible it is necessary that they be housed in hangar accommodation and that the expertise of the groundcrew should embrace the Lancaster as well as the Spitfires and Hurricanes. Regrettably the formation of a further Jaguar Squadron in late 1976 will mean that suitable accommodation will no longer be available at Coltishall.

Fortunately hangarage will be free at Coningsby which, with insignificant works services, can provide sufficient accommodation to allow the aircraft to be permanently displayed when not flying. The move to Coningsby meets the long term aim of returning the Spitfires and Hurricanes to the control of No 11 Group with whom they served during the Battle of Britain as well as returning the Lancaster to Lincolnshire where experienced heavy piston engined aircraft crews are now only available with the Hastings Flight at Scampton. It also places the Flight closer to the 'centre of gravity' of the area covered by flying displays with a consequent saving of precious flying hours from purely transit flying.

A brief for the US of S(RAF) in readiness for a meeting on 21 October 1975 with Norfolk MPs who were objecting to the move was drafted as follows:

### INTRODUCTION

1. The Battle of Britain Memorial Flight was formed at RAF Biggin Hill in 1957. In 1958 the Flight moved first to RAF North Weald and then on to RAF Martlesham Heath until 1960 when it moved to RAF

*AB910 undergoing maintenance at Coltishall. (Harry Martin/BBMF Archives)*

Horsham St Faith and thence to RAF Coltishall in 1964. The Flight is now due to move to RAF Coningsby in March, 1976. This impending move has generated some local feeling and letters have been received from local MPs and the Chief Executive of the Norfolk County Council. A historical note on Norfolk airfields during the war is at Annex A.

## REASONS FOR THE MOVE AND RELOCATION OF THE FLIGHT

2. The historic aircraft of the Flight need to be housed in heated accommodation, in order to preserve them as long as possible. Unfortunately, the hangar in which the aircraft are now housed at RAF Coltishall will be required for a further Jaguar Squadron which is due to form there next year and no suitable alternative accommodation will be available on the station to house them.

3. Apart from RAF Coltishall, the only active RAF flying station in Norfolk after March 1976 will be RAF Marham; this will be fully utilised and unable to provide suitable accommodation for the Memorial Flight. The other RAF airfields in Norfolk are Sculthorpe, Watton and West Raynham. The first of these is a reserve base for the USAF and the others will have no flying activity or facilities; they are not therefore suitable for the Memorial Flight.

*LF363 is seen about to touch down at Coltishall after a sortie. Note that in those days the pilots still wore traditional World War Two leather flying helmets. (via Martyn Chorlton)*

4. On the other hand, suitable hangarage and facilities will be available at RAF Coningsby and a move to that station will not only provide adequate accommodation but will also offer the following additional advantages:

a. it returns the Lancaster to Lincolnshire;

b. it returns the Spitfire and Hurricanes to No.11 Group under which they served during the Battle of Britain;

c. the aircraft will be more centrally located for flying displays and therefore fewer of the very strictly limited flying hours will be spent on purely transit flying.

*PM631 breaks away from LF363 in this photo taken in 1975. (BBMF Archives)*

## EMPLOYMENT

5. As there are no civilian posts at RAF Coltishall specifically related to the Flight its move will not entail any redundancies. Eventually a few more industrial posts may be required to support the additional Jaguar Squadron.

## APPEARANCES AT DISPLAYS

6. In his letter of 24 July, the Chief Executive of the Norfolk County Council asked for priority treatment to be given to Norfolk in so far as requests for the Flight to appear at displays are concerned. In his reply of 19 August, US of S(RAF) explained to the Chief Executive that the number of flying hours available for these aircraft was strictly limited and that he believed it would be indefensible to allocate priority to any particular area of the country. However, there was no reason to suppose that the move of the Flight would diminish the number of appearances at displays and functions in Norfolk.

7. All requests for RAF participation at air displays and functions are referred to the Participation Committee who, bearing in mind the numbers and locations of displays to which the Memorial Flight are asked to appear, consider the publicity and recruiting value to be expected from each. The move of the Flight should not of itself, affect

*Spitfire PM631 undergoing maintenance inside the hangar at Coltishall in August 1973. (BBMF Archives)*

*Air Vice-Marshal Harold Bird-Wilson after his last Spitfire flight in the early 1970s – in the Flight's Spitfire Mk.IIa P7350. From 2006 the Flight's LF363 has worn the markings of this pilot's Hurricane, which he flew during the Battle of Britain. (BBMF Archives)*

the number of appearances in Norfolk.

## CONCLUSIONS

8. There will be no suitable accommodation available for the Flight at RAF Coltishall or elsewhere in Norfolk after March 1976 (Paragraphs 2 and 3).

9. Suitable accommodation will be available at RAF Coningsby which, incidentally, offers some additional advantages (Paragraph 4).

10. It is indefensible to allocate priority for participation in air displays to any particular area of the country (Paragraph 6).

11. Norfolk was predominantly a 'bomber' county during World War II and cannot therefore justify any special case for having the Battle of Britain Memorial Flight (Annex A).

## RECOMMENDATIONS

12. In the light of the above, US of S(RAF) is recommended to reply to the delegation that while he understands their strong feelings on this

matter, he sees no reason to reverse his earlier decision to move the Flight to RAF Coningsby in March 1976.

The meeting between the US of S(RAF) and the Rt Hon David Ennals MP and Mr Ralph Howell MP held in the House of Commons on 21 October concerning the move of the Battle of Britain Memorial Flight was recorded as follows:

**Present:**

| | | |
|---|---|---|
| Mr Brynmor John MP | - | US of S(RAF) |
| The Rt Hon David Ennals MP | | |
| Mr Ralph Howell MP | | |
| Mr G Gammon | - | Head of S9 (Air) |
| Gp Capt F F Mossman | - | DD Ops (A Def & O) |
| Mr R Murgatroyd | - | APS/US of S(RAF) |

After welcoming the two MPs, US of S(RAF) suggested they might like to start by raising with him any particular points which had not so far been made in the exchange of correspondence.

*An incredible addition to the Flight in November 1973, Lancaster I PA474 arrives for landing at Coltishall. (via Martyn Chorlton)*

*Bearing its* City of Lincoln *name and coat of arms on the port side, PA474 is seen parked up at Coltishall. (via Martyn Chorlton)*

Mr Ennals said that since the MOD announcement about the impending move of the Memorial Flight from Coltishall to Coningsby there had been a great deal of pressure put on the Norfolk MPs to have the decision reversed. Both MPs said that their constituents were somewhat sceptical of the reason given publicly to the effect that the aircraft needed to be kept in heated accommodation – which was available at Coningsby but not Coltishall. The general feeling was that we were simply giving in to pressure from Lincolnshire.

US of S(RAF) said that the move of the Memorial Flight to Coningsby was not in any way meant as a sop to placate the Lincolnshire 'Lancaster' enthusiasts. The accommodation consideration was certainly valid but the real reason – which had yet to

*Led by PA474, five of the Flight's aircraft are seen* en route *to their new base at Coningsby having left their home of eleven years at Coltishall on 1 March 1976. With the Lancaster are PM631, PS853, P7350 and LF363. AB910 and PZ865 were to follow them later. (BBMF Archives)*

be announced, and was therefore confidential at this stage – was that the RAF proposed to form a third squadron of Jaguars at Coltishall next year [41 Squadron – JC]. Thus we would require the hangar presently used to house the Memorial Flight. There was no suitable alternative accommodation at Coltishall so therefore they had to move elsewhere.

Continuing, US of S(RAF) explained that the only active RAF flying station in Norfolk after March 1976 would be RAF Marham; this would be fully utilised and was unable to provide suitable accommodation. The other RAF airfields in the county were not suitable for various reasons. On the other hand, suitable hangarage and facilities are available at Coningsby and the move there would have certain additional advantages. One of these was that it would return the Spitfire and Hurricanes to 11 Group under which they served during the Battle of Britain. Secondly, the aircraft would be more centrally located for flying displays and therefore fewer of the very strictly limited flying hours would be spent on purely transit flying – this would extend the usable life of the aircraft.

The Minister mentioned too that the move would not entail any civilian redundancies since none were attached to the Flight. There was a possibility that the Jaguar Squadron might generate a few jobs; but this was not known yet.

US of S(RAF) said that the Norfolk County Council had suggested in a letter to him that Norfolk should be given some priority in the allocation of the Flight for displays. The Minister said, all things considered, the MOD could not accept this since the Flight was part of the country's heritage as a whole and he felt it would be indefensible to allocate a priority to any given area. However, there was no reason to suppose that the move of the Flight would diminish the number of appearances at displays and functions in Norfolk, but he added if East Anglian stations have Open Days etc there should be no difficulty in arranging participation by the Flight.

In conclusion both MPs thought that the Minister's arguments were telling, especially the formation of the Jaguar Squadron. They felt that once this became public the 'lobbying' would cease and wondered when it would be possible for them to use this information. US of S(RAF) said he would find out what the position was regarding this and would write to them as soon as he possibly could.

A local newspaper reported the following:

### SPITFIRE FLIGHT TO BE MOVED

The Battle of Britain Memorial Flight of four Spitfires, two Hurricanes, and a Lancaster is to move to RAF Coningsby, Lincs, next March. Norfolk County Council and MPs had backed an appeal for the Flight to stay at RAF Coltishall, Norfolk, where it has been for the last 11 years.

The Ministry of Defence, however, is going ahead with the transfer and says that a new Jaguar squadron for Coltishall will need the space taken by the Memorial Flight.

Despite all the public outcry from those in Norfolk, the move went ahead and on 1 March 1976 the Flight's aircraft began to make their way to Coningsby. This of course delighted the folk of Lincolnshire, as they were getting their beloved and adopted Lancaster back in the county! This too had of course added to the controversy as it was felt that the move had come about as a result of the petition made by the Lincolnshire Lancaster Appeal. However, although this was not the case and the move was of an operational nature, not everyone was convinced!

There is no doubting that after a succession of troubled times it was while at Coltishall that things changed for the better for the Flight. It had arrived with two wartime era aircraft, and left with seven – including at the time the world's only airworthy Lancaster – plus a dedicated engineering team.

*Overhead view of the BBMF pan at Coningsby in 1976. (BBMF Archives)*

# CHAPTER 5

# Continuing the Tribute at Coningsby

Since its arrival at Coningsby in Lincolnshire, the Battle of Britain Memorial Flight has continued to go from strength to strength. It has increased its fleet of aircraft, though some have gone too, and since 1986 has been made available to the public during weekdays – which is an incredible gesture of goodwill by the RAF authorities.

Not long after the Flight had arrived at Coningsby though, a major review of its justification and operations – which was due for March 1978 – was brought forward. Extracts from it include:

## AIR FORCE BOARD

## THE BATTLE OF BRITAIN MEMORIAL FLIGHT

### INTRODUCTION

The concept and operation of the Battle of Britain Memorial Flight (BBMF) was last examined in 1975 against the background of the Defence Review and the public relations value of the Flight. The AFBSC agreed that the BBMF should continue subject to further review in March 1978.

*RAF Coningsby Open Day on 4 June 1977, with Hurricane PZ865 tucked in formation off to the Lancaster's starboard side. (BBMF Archives)*

*LF363 tucks up close behind the Lancaster PA474's rear turret, with P7350 slightly further back. (© Crown Copyright/MOD)*

Because of continuing financial constraints, it has been decided to bring forward the review scheduled for March 1978 and reconsideration of the continued operation of the BBMF forms the subject of this paper.

## ACTIVITIES OF THE BBMF SINCE 1975

The BBMF moved, as planned, from Coltishall to Coningsby in March 1976, and is now under the operational command of AOC No.11 Group.

Details of the hours flown and displays given by the BBMF are set out at Annex A and these show that by undertaking fly-pasts while in transits to other events, an increasing number of displays have been given within the current flying task. In 1976 it was estimated that the total audience watching BBMF displays was $2^1/2 - 3$M.

## JUSTIFICATION FOR THE BBMF

Participation by the Royal Air Force in public events fulfils two primary purposes:

a. To foster a more appreciative public awareness of the RAF, its role and purpose.

*PA474 leads all the Flight's seven fighters in an incredible formation during 1990 to commemorate the fiftieth anniversary of the Battle of Britain in fine style. (Geoff Lee/British Aerospace)*

*Inside the Flight's hangar in 1983, with PS853 'under wraps' to the fore. A sign on its fuselage side reads 'Hibernating Spitfire – Do Not Disturb'. PS853 was grounded from 1980 to 1989 while trials were conducted to fit a Griffon 58, used for Avro Shackletons, to a Spitfire XIX as the Griffon 66s were reaching the end of their lifed hours. PS915 was delivered from the gate at Brawdy in 1977 for the trials, as the Mk.66 availability problem had been foreseen some years previously. Behind PS853 are PM631 and AB910. In the centre is Chipmunk WK518, wearing the standard RAF red and white training scheme of the time, with the two Hurricanes in the far right corner. (Duncan Cubitt/FlyPast)*

       b. To promote recruitment to the Service. When considering participation, many factors are taken into account such as crowd size, TV and Press coverage, recruiting value and economy.

Links between any fighting Service and the general public are of fundamental importance. The general public needs constantly to be reminded of the Service and its great achievements if they are to be sympathetic to the allocation of resources to preserve the country's security. Conversely, the Armed Forces need to maintain close touch with the views and attitudes of the public.

    Flying displays are the most popular and impressive form of RAF participation permitted by security and available resources. The BBMF combines to a notable degree the public appeal of a flying display with a reminder of the part played by the RAF in the defence of the country. Its value cannot be precisely assessed, but it is worth reflecting on what an advertiser would have to pay for the media coverage given to a single historical aircraft flying over London – at least twice the current annual running cost of the Flight. Appearances by the Flight are cheap compared with what it would cost to provide operational aircraft. The Flight can in any case meet commitments where no other form of participation could conveniently be provided and 14 such appearances are planned for 1977. The BBMF thus provides a cheap and extremely effective form of RAF presence with the least detriment to front-line operations.

There are other benefits to the Service from the Flight. To the general public the BBMF is a living reminder of a victory of which all who have served in the RAF have just cause to be proud. To the Service it is a major Battle Honour and one on which we are glad to be able to base our traditions.

Disbandment of the Flight would directly affect the RAF's ability to appear at displays. Either front-line aircraft would have to substitute for the BBMF, with increased costs and interference with operational training; or the lever of participation would fall with effects greater than would be justified by the cost saving.

If, despite everything, the Flight had to be disbanded the aircraft could be accommodated by the RAF Museum, at an RAF Regional Collection, or as 'gate guardians', and there would be no significant maintenance costs falling on Defence Votes. But static aircraft cannot reach such a wide public as flying displays, and there is already a fair number of Second World War aircraft on static display throughout the country. The special attraction of the BBMF lies in the fact that its historic aircraft can, and do, still fly.

Disbandment would also attract the widest public dismay. Quite apart from local reaction in the Lincoln area to the grounding – or removal – of the Lancaster there would be a more widespread public reaction for what could be regarded as an unjustifiable economy.

In summary, I believe that the BBMF represents a cheap and effective means of achieving the two principal purposes of our participation programme, and is of good value for that reason alone. There are other less tangible, but nonetheless extremely important, benefits. The saving we would realise by disbandment would fall far short of the cost of the compensatory efforts we should need to make in our participation programme to balance its loss – quite apart from the adverse public reaction which could ensue.

*Squadron Leader Paul Day carries out a flypast of Big Ben in Spitfire PR.XIX PM631 at precisely 11:00 on 5 March 1986. This event was notable for a number of reasons. Firstly, it was the first time one of the Flight's Spitfires had flown over London since being 'banned' in 1959. The flypast itself was carried out to celebrate the fiftieth anniversary of the first flight of the Spitfire, which took place at Eastleigh (Southampton) on 5 March 1936. Also, PM631 was scheduled to be at Big Ben at 11:00 as tribute to 11 Group, which had born the brunt of fighter operations during the Battle of Britain and which the BBMF was part of.*
*(11 Group RAF via Paul Day)*

*Devon VP981 in the Flight's hangar shortly after its arrival in 1985. (Duncan Cubitt/FlyPast)*

The Flight's future secure, attention next turned to the aircraft's markings:

No MOD policy has ever been established for the allocation of individual markings to aircraft. Of the seven, six saw war service, but so far as can be established only one of them – a Spitfire Mark II (P 7350) – bears its original wartime markings. The markings of the others have been influenced by their restorers, their donors or their controlling Headquarters. The markings appear to have been selected for sensible commemorative reasons and the basis for the choice is defensible in each case.

The principal objection to changing the present markings is, of course, that changes would be immediately noticed by enthusiasts and publicised. Moreover the presently widely accepted basis of selection would be broken and successive markings would be greeted with acrimony however meticulously they were chosen. The cost of repainting would not be an additional cost if done when repainting was needed, but changes made by this means would be infrequent and thus not a very effective way of honouring others. Out of place repainting would be costly and every change will cause aircraft markings to be at variance with the BBMF illustrated handbook. The cost of changing the markings would be about £1,200 for a Spitfire and £4,000 for the Lancaster. If complete stripping and repainting was involved the costs would be £4,000 and £12,000 respectively.

Conclusion

    a. Leave things as they are.

    b. Changing markings when repainting.

    c. Stick with constant markings, but different from what they are now.

Another review on the way forward for markings set out the following points:

Following the Air Force Board's agreement (AFB 6(77)) to the continued operation of the Battle of Britain Memorial Flight subject to the periodic change of the aircraft markings, I immediately set in hand an examination of the aircraft's refurbishment programme, as well as of possible cheaper forms of markings such as that suggested by CAS. The results of this investigation are set out below.

*Above: Seen during the early 1990s is Spitfire PR.XIX PS853 after its return to flight fitted with a Griffon 58 in the company of Tornado F.3 ZE785 of 226 Operational Conversion Unit, then based at Coningsby. (Geoff Lee/British Aerospace)*

*Left: This is a typical BBMF three-ship air show appearance, with the Hurricane, Lancaster and Spitfire all represented. This formation at the Royal International Air Tattoo at RAF Fairford in July 1996 comprises PZ865, PA474 and P7350. (Duncan Cubitt/FlyPast)*

*Hurricane IIc PZ865 is seen here being refuelled at Coningsby after a sortie. The fuel used is AVGAS 100LL. Nowadays the engines are operated with 100 octane petrol (low lead), whereas towards the end of World War Two and after there was the benefit of ratings up to 150 octane using tetraethyl lead to boost the octane. However, the way that the Flight uses the engines, at only relatively low boost settings (approximately half of what is available), detonation or 'pinking' caused by high boost pressures with low octane fuel is not a problem; the high boosts that were used operationally are not needed to fly the Flight's aircraft for its display and commemorative duties. (Author)*

Taking the suggestion of transfers first, these are used on some aircraft for safety, ground handling and engineering markings. They have also been used in the past for roundels, but this was discontinued several years ago. As the storage life of these transfers is only about one year, the order of quantities for the letters required for squadron markings would be small and the cost would be high. In view of this, the painting of markings is considered more cost-effective.

Turning to the aircraft's refurbishing programme, each aircraft is given a partial repaint at four yearly intervals in conjunction with its Major Servicing. For planning purposes, we allow for touch-up and over-spray of the aircraft's basic finish to the existing pattern and colours, together with renewal of the markings. In practice, the work required on individual aircraft is determined by its state at the time of its Major Servicing; frequently only touching-up is required completely. We try to keep the weight of paint applied to a minimum and are particularly reluctant to respray the Hurricane unnecessarily as each doping softens the fabric and hastens its eventual deterioration.

Provided changing the markings did not involve changing the aircraft's basic colour scheme, it would be regarded as a 'no cost' action when carried out with the partial repaint following a Major. If, however, for reasons of historical accuracy the aircraft's whole paint scheme were to be changed a full repaint would be involved and the extra costs are assessed to be 150 man hours for the Hurricane and Spitfire and 600 man hours for the Lancaster; in cash terms £1,200 and £4,800 at marginal rates.

In view of the above, I suggest that the markings should be changed on the occasion of an aircraft's Major Servicing, which would involve three aircraft every two years. The first change could be made at the end of the current season when two aircraft (one Hurricane and one Spitfire) would be completed. This timing also has the merit of giving sufficient notice for AMP's staff to decide on which individuals and squadrons to honour, as well as for the handbook to be amended.

The new policy for markings soon made its impact when after their winter services of 1977-8 P7350 and PZ865 emerged in two noteworthy new liveries. For the 1978 season 'P7', as the fighter is called by its pilots, was wearing the QV-B code of 19 Squadron – this was the first RAF squadron to receive the Spitfire. Meanwhile PZ865's new paintwork saw it with the 111 Squadron code JU-Q – and that was the unit that first took delivery of the venerable Hurricane.

But while 1978 began on this positive note, a serious accident was to follow later in the year. On 21 August AB910 was just beginning its take-off run at Bex in Switzerland when another aircraft turned onto the runway. The Spitfire V was seriously damaged, though fortunately its pilot escaped unhurt (see Chapter 7 on Spitfires for more details).

During the 1980s the Flight was to gain several more aircraft. At the end of 1975 DHC Chipmunk T.10 WP855 had joined the Flight at RAF Coltishall. It continued to operate with the Flight as the main trainer until 1983, when in April WK518, another Chipmunk, was allotted to the Flight. In mid-1983 WP855 moved to No. 1 Air Experience Flight at RAF Manston in Kent, where it continued to operate until March 1996 when it moved to RAF Newton, Nottinghamshire, to await disposal.

In 1985 the Flight gained DH Devon VP981. Extracts of the case study for its acquisition make interesting reading.

It was announced on 6 February 1984 that the DH Devons operated by 207 Squadron at Northolt, Greater London, were to become available as the unit was to disband on 30 June that year. Discussions indicated that between five to eight of the aircraft would be disposed of by sale to the public, one would go to a museum, one to MOD PE at West Freugh and two for fire-training hulks. It was suggested that there would be considerable merit in having a Devon attached to the Flight when 207 Squadron disbanded, as the advantages would be many. Discussions between HQ Strike Command and OC AEF at RAF Wyton, Cambridgeshire, suggested that the short-term engineering costs would be minimal. OC BBMF advised HQ Strike Command and HQ 11 Group that the Flight would be submitting a case for the retention of a Devon.

*Prior to a sortie, Group Captain Bob Judson adjusts the mirror on 'PZ'. (Author)*

Its benefits were outlined as such:

Airborne Escort and Logistics Support. There were at the time five to six displays a year for which BBMF required airborne support, both for airborne escort or logistic reasons, when the fighters were not accompanied by the Lancaster. In the airborne escort role the Devons at the time had provided navigational assistance over water, in controlled airspace and areas with which the fighter pilots were not familiar.

In the airborne escort role the Devons provided:

1. Navigational assistance in controlled airspace, over water and into areas where pilot navigation is not relatively easy and where the fighter pilots were not familiar with the terrain.

2. A flexible radio fit. The Spitfire and Hurricane had 720 channel VHF radios, however several agencies specified a two radio capability, and more significantly transmission and reception especially in the Hurricane was bad.

3. An IFF/SSR capability.

4. Safety cover over water.

5. Navigation cover in the event of diversion.

6. A reliable instrument platform and lead aircraft in the event of poor weather or being caught in instrument flying conditions.

7. Familiarity with the whole process of Customs, Flight plans and overseas air traffic procedures.

The very presence of the Devon crew would considerably ease the work load and stress on the BBMF display pilots and ultimately ensure safer operation. On land-away sorties

*Devon VP981 near the end of its time with the Flight, seen at Blackpool in 1993. (FlyPast)*

*Inside the Flight hangar on 10 April 2001, with the Dakota outside awaiting flying duties allowing for a clear view of the neatly positioned aircraft. (Author)*

*Multi-theatres represented in 1994, with PZ865 in desert camouflage to the fore, PM631 in South East Asia Command colours next and then the Lancaster in its 9 Squadron 'Johnny Walker' identity as worn by W4964 WS-J while based at Bardney in Lincolnshire. (Duncan Cubitt/FlyPast)*

the fighters have to be serviced by BBMF groundcrew because of the vagaries of the aircraft, so the groundcrew had to be transported in the BBMF Sherpa or by air. Normally the groundcrew would travel in the Lancaster or, if that was not available and a simple single aircraft turn-round service only was required and there was no pressure for the recovery of the fighter, a single member of groundcrew was taken to the venue in the Chipmunk. The latter, however, was not suitable if specialist oils, tools, towing arms or overnight kit was required; on these occasions Devon support was required and up to four BBMF groundcrew could be carried. Airborne ground support frequently permitted a longer detachment over a weekend than could be supported by ground transported personnel. On several occasions spares had been needed from base for aircraft on Category 1 displays and the only method of getting them there was the Devon.

The Devon would also benefit with continuation training. At the time the Lancaster captain received no formal continuation training in the aircraft between April and the end of the display season some 70 flying hours later. Prior to the season he received approximately five hours flying on the Shackleton; this flying being predominantly

*This photo shows an incredible formation out of Coningsby. Nearest the camera is Tornado F.3 ZH552 of 56 Squadron, with LF363 above that in the same unit's markings. The second Tornado is F.3 ZH555 of 5 Squadron, with PZ865 at the rear of the formation wearing an SEAC paint scheme of that unit. (Steve Witty/© Crown Copyright/MOD)*

oriented towards circuits, practice emergencies and some instrument flying. The only other BBMF flying the Lancaster pilot got was some flying in the unit's Chipmunk.

The Lancaster co-pilots were not entitled to any formal continuation training or pre-season Shackleton flying, although this was normally 'found' on a non-interference basis. At the time the three Lancaster co-pilots were all on ground tours, whereas a few years previously they were all full time Handley Page Hastings pilots and the similarity of aircraft type meant that the lack of familiarity with heavy multi-engined aircraft was not so acute.

It was thus considered that a Devon on the BBMF establishment would provide year-round multi-engined flying and would enable all the Lancaster pilots to be fully air-wise and allow the captain to get, and maintain, an instrument rating. The Devon instrumentation was of a compatible era to that of the Lancaster. The aircraft could also be used for the early conversion training of co-pilots as two of the last three volunteers had no multi-piston experience. Several of the fighter pilots also had no piston-engined experience before flying with BBMF, and it was thought that the Devon could be used to show basic engine handling techniques on an engine somewhat more complex than the Chipmunk's.

There would be considerable benefit for the Lancaster navigators too. Most were current navigators on McDonnell Douglas Phantoms which had totally different navigation systems – and because of their operating roles required totally different navigation techniques. It is by no means a simple task to revert to very basic navigation at 150 knots. Again shortage of flying time on the Lancaster precludes any navigation continuation training. The system was for a new navigator to fly one tutorial sortie, one monitored sortie and he was then on his own. In display flying accuracy in transit timing is essential and the small speed range of the aircraft is small, thus the navigator has to be on top of his task. Greater allowances have to be made at the start of the season than later when a 'newcomer' was in practice, and this was wasting precious flying time. A Devon to fly all year round would resolve this problem.

It was also anticipated that any continuation flying done by the Devon could, in part, be tied in with station or group tasks and thus be mutually beneficial and ease the load on whatever communications flight aircraft remain. There were several occasions, for instance, when Phantom crews had to be transported to and from aircraft at Maintenance Units or detachments. Spares too could be carried and aircraft recovery should one divert elsewhere through unserviceability could be simplified somewhat. Crews and spares were sometimes sent by road or rail, taking considerable time and causing a great deal of inconvenience. OC 228 Operational Conversion Unit (OCU) confirmed that he would have a use for a Devon in the above role about once a week. It was assessed that the Devon task for Flight support would be approximately twenty-five hours per year and that a further fifty hours a year would be needed for continuation and training, and it was concluded that this could be largely tied in with station tasks.

The case was strong, and it was consequently recommended that a surplus Devon, with appropriate airframe life and a recently completed minor servicing, be allocated to the Flight to meet the support aircraft requirement and to maintain a limited communication facility. VP981 joined the Flight in April 1985.

An 'old friend' was to rejoin the Flight in 1987. Rebuilt to airworthy condition by British Aerospace at Salmesbury, Lancashire, PS915 was generously gifted to the Flight. Its first post rebuild flight was carried out by Squadron Leader Paul Day out of Warton, Lancashire, on 16 December 1986. Movement back to the Flight occurred on 7 April 1987. Almost thirty years after being delivered to Biggin Hill in poor order by Wing Commander Peter Thompson, 'PS' had returned 'home' in pristine condition to once again take up its rightful place with the Flight and increase its fighter strength to seven.

The next major event in the Flight's history was somewhat less fortunate than the

*A typical year will see the Flight's pre-season work-up well under way during March, with PA474 having usually flown its first air test of the year sometime around the middle of the month. Any minor 'snags' arising during the test flight are rectified soon afterwards. The Air Officer Commanding's Public Display Approval check is then generally scheduled for mid to late April, when the Flight carries out its display routines for each type. Once happy with this the AOC will then give the Flight the necessary authorisation for the season's displays. All being well the Flight will usually begin making public appearances during late April, and traditionally finish the scheduled events during late September. During the AOC's PDA practice day on 25 April 2005, a three-ship formation comprising PA474, P7350 and PZ865 was photographed taxiing out at Coningsby for take-off. (Author)*

*Above: AB910 and LF363 close in on the Lancaster in dramatic style. (RAF Coningsby/© Crown Copyright/MOD)*

*After displaying at Biggin Hill on 8 June 2003, Wing Commander Paul Willis is seen having just taxied Spitfire Vb AB910 up to the temporary BBMF hangar at Barkston Heath. This was the first day of the Flight's temporary relocation to this airfield for the 2003 flying season, as Coningsby's runway was refurbished in readiness for the RAF's new Eurofighter Typhoons. Note the RAF Police dog handler – regular patrols were stepped up while the Flight's aircraft were on site. (Author)*

gaining of the lovely Devon and one of its founding Spitfire PR.XIXs. In September 1991 Hurricane LF363 suffered a major accident while attempting to land at RAF Wittering after an engine failure *en route* to Jersey. This put it out of service for seven years as it had been destroyed by fire and needed a major rebuild (see Chapter 6 on Hurricanes for more details).

During 1993 another review of the Flight was also carried out. But a statement put out by RAF Strike Command was felt necessary to be given ahead of the review's findings as rumours were rife in the media: 'Battle of Britain Memorial Flight is an important part of the nation's heritage. It is a memorial to the sacrifice of airmen past and present and brings many thousands of the public pleasure each year. These factors will have an important bearing on the outcome of the review underway.'

Also in 1993 the Flight was to gain another aircraft, as on 20 July Douglas Dakota III ZA947 arrived. Not only would the Dakota be an ideal training aircraft to keep the Lancaster crews current on multi-engine tailwheel types and as a transport and support ship, but it would offer the Flight a new display aircraft in its own right. It also arrived at a good time, as the following year would mark the fiftieth anniversary of the Arnhem airborne forces operations and the Dakota would be in high demand to commemorate this.

When ZA947 joined the Flight though, the Devon's role became superfluous and the aircraft was put into storage at Coningsby. After being later put up for sale, VP981 was acquired by the Air Atlantique Historic Flight and ferried to Coventry. The Devon joined Air Atlantique Historic Flight's 'all-British' fleet of Avro Anson C.21 WD413 (G-VROE), DH Dragon Rapide G-AIDL, Percival Prentice VR259 (G-APJB) and SAL Twin Pioneer XT610 (G-APRS). It is still there wearing an RAF Transport Command colour scheme.

*The Flight's three founder Spitfire PR.XIXs make a return flight over Biggin Hill to celebrate the BBMF's fortieth anniversary in 1997. Leading is PS853, with PS915 nearest the camera and PM631 furthest away. (Duncan Cubitt/FlyPast)*

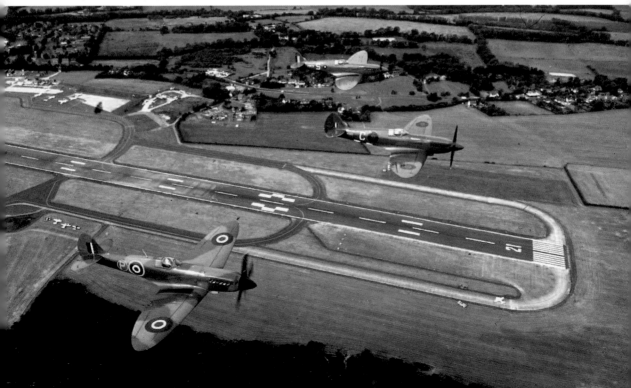

*OC BBMF Squadron Leader Paul Day (standing left) and Squadron Leader 'Shiney' Simmons observe a new BBMF pilot's first display practice from the RAF Coningsby control tower in April 2002. (Author)*

Another aircraft was lost to the Flight in 1994, though this was to be a more emotional and controversial departure. To raise capital for the restoration of LF363, it was decided to sell Spitfire PR.XIX PS853. The arguments to rebuild 'LF' were strong; not only had it been in continuous RAF service since 1944, but it was also a founder member of the Flight. However, the cost of its rebuild could not dip into the public purse. Therefore it was reluctantly decided to put up one of the Flight's more numerous Spitfires for tender, and with the funding plans made earlier in the year, the MOD had invited tenders from civilian companies to carry out the considerable restoration work. The contract was won by Historic Flying Ltd, a highly respected warbird company especially well-known at the time for its Spitfire restorations. The sad remains of 'LF' went to Historic Flying's workshop at Audley End in Essex in September 1994.

News of the Spitfire being offered for sale caused some controversy. Much of the objection had been raised by a councillor who wrote to the Prime Minister and also had correspondence with MPs and the Department of National Heritage. The sale made headlines in the national papers, some of which carried the title 'Battle of the Spitfire'.

PS853 was entered into a Sotherby's auction on 26 November 1994. For the second time this founder member of the Flight had been lost from its charge, and this time it wasn't to return. It raised £410,000 at the auction, though the original sale eventually fell through. It was subsequently purchased by Euan English and moved to one of its old haunts in the shape of North Weald. The Spitfire was delivered to North Weald on 17 February 1995. Sadly, before he had the chance to fly the Spitfire its new owner was killed in a tragic flying accident in his Harvard.

In 1995 the Flight was to gain a second Chipmunk. Having formerly served in an 'operational' role at Gatow, Berlin, during the Cold War, WG486 was delivered to the Flight in June 1995. Having two Chipmunks on strength would allow for more availability of the classic trainers when one was unserviceable or undergoing maintenance.

In November 1997 there was a major addition to Flight's inventory, when the BBMF took delivery of a newly restored Spitfire. Incredible enough already, this had the additional and significant benefit of adding a fresh mark of R J Mitchell's famous design to its fleet.

Spitfire LF.IXe MK356 had been restored to flying condition by technicians at RAF St Athan in Wales, and the fighter made its first flight since 1945 on 7 November 1997 in the hands of the then Officer Commanding, Squadron Leader Paul Day OBE AFC. Following the air test some minor adjustments were carried out and completed by the next Friday, and the 'Major' subsequently flew the aircraft to its new home at Coningsby on 14 November.

This was the first time in the Flight's history that a Spitfire IX had been on its 'flying strength' and the addition of this new airframe gave the BBMF a wonderful collection

*For the first time in many years, during the 2004 display season the Flight revived its splendid Hurricane/Spitfire synchro routine at some air shows, which offered a different sight to the more familiar consecutive solo displays. Here Spitfire IX MK356 and Hurricane IIc PZ865 are caught during a pass on the Sunday of the Waddington International Air Display on 27 June that year. MK356 and Spitfire PR.XIX PS915 carried out a Spitfire synchro routine on both days of that year's Flying Legends at Duxford on 10 and 11 July. Afterwards the massive crowd burst into a spontaneous round of applause in appreciation of this spectacular sight. (Steve Fletcher/FlyPast)*

*PM631 and MK356 taxi away from the BBMF pan for a Spitfire synchro display practice as the three-ship formation comes in for a flypast during the AOC's Public Display Approval practice on 25 April 2005. (Author)*

*Viewed from the tail gunner's turret is Hurricane IIc PZ865 (centre) and four Spitfires (from left to right: LF.IXe MK356, Mk.IIa P7350, Mk.Vb AB910 and PR.XIX PS915) caught flying over the BBMF hangar at Coningsby in September 2004. (JT Chris Elcock/© Crown Copyright/MOD)*

representing the type's evolution and major marks – IIa, Vb, IXe and PR.XIX. MK356 came with fine provenance – it had flown during the D-Day period in June 1944 supporting the invasion of occupied France.

After a comprehensive four-year rebuild, 'LF' flew for the first time in seven years on 29 September 1998 and was returned to the Flight. OC BBMF Squadron Leader Paul Day was the Hurricane's pilot, and after a scheduled landing at Cambridge Airport the fighter returned to Coningsby at 17:30 – looking somewhat different to when it had left four years previously!

In January 2001 the BBMF took delivery of two Spitfire Mk.XVIs – TB382 and TE311 – which had been placed on the Flight's strength following many years with the RAF's recruitment 'road show'. The brace of Mk.XVIs had previously been stored in one of Coningsby's hardened aircraft shelters since October 1999.

Their Rolls-Royce Merlins were soon removed and one was refurbished for use in another Flight aircraft. This fitted ideally with the intention to use the two Mk.XVIs for spares reclamation where necessary to keep the Flight's other charges airworthy. Facing fairly uncertain futures, TB382 and TE311 were structurally examined. While TB382's skin was in poor condition, TE311's bodywork was in remarkably good shape. The poor condition of TB382 meant that it was dismantled for spares and struck-off charge.

TE311 was initially retained as a spares recovery programme, but work to restore the fuselage as a 'spare' began in October 2001. It was, however, required to be carried out at no cost to the MOD. This resulted in the two technicians principally responsible for the project, Chief Technician Paul Blackah and Corporal Andy Bale, carrying out the work in their spare time. Generous help has also been given to the project by several companies and other BBMF engineers along the way. Because of the standard and extent of the work carried out, official approval was granted to complete a full restoration to flying condition (see Chapter 7 on Spitfires for more details).

For the 2003 flying season, the Flight's aircraft had temporarily to relocate from Coningsby to Barkston Heath, Lincolnshire. The move was necessary due to the impending refurbishment of Coningsby's runway in readiness for the Eurofighter Typhoon, a move that in RAF parlance is called a 'Bolthole'. The Flight's first choice of the three possible bases in a shortlist was to move to Waddington, especially so as it would keep them within Strike Command, which would have made matters far simpler. However, the base could not accommodate them. They then looked at Scampton, Lincolnshire, but the available hangar there was in poor condition and would have needed a great deal of refurbishment, plus the airfield was effectively too large for the Flight's operations – for example, the Spitfires may have had overheating problems whilst taxiing about.

It was consequently decided that Barkston Heath, approximately 25 miles away from Coningsby, offered the best facilities. By the time the aircraft arrived the airfield had three runways in use, and the hangar available to the Flight was in good condition and needed only minor work to ready it. This included the provision of a tie-down point for running up the fighters on the ground.

Barkston Heath was mostly civilian-manned, so the Flight had to take RAF air traffic controllers and fire crews with them to make the operation viable. Only the aircraft went to Barkston Heath though, as the hangar used was just large enough to house them with no available space for other facilities. BBMF Ops, administration and maintenance

*Accompanied by a Spitfire on each side, the BBMF Lancaster carries out its D-Day sixtieth anniversary poppy drop over the MV* Van Gogh *on 5 June 2004. (© Crown Copyright/MOD)*

remained on site at the Coningsby HQ.

During early June the Flight's aircraft began their temporary relocation to Barkston Heath, just north-east of Grantham. First to arrive at the airfield was Hurricane PZ865 and Spitfire IIa P7350, which made the move on 8 June. These were joined later the same day by Lancaster I PA474 and Spitfire Vb AB910, both arriving directly after displaying at the Biggin Hill International Air Fair that weekend (Hurricane LF363 temporarily remained at Biggin Hill with a technical problem). The Flight's other aircraft arrived at Barkston Heath the following week, though Dakota III ZA947 remained at Coningsby awaiting the arrival of a replacement engine from the USA. Also, one of the Flight's Chipmunks remained on site at Coningsby to operate from

*As well as continual tireless efforts both in and out of the flying season carrying out scheduled maintenance, the dedicated BBMF ground crew are always there to deal with minor snags that can happen at any point. Here Corporal Andy Bale hands Chief Technician Paul Blackah (far left) the necessary tool to deal with a problem that arose shortly before a sortie with PS915. Chief Technician Keith Brenchley inspects the canopy. (Author)*

*BBMF aircraft don't just turn up on time at a scheduled venue by chance. This is a typical pre-sortie briefing led by Lancaster Captain Flight Lieutenant Ed Straw (centre) in August 2006. OC BBMF Squadron Leader Al Pinner is seen left, and Navigation Leader Squadron Leader Jeff Hesketh is pictured right complete with map in hand. All involved in the sortie will be present in the BBMF Briefing Room for this, and every aspect will be discussed, so that everyone knows each detail of how the flight will be carried out. And prior to the briefing weeks of planning will have been undertaken, all to make sure the aircraft is exactly where it should be, exactly when it should be. (Author)*

the grass for various Flight purposes. At Barkston Heath the Flight aircraft joined the fleet of Slingsby T-67 Firefly two-seat training aircraft that operate from the airfield.

After spending the majority of the 2003 flying season out-based at Barkston Heath, the Flight's aircraft returned to their permanent home on 5 October. The only aircraft not to return to Coningsby on the day were the Flight's two Spitfire PR.XIXs, with PM631 remaining at Barkston Heath until 8 October and PS915 flying to Duxford, Cambridgeshire, for maintenance and a repaint also on 8 October.

In June 2004, the Flight's part in commemorating the sixtieth anniversary of D-Day was broadcast live on national television. It involved a complex five-day operation, which included the Lancaster, Dakota and Spitfires Vb AB910 and LF.IXe MK356. Of particular note, both these Spitfires actually took part in the D-Day operations – making their role to commemorate the sixtieth anniversary all the more poignant.

On 4 June, the Lancaster and two Spitfires set off from Coningsby to pre-position at Southampton, Hampshire. On the same day the 'Dak' pre-positioned at Lyneham, Wiltshire.

As 5 June dawned, the Lancaster and Spitfires carried out a morning display over Portsmouth Harbour, from where a flotilla of vessels set sail to make their way to

*Arguably the ultimate BBMF three-ship combination, with Lancaster PA474 at the top of the formation, Battle of Britain combat veteran P7350 below it and founder Hurricane LF363 in a Battle of Britain era paint scheme nearest the camera. Current policy for the Flight is to keep P7350 and LF363 in representative Battle of Britain era paint schemes. 'LF' wears a 17 Squadron identity, while 'P7' is outshopped in 603 (City of Edinburgh) Squadron Royal Auxiliary Air Force paintwork. (Geoffrey Lee/Planefocus)*

During 2006 the Flight's Spitfires were in high demand to celebrate the seventieth anniversary of the first flight of the legendary type. Such was the case at the Waddington International Air Display on 27 June, where rather than the traditional three-ship combination two Spitfires were in attendance for the occasion. PR.XIX PS915 and Mk.IIa P7350 join PA474 for a flypast before the Spitfires and Lancaster split to carry out their respective display routines. (Author)

A sight and sound to stir the emotions, as the Lancaster leads four Spitfires and two Hurricanes over Coningsby on 24 September 2006. (Author)

...And the same formation after having passed overhead. (Author)

To celebrate the fiftieth anniversary season, the founding four aircraft of the Flight were reunited in formation. Leading is Squadron Leader Al Pinner in PS915, with Wing Commander Russ Allchorne in PM631 to his starboard and Phil O'Dell in PS853, nowadays very appropriately operated by Rolls-Royce, to his port. At the rear of the three Spitfire XIXs is Squadron Leader Ian Smith in Hurricane LF363. (Author)

Normandy, France, in a symbolic crossing of the Channel. These included cruise ships, historic vessels and multi-national Naval ships. The same morning Dakota III ZA947 headed to Le Havre, France, where the Flight would be based for its 'detachment', ready to load paratroops for a para-drop later in the day.

In the afternoon the Lancaster and Spitfires carried out another display, this time at the air show being held at Sandown on the Isle of Wight. After the display, the three Flight aircraft continued on to carry out the poppy drop over the cruise liner MV *Van Gogh*.

Chartered by the Royal British Legion, the *Van Gogh* had on board some 450 veterans who would take part in a memorial service *en route* to France. As the ship approached the French coast, at 15:00 the Service of Preparation was relayed live on television. The service included a two-minute silence and culminated with wreaths being laid in the Channel from the ship's side. As a finale, at 16:30 PA474, which had the two Spitfires in formation to each side, dropped a staggering one million poppies from its bomb bay alongside the ship.

The poppies were supplied by the Royal British Legion and work to get them in place had taken the BBMF ground crew around a week. Preparations included the requirement to line the Lancaster's bomb bay with a protective sleeving to safeguard the mechanical workings, before the poppies could be loaded – one million, by hand!

On the same afternoon, ZA947 headed a stream of aircraft for a para-drop over Ranville 'DZ' (Drop Zone). On board the BBMF 'Dak' the paratroops were sat in authentic para seats, which had been obtained from the US in time to be fitted for this special occasion. The stream also included RAF Lockheed Hercules transports dropping more paratroops.

There were further appearances by the Flight's aircraft on 6 June, the anniversary day itself. The highlight was the participation of all four of the Flight's aircraft that had been deployed to France in a major flypast by British and French air forces – which included the RAF's Red Arrows – over the main anniversary ceremony at Arromanches. In attendance at this ceremony were seventeen heads of state, including Her Majesty Queen Elizabeth II. There was another flypast involving all four aircraft on 7 June over Sannerville, before the Flight returned to base the following day.

Since its formation the Flight has emerged as one of the world's best-known and most respected collections of historic aircraft. Nowadays the Flight's display aircraft comprise the Lancaster, Dakota, two Hurricanes and five Spitfires. Recent years have additionally seen Spitfire Mk.XVI TE311 undergoing restoration for the Flight.

From the outset in 1957 its aircrew have been volunteers, all of whom nowadays perform primary duties on front-line types such as the BAe Harrier GR.7 (gradually being upgraded to GR.9s), Eurofighter Typhoon F.3 and Boeing E-3D Sentry. The only exception to this is the BBMF's Officer Commanding, who with the additional demands of overseeing operations, administration and engineering, needs to be full time on the Flight. OC BBMF is assisted by a Reserve Officer as Operations Officer/Adjutant and a civilian Administrative Officer.

Early on in the Flight's history the engineers, like the aircrew, made themselves available on a voluntary basis. However, with the expansion of the Flight in the mid-1970s, there was a need for a more formal engineering structure and nowadays the Flight has twenty-five full-time personnel under the control of a Warrant Officer as Engineering Officer, supported by a Chief Technician as Engineering Controller. These personnel handle all aspects of the maintenance of the fleet, not only at Coningsby but also out on the display circuit. The only aspect that is usually contracted out to industry is scheduled major servicing.

For many years after its formation the Flight carried out relatively low-key operations, generally performing around fifty to sixty displays a year up until the mid-1960s. This gradually grew and by 1992 the participations had risen to about 150 per season, which rose further to 200 in 1995 and numbered over 500 appearances for the 1996 season. During the 2002 and 2003 seasons, the Flight amassed an incredible tally of over 600 individual aircraft appearances. At the start of the 2004 season this already impressive commitment had risen to a planned 700-plus individual appearances, with the Flight booked to display at over sixty air shows plus 300 other events – and remember this is with just nine display aircraft! This level of commitments continued unabated for 2005, and during the 2006 season there were more than 760 individual appearances planned on the board! The aircraft's appearances can be at locations throughout the UK mainland and surrounding islands; from Cornwall to Scotland, Jersey and Guernsey, Northern Ireland and occasionally even the near Continent in countries such as France and The Netherlands.

Flying hours are restricted very carefully. The Lancaster can fly no more than 100 hours per season, while the Dakota can fly no more than 200 in any one year. The Spitfires are limited to 180 hours *in total* each season, and that's the total for all five, not each. There is a total of 100 hours imposed on the Hurricanes, and similarly to the Spitfires that allowance is split between the two aircraft.

It is incredible that from such constrained beginnings our nation now has this national treasure offering the public so many appearances by priceless aircraft that helped achieve the freedom we enjoy today. And as for the brave souls who never lived to see the fruits of their endeavour, 'Lest We Forget'…

*Back in the air, LF363 emerged like a 'phoenix from the ashes' in a 56 Squadron paint scheme as US-C. (© Crown Copyright/MOD)*

# CHAPTER 6

# Hurricanes

## LF363

Hawker Hurricane Mk.IIc LF363 is believed to be the last Hurricane to enter service with the RAF, and certainly went on to achieve the longest continual service of its type. It first flew on 1 January 1944, and was delivered to 5 Maintenance Unit at Kemble, Gloucestershire, on the 28th of that month.

The first unit to receive the aircraft was 63 Squadron at Turnhouse, Scotland, which took delivery of LF363 on 30 March 1944. It remained with 63 Squadron for only two months before being transferred to 309 (Polish) Squadron at Drem, Scotland, from 23 May 1944. There it was given the squadron code WC-F. Then, after a return to 63 Squadron on 2 November 1944, the fighter went to 26 Squadron, which was based at Tangmere, Sussex, a few weeks later on 30 November. Before war's end it was with 62 Operational Training Unit at Ouston, Durham. The war over, LF363 was placed on the charge of RAF Middle Wallop in Hampshire from 30 August 1945.

The next entry on LF363's movement card is for 21 June 1947, when the Hurricane is annotated as being 'Presumed Struck-off Charge', but by 14 August the fighter was on the strength of the Fighter Command Communication Squadron at Northolt.

In February 1948 LF363 was with the Station Flight at Thorney Island and in a bit of a sorry state, being classified as U/S (unserviceable) and awaiting spares. Following

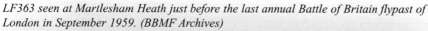
*LF363 seen at Martlesham Heath just before the last annual Battle of Britain flypast of London in September 1959. (BBMF Archives)*

repairs in September 1948 it took part in the Battle of Britain flypast over London. Soon after, LF363 had to force-land at an unknown RAF station somewhere in the London area as a large inspection panel situated just below the cockpit was blown off. It was sent to Hawkers at Langley.

In the summer of 1949 an experienced Hurricane fitter was sent to Langley to make LF363 airworthy ready for a return to Thorney Island, where it would undergo a full refurbishment for Air Commodore Vincent of 11 Group, Fighter Command, to again fly in the annual London flypast that September.

LF363 was not in great shape though, it needed attention in several areas including the oleos, tyres and the batteries, which were flat. The guns and radio had disappeared as had its Form 700 and other documents and it was in need of some major cosmetic attention too. The staff at Hawkers gave the project assistance in every way they could. The oleos, tyres and batteries were all as good as new after some attention, and basic servicing checks were carried out before it was taken out of the hangar for a ground run. The Merlin fired-up at the first attempt.

*Left: 'LF' wearing the markings of Douglas Bader's Hurricane, pictured circa 1974. (BBMF Archives)*

*Below: LF363 breaks away from the camera ship in 1974. (Harry Martin/BBMF Archives)*

*Legendary wartime ace Sir Douglas Bader in the cockpit of LF363, wearing the markings of his fighter during the Battle of Britain, as Lady Bader looks on. (BBMF Archives)*

After various tests had been completed LF363 was ready for the ferry flight back to Thorney Island. On reaching its destination though, the Hurricane's pilot had to carry out a wheels-up landing on the grass beside the runway as he could not get the undercarriage down.

Air Commodore Vincent was determined to have a Hurricane for the Battle of Britain flypast that September and so LF363 was repaired. In just six weeks or so of very hard work the Hurricane was airworthy again. The flypast of London was carried out and 'LF' was proudly applied with an Air Commodore's pendant and the crest of 11 Group.

In May 1950 'LF' was transferred to Flying Training Command (FTC) and later moved to Waterbeach, Cambridgeshire. A year later it was with 61 Group at Kenley. On 10 August another transfer saw the Hurricane at Biggin Hill and a few days later it was recorded as being with 41 Squadron, which was based there at the time flying DH Hornet F.3s.

On 6 November 1951 the fighter moved back to Waterbeach with the Station Flight. In September 1955 LF363 went to Hawkers for a major rebuild. It returned to Biggin Hill resplendent in an all-over silver paint scheme on 10 June 1956 and was placed under the care of the Station Flight, designated as an exhibition aircraft. In June 1957 LF363 became the founder member of the soon-to-be established Historic Aircraft Flight.

Some of LF363's early high-profile events include its participation in a flypast with a Spitfire in 1965 over the interring of Sir Winston Churchill at Bladon. In 1967 LF363, along with the Lancaster and a Spitfire, took part in the ceremony for the closing of Fighter Command at Bentley Priory. Film work has also seen this Hurricane appear in the 1969 aviation classic *Battle of Britain*, with other movie appearances including *Angels One Five* and *Reach for the Sky*.

In its time with the Flight LF363 has worn seven principal paint schemes, not including those applied for film work. While it was wearing all-over silver when first returned to Biggin Hill, by the time the Historic Aircraft Flight was formed in July 1957 the Hurricane had been painted camouflage, though with no squadron codes.

Following its appearance in the film *Battle of Britain*, in April 1969 'LF' was given its first representative identity when it gained the 242 Squadron code LE-D, to portray the Hurricane of Squadron Leader Douglas Bader during the Battle of Britain. Features included a red tip to its spinner and a Squadron Leader pendant on the fuselage underneath the canopy. Its code letters were first painted in a thin style, but for the 1973 season onwards thicker LE-D lettering was applied.

Douglas Bader flew two different Hurricanes while with 242 Squadron at Coltishall and then Duxford; P3061 in which he shot down seven aircraft and V7467 in which he scored 4$^{1}/_{2}$ victories. Years later Sir Douglas Bader was reunited with 'LE-D' courtesy of the Flight's LF363.

Its next scheme was GN-F, representing a Hurricane of 249 (Gold Coast) Squadron, which was in the thick of the Battle of Britain at North Weald, Essex, by 1 September 1940. 'LF' wore this scheme from the 1979 season.

Over the winter of 1982/3 LF363 was repainted into all-over black with the 85 Squadron code VY-X. This was a night-fighter scheme, again from the Battle of Britain period, at which time 85 Squadron was based at Debden, Essex.

NV-L coding was applied in 1987. This gave 'LF' the identity of a 79 Squadron Hurricane, the unit being based at various airfields during the Battle of Britain, including Biggin Hill and Hawkinge.

In readiness for the fiftieth anniversary of the Battle of Britain in 1990, LF363 was repainted to portray Hurricane I P3576 GN-A, which was flown by Flight Lieutenant James Nicolson, Fighter Command's only Victoria Cross winner. This was LF363's second 249 Squadron identity. The scheme was most apt for the year's commemorations, as James Nicolson's bravery in the air was a shining example of the fighter pilots' spirit to defend the country at that time.

It was in this paint scheme that LF363 was to suffer its crash at Wittering on

*A 249 Squadron GN- code has been worn twice by LF363. (Duncan Cubitt/FlyPast)*

*For the 1983 to 1986 seasons LF363 wore an all-over black night-fighter scheme of 85 Squadron. It is seen on its old stamping ground at a North Weald Fighter Meet. (Duncan Cubitt/FlyPast)*

11 September 1991. While *en route* from Coningsby to Jersey in a three-ship formation with the Lancaster and a Spitfire, the Hurricane's engine started running rough. This became so bad that smoke began to pour out of all twelve exhaust stubs, so the pilot, Squadron Leader Allan Martin, called an emergency and attempted to land at the nearest available airfield – Wittering in Cambridgeshire. However, the engine then totally failed and the Hurricane

*The cockpit of LF363. (Author)*

crash-landed on the airfield. Fortunately the pilot escaped, though he did sustain a broken ankle during the landing and suffered minor burns before he could exit clear.

As Squadron Leader Martin later described the incident:

> Shortly after the formation of the Lancaster, Spitfire and myself in the Hurricane entered the RAF Wittering air traffic zone at 2,500 ft, there was an almighty bang and the engine started running roughly. I tried changes of boost and fuel mixture on the engine to try to restore smooth running, and got the best I could, but it was clear that I was not going to be able to maintain height. I immediately headed for RAF

Wittering to try to put the aircraft down.

Right up to the last moment I was confident that I was going to be able to land the Hurricane safely, but in retrospect I must have over estimated the aircraft's height and the engine gave its final cough as I was lining up with the main runway. I'd actually 'changed hands' to select undercarriage down when I felt the right wing drop and realised that I'd stalled the aircraft. I then thought that I'd flip upside down and that would be the end of me and the Hurricane, but as it transpired the aircraft hit the runway and slid backwards down it. I can remember looking down through the Perspex panel in the floor and seeing showers of sparks going down the fuselage.

We came to a halt and the cockpit immediately erupted in flames. Fortunately, the escape hatch on the starboard side of the Hurricane had fallen off with the initial impact and I just unstrapped and legged it over the side.

The Hurricane was quickly turned into a blackened wreck as flames rapidly engulfed it, even though the Wittering fire crews were on the scene immediately. The fire destroyed virtually all the wooden structure of the airframe, and some of the metal too. The situation was worsened by the fact that the Hurricane was heavily laden with fuel as it was flying with full tanks for the long transit to Jersey, and was not far from the beginning of its journey. This accident was the most serious in the Flight's fifty-year history and we can only hope that the likes of it never occurs again.

LF363 was moved back to Coningsby by road in its desperately sad state on 13 September and was then the subject of a board of inquiry. It was subsequently discovered that the cause of the engine failure was a broken camshaft.

The wrecked Hurricane remained in the BBMF hangar for three years while its future was decided. As things turned out no public funding would be made available for its rebuild, so reluctantly PS853 was put up for sale to defray the costs – see Chapter 5 for more details. But on a positive note the rebuild of the Hurricane by Historic Flying Ltd (HFL) at Audley End, Essex, did finally begin three years after its crash. This company

*The sad remains of 'LF' after its crash-landing at Wittering on 11 September 1991. (RAF Wittering/© Crown Copyright/MOD)*

had a proven track record of putting warbirds back into the air, and sure enough 'LF' became airborne again in the autumn of 1998, some seven years since that disastrous day. It returned to RAF Coningsby on 29 September 1998. The Hurricane arrived at HFL in September 1994, with work starting in early 1995 to ascertain just how much of the aircraft's original structure could be used in the restoration. It soon became apparent that relatively little was of use for the rebuild, which can be highlighted by the fact that only six original tubes remain in the fuselage.

The fuselage was then sent to an outside company, Retrotec, for the rebuilding of the tubular structure. The wings and centre section of the Hurricane were rebuilt on site at HFL. Although many drawings were available to help with the construction, others were not, so parts from LF363, and another recovered Hurricane, were used as patterns to replicate new parts. The centre section was one of the most complex areas on the aircraft, housing a great deal of panelling, which fairs on both the wing and undercarriage when retracted.

The biggest job on the centre section was the replacement of the front spar, which meant sourcing a supply of twelve-sided spar tubing – something that only Hawker used in aircraft production. Fortunately, HFL was not the only organisation involved in restoring Hurricanes, and the appropriate tubing was able to be supplied by Hawker Restorations Ltd based in Essex, which had just manufactured a large batch for its own Hurricane projects. Reference was also made to a number of other surviving Hurricanes and it turned out to be a lengthy and very complicated job.

Every steel part on LF363 was cadmium-plated for protection against corrosion and all aluminium parts were anodised. Using modern technology, HFL ensured that LF363 would remain in excellent condition for many years to come.

The aircraft's tailplane was also badly damaged and this was compounded by a modification carried out some years previously to improve the life of the Flight's Hurricanes. The twelve-sided tube had been replaced by a plain tube, as the original had become too corroded for further use. However, this modification had added considerable weight to the rear of the Hurricane, so again with the help of Hawker Restorations, new twelve-sided tubing was installed. The fin and rudder were of almost entirely new construction, with the exception of some parts of the spar and the trim tabs. All of the Hurricane's engine cowlings were destroyed by the fire and replacements had to be fabricated.

During the long rebuild process, the opportunity was taken to return everything on the Hurricane to its original manufacturer's specifications, so parts worn in service were also replaced. The systems team at HFL were responsible for the fitting of the engine and propeller, though these were supplied by the BBMF. During the work the HFL team re-made the myriad of hydraulic, pneumatic and fuel pipes.

The Hurricane's woodwork was replaced by Westley Aircraft. This organisation also recovered the fuselage with the correct grade of Irish linen, while Vintage Fabrics re-covered the flying controls and tailplane.

The new paintwork chosen was very apt, especially considering what the Hurricane had gone through since its accident. It now wore the US-C code of 56 Squadron, which also appropriately was at the time based at Coningsby with its Tornado F.3s. No. 56 Squadron's badge just so happens to feature a phoenix rising from the fire, just as LF363 had done.

After considerable work, LF363 was ready for collection at Audley End on 29 September 1998. OC BBMF at the time, Squadron Leader Paul Day, took the fighter aloft for the first time in seven years, with Allan Martin there to witness the momentous occasion. During the thirty-five-minute flight to Cambridge Airport the 'Major' carried out 75 per cent of the air test, which was adequate to ascertain that the Hurricane was in a fit state to be accepted back into the RAF. On landing at Cambridge, a party of BBMF engineers gave the aircraft a once over, after which Paul flew LF363 back to its home base, carrying out the remainder of its air test *en route* and arriving back at Coningsby at 5:30 pm.

'LF' soon made a very welcome return to the display circuit, when it appeared at Duxford's Autumn Air Day a couple of weeks later on 11 October. Flown by Air Marshal Sir John Allison, the Hurricane was understandably the centre of attention at the air show.

LF363's 56 Squadron identity remained until 2005, when it went for an equalised maintenance programme and repaint by the Aircraft Restoration Company at Duxford, Cambridgeshire, between October that year and March 2006. The company won the contract from the Ministry of Defence under competitive contract rules, having conducted similar work on the Flight's other Hurricane, PZ865, the previous winter.

LF363 emerged in 2006 wearing a new colour scheme faithfully replicating Hurricane I P3878 YB-W of Flying Officer Harold 'Birdy' Bird-Wilson. The story behind LF363's current scheme is a fascinating one, and highlights perfectly the kind of courage and sacrifice that the Flight's aircraft pay tribute to. It is told here by Squadron Leader Clive Rowley who carried out this detailed research:

At the height of the Battle of Britain, 21-year-old Flying Officer Harold 'Birdy' Bird-Wilson was flying his personal aircraft, Hawker Hurricane I P3878 YB-W, leading Green Section as part of a 17 Squadron formation on yet another scramble

*'LF' pictured during its first pre-season engine ground run on 11 March 2003. As a testament to the work of the BBMF engineers, when its engine was fired up for the first time since September the previous year it kicked straight into life and ran sweetly. (Author)*

*Above: LF363 undergoing repairs at Coningsby in January 2005. (Author)*

*Left: A timeless view of LF363 in the skies over England. (Author)*

to engage the raiding enemy formations. It was September 24th 1940.

On this morning the *Luftwaffe* made two major attacks over the Thames Estuary and Kent, one at about 08:30 and the second at about 11:15, with around 200 enemy aircraft involved in each raid. Some fifteen RAF fighter squadrons had been sent up to engage them on the first attack and eighteen scrambled against the second.

The 17 Squadron formation was flying over the Thames Estuary, east of London, near Chatham, and was being vectored under ground control in a stern chase onto some 'bandits'. As the German bomber raid withdrew, the Hurricanes were bounced from above by unseen Messerschmitt Bf 109s of JG26, diving down on them from out of the blue.

Momentary confusion and mayhem ensued and, almost before he could react, 'Birdy's' Hurricane was hit by cannon shells. It was critically damaged and immediately burst into flames. Other pilots in the formation, busy fighting for their own lives, heard him transmit on the radio, 'Mayday, Green 1 on fire,' just before he baled out of his burning cockpit.

The voice of his colleague and friend David Leary was then heard on the R/T: 'He's out. There's a parachute. I'm going to circle him to guard him down.' Unbeknown to him at the time, 'Birdy' had just become the 40th victim of the renowned and high-scoring German fighter ace, Adolf Galland.

Hurricane P3878 plummeted in flames into the water and 'Birdy' parachuted down into the Thames with shrapnel from the guns of Galland's Bf 109 embedded in his body and suffering from burns for the second time in his flying career. Fortunately, he was soon rescued by Royal Navy Motor Torpedo Boat MTB-104 and taken to a hospital in Haywards Heath, Sussex.

Ironically, he was gazetted for the award of the Distinguished Flying Cross on the same day that he was shot down, the citation stating: 'Flying Officer Bird-Wilson has shot down six enemy aircraft and shared in the destruction of several others. He has shown fine fighting qualities and determination in his attacks.'

Affectionately known throughout his career as 'Birdy', Harold Bird-Wilson joined the RAF in 1937, straight from school, being awarded a short-service commission in September 1937. After completing training he commenced his operational career with 17 Squadron at Kenley, Surrey, flying Gloster Gauntlets.

Shortly after joining the squadron, he was sent on a navigation course at Brough, near Hull. While on this, in September 1938, he crashed in a BA Swallow after being caught in bad weather near Cranwell, Lincolnshire. He was fortunate to survive the accident in which the other pilot in the aircraft was killed.

'Birdy' was badly burned and lost his nose. He underwent plastic surgery at the Queen Victoria Hospital, East Grinstead, and was one of the earliest aircrew 'guinea pig' patients of the famous, pioneering plastic surgeon, Sir Archibald McIndoe. For some months 'Birdy' walked around without a nose while McIndoe rebuilt it for him. He became the second member of the famous 'Guinea Pig Club'.

By April 1940, 'Birdy's' face was restored and having regained his fitness he quickly returned to operational flying with 17 Squadron, which by this stage had re-equipped with Hurricanes. In May and June 1940, the squadron was involved in the heavy fighting over the Netherlands and Belgium, deploying to French airfields to cover the retreat of Allied troops from France via Dunkirk, and moving to Brittany in June, as the remnants of British Expeditionary Force and RAF units in France were evacuated.

During this time, 'Birdy' was involved in several combats and shared in the destruction of two enemy aircraft as France was overrun by the Germans. Surviving 17 Squadron aircraft and pilots, including 'Birdy', escaped back to England from Brittany at virtually the last opportunity, operating from the Channel Islands for two days, before they became the only British territory to fall into enemy hands.

Throughout the Battle of Britain 17 Squadron and 'Birdy' flew in action over southern England. Mainly based at Debden in Essex, and Tangmere in Sussex, the unit was heavily involved in the fighting. Unlike many others, 17 Squadron was never rested but fought all the way through the period of the Battle and into November 1940.

In later years 'Birdy' retained vivid memories of attacking formations of more than 100 enemy aircraft as one of a force of only twelve Hurricanes: 'Your throat dried up as you got nearer. I don't believe any man who said he wasn't afraid. We just went ploughing in, picked our target and fought.'

He also said later that he was shocked when the Battle of Britain ended in the autumn of 1940 to realise that: 'There was hardly anybody left of the pilots who started out with me – all one's friends had gone.'

In a photograph of 'Birdy' standing by a Hurricane with other 17 Squadron pilots taken in the summer of 1940, apart from him, all his friends and colleagues in the line-up lost their lives during the war. Three of them (Dennis Wissler, CO Cedric Williams and David Leary) had been killed by the end of 1940 and the fourth (Jack Ross) was killed in November 1942. 'Birdy' was the only one to survive the war and he later said about his feelings during the conflict, 'There was no time for tears, only sorrow and off into the next scramble.'

During the Battle of Britain, 'Birdy' shared several victories against enemy aircraft with other pilots of 17 Squadron and was credited with two personal 'kills' and numerous enemy aircraft 'probably destroyed' or 'damaged'. On Wednesday August 21st 1940, 'Birdy', now a section leader flying as *Green 1*, shot down a Junkers Ju 88 and saw it force land on the very tip of Selsey Bill. After landing he went off to inspect it and returned later with a trophy for the squadron, part of the tailplane, which he nailed up to the B Flight dispersal hut at Tangmere.

The next day he had an emblem painted on the cockpit escape door of P3878 – three vengeful swords flying towards a Nazi eagle and swastika symbol. On the reverse of his own photograph of this cockpit art he wrote 'A logo painted on my Hurricane YB-W at Tangmere during the Battle of Britain August 1940. Thought up at the spur of the moment in the 601 Squadron dispersal hut... scrambled thereafter.'

Like many, many other Hurricanes during the Battle, YB-W's luck was to run out on September 24th 1940, while 'Birdy's just about held. Having been shot down in flames, baled out with shrapnel and burn injuries, and being rescued from the water by an MTB, this was the end of the Battle of Britain for 'Birdy', as it was not until November that he was able to return to flying duties.

This was certainly not the end of the war for this courageous fighter pilot though. By 1941 he was a Flight Commander flying Spitfires with 234 Squadron, and subsequently led 152 and 66 Squadrons, both also equipped with Spitfires. Later he commanded 122 Wing.

After a long and distinguished post-war career, he eventually retired from the RAF in 1974 as an Air Vice Marshal having been awarded the CBE, DSO, DFC* and AFC*. He had flown various jet types and been Commandant of the Central Flying School who endorsed the formation of the Red Arrows as the RAF's official display team. He died in August 2000 at the age of 80.

LF363's current paint scheme is once again a very appropriate choice. No.17 Squadron is currently the 'numberplate' of the Typhoon Operational Evaluation Unit based at RAF Coningsby alongside the BBMF; the unit's Eurofighter Typhoons proudly wearing the mailed gauntlet emblem from the squadron crest. Coningsby is, therefore, home to two types of aircraft operated by 17 Squadron during its history, and separated by over 65

*Hurricane IIc LF363 wearing its new 17 Squadron colour scheme on the return ferry flight from Duxford to its home base at Coningsby on 6 April 2006, flown by OC BBMF Squadron Leader Al Pinner in the company of a 17 Squadron Eurofighter Typhoon flown by Squadron Leader Al Seymour. (Author)*

*The Eurofighter breaks away from LF363 – representing RAF fighter history spanning over sixty-five years! (Author)*

years.

Therefore, when LF363 was to make its ferry flight from Duxford back to Coningsby on April 6 2006 the opportunity was taken to rendezvous with a 17 Squadron Typhoon that would be returning to base at the same time as the Hurricane. The sortie was to comprise a ferry flight to Duxford in the Dakota, which would take the Hurricane's pilot OC BBMF Squadron Leader Al Pinner there to pick up the fighter, then it would act as camera ship for the BBMF to get some air-to-air photos of the new scheme for publicity purposes. The Hurricane was to be joined by the Typhoon at Whittlesey, Cambridgeshire.

Three Typhoons were in the 17 Squadron sortie, therefore although only one was to formate on the Hurricane all three pilots attended the briefing. The plan was for the Dak and Hurricane to transit at 2,000 ft at 140 knots, so the Typhoon pilot who was to take part in the formation, Squadron Leader Al Seymour, was asked if this speed was acceptable. When this formation was first considered, there was some concern that the jet may not be able to maintain the relatively low speed to hold in formation with the Hurricane and would instead have to carry out a gentle overtake. However, its pilot soon made it clear that it wouldn't be a problem.

The Dakota made its way to Duxford and delivered OC BBMF to collect LF363 without a hitch. After take-off from Duxford, all went to plan for Serial 1 of the air-to-air

sortie, which was for the Hurricane to position itself in echelon left of the Dakota and transit to Whittlesey. Serial 2 of the sortie involved a right-hand orbit at Whittlesey awaiting the call from the Typhoon that it was in the area for the 'RV', and then that it had a visual on 'Memorial Flight' as the two BBMF aircraft were callsigned.

Serial 3 involved the Typhoon joining the Hurricane in echelon left outside, where the remarkable 'heritage flight' formation could be recorded in still photography and video footage by BBMF and RAF Coningsby photographers. Once the close formation photographs were 'in the can', the Typhoon pilot called 'Typhoon ready Serial 4.'

Serial 4 involved a formation break of the two fighters, and the call 'Break, break, go' from the Typhoon saw the jet turn and break followed by LF363 once the Typhoon was clear.

The results were a world first formation and one of the most appropriate pairings to pay tribute to the RAF's heritage. When considered, it is simply marvellous that one of the BBMF's founding aircraft, wearing the paintwork of an era that represents a crucial period in the nation's history, found itself involved in such a high profile formation with its modern day equivalent demonstrating the cutting-edge technology of the 21st Century.

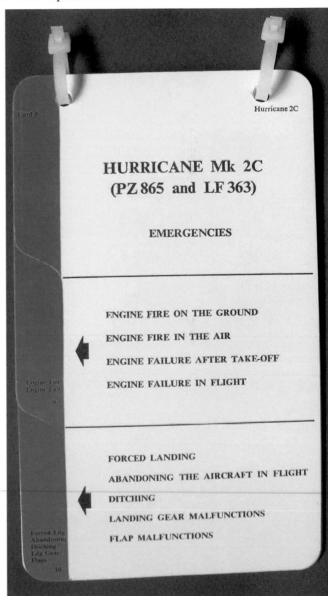

Card 8

Hurricane 2C

# HURRICANE Mk 2C
## (PZ 865 and LF 363)

### EMERGENCIES

ENGINE FIRE ON THE GROUND

ENGINE FIRE IN THE AIR

ENGINE FAILURE AFTER TAKE-OFF

ENGINE FAILURE IN FLIGHT

FORCED LANDING

ABANDONING THE AIRCRAFT IN FLIGHT

DITCHING

LANDING GEAR MALFUNCTIONS

FLAP MALFUNCTIONS

### PZ865 *The Last of the Many!*

Completed at Hawker's factory at Langley, Buckinghamshire, on 27 July 1944, Mk.IIc PZ865 was the last of the more than 14,500 Hurricanes that had been built. To mark this, the fighter had The Last of the Many! adorned on both sides of its fuselage, just aft of the cockpit.

PZ865 was rolled out bedecked with banners listing notable campaigns during the type's service career – including the Battle of France, Dunkirk, Battle of Britain, Malta, Africa, Burma, Italy and Normandy. The fighter then carried out its maiden flight in the hands of Hawker's chief test pilot, Group Captain P W S 'George' Bulman, who had flown prototype Hurricane K5083 for its first flight on 6 November 1935.

The last-built example didn't see squadron service; at the time there were more than enough Hurricanes to see the RAF through to war's end. Instead, it was bought back from the Air Ministry and used by Hawker as a communications and test aircraft.

On 1 May 1950, the fighter was placed onto the civil register as G-AMAU. With its weapons removed, it was repainted into an overall royal blue paint scheme, complete with gold trim. It went on to participate in a number of air races, including the 1950 King's Cup – sponsored by HRH Princess Margaret – and was flown into second place by Battle of Britain veteran Group Captain Peter Townsend.

The Hurricane later appeared in the well-known 1952 film *Angels One-Five*, for which it was painted back into military colours wearing the serial number P2619 and the code US-B to represent an aircraft of 56 Squadron. In 1960 Hawker decided to refurbish PZ865 and on completion of this work it reappeared in military colours, wearing its RAF serial number with its civil registration tucked away underneath the tailplane.

Next the Hurricane was employed at Dunsfold as a chase plane, initially for Hawker

*PZ865, the last Hurricane built, is seen carrying out a flypast over the British Aerospace factory at Weybridge (Brooklands), Surrey, in 1985 to mark the fiftieth anniversary of prototype Hurricane K5083's first flight on 6 November 1935 at Brooklands, when it was piloted by Flight Lieutenant P W S 'George' Bulman. (British Aerospace)*

*'PZ' was photographed in 1974 wearing the DT-A code of the 257 (Burma) Squadron Hurricane of Squadron Leader R R Stanford-Tuck during the Battle of Britain. (BBMF Archives)*

Sea Fury T.20S target-tug trials and later for the Hawker Siddeley P.1127 prototype; forerunner of the Harrier 'jump jet'. The Hurricane's low-speed envelope was found to be ideal for monitoring the P.1127 during its transition between conventional flight and jet-borne lift.

PZ865's next cosmetic makeover was for another movie appearance, this time the 1969 classic *Battle of Britain*. As one of the airworthy Hurricanes in the film, PZ865 was given various identities, including 'OK-1' to portray the personal aircraft of AOC 11 Group Air Vice-Marshal Sir Keith Park.

A period of static display at Dunsfold as part of the company's unofficial 'museum' collection followed, before the Hurricane was restored back to flying trim in 1971. Hawker presented the fighter to the Battle of Britain Memorial Flight on 30 March 1972 while it was based at Coltishall, Norfolk.

During its career with the Flight to date, PZ865 has worn seven schemes. It was delivered in its *The Last of the Many!* scheme, but a few months later this was replaced with the identity of Hurricane I V6962 DT-A, which was the aircraft of the then Squadron Leader Robert Stanford-Tuck, OC 257 (Burma) Squadron, while based at Debden during the late summer of 1940.

[Personal note: The Author feels privileged to have met Robert Stanford-Tuck during an Air Training Corps summer camp to RAF Manston in 1982. The occasion was a visit to the then newly opened Spitfire Memorial Building, and who better to show a group of keen aviation-minded cadets around a Spitfire than a legendary wartime fighter ace such as this! JC]

This paint scheme saw the Hurricane applied with a black underside on its left wing.

*Rare colour photo of PZ865 in its 111 Squadron JU-Q paint scheme, which it wore from 1978 to 1981. This identity was chosen as 111 was the first RAF squadron to operate the Hurricane. Note the early-style half black, half white (port and starboard respectively) undersides.*
*(BBMF Archives)*

Stanford-Tuck's Hurricane was unusual to have retained this early war paintwork at that stage. The scheme was retained until the end of the 1977 season, when PZ865 went for its next major service.

PZ865's next paint scheme saw it emerge for the 1978 season wearing the code JU-Q to represent an aircraft of 111 Squadron. This was the first RAF squadron to receive the Hurricane, and PZ865's new paintwork featured early war half-black, half-white undersides (port and starboard respectively), though this time extending all the way from the nose to tail.

*'PZ' wearing its 303 (Polish) Squadron RF-U markings of the early 1980s.*
*(Duncan Cubitt/FlyPast)*

*Unusual high-angle view of* The Last of the Many! *undergoing maintenance at Coningsby in 1985. (Duncan Cubitt/FlyPast)*

For the 1982 season 'PZ' was returned to its familiar *The Last of the Many!* identity, which it kept until 1988. For the 1989 season it gained the identity of Hurricane I P3975 RF-U, the 303 (Polish) Squadron mount of Sergeant Josef Frantisek. This pilot claimed seventeen victories in the month of September 1940, but he was killed on 8 October in a different Hurricane, which crashed while landing at Northolt. Sgt Frantisek, who was actually Czech, was the highest scoring pilot during the Battle of Britain, and thus this scheme had been chosen as being appropriate for the following year's fiftieth anniversary commemorations.

*In 1993 'PZ' took on the identity of 261 Squadron's Hurricane I P3731 J in desert paintwork, representing one of the first twelve Hurricanes delivered to Malta in September 1940. (Duncan Cubitt/FlyPast)*

Initially the aircraft had Czech insignia below the canopy and a red spinner. However, this caused some debate amongst Polish veterans and it was later changed to feature a 303 Squadron badge positioned high on the fuselage, in line underneath the aerial mast. It was also given red and white Polish 'chessboards' on the forward lower engine cowlings.

Next, for the start of the 1993 flying season, 'PZ' took on the totally different identity of 261 Squadron's Mk.I P3731 J in desert paintwork, one of the first twelve Hurricanes delivered to Malta on board the carrier HMS *Argus* as part of Operation *Hurry* in September 1940. It was while in this paint scheme that the aircraft was also refitted with 20-mm Hispano cannon on its wings, giving it the appearance of a desert 'tank buster'.

Following a major servicing over the winter of 1997/8, 'PZ' emerged in the colours of a 5 Squadron aircraft from the unit's time in South East Asia Command, coded Q. At the

*There's no mistaking the ownership of this set of chocks while the 'Hurri' was out on a sortie! (Author)*

*From the 'desert' to the 'jungle', as in 1998 'PZ' emerged in the colours of a 5 Squadron aircraft from the unit's time in South East Asia Command. (Neil Clegg/© Crown Copyright/MOD)*

time this new paintwork was applied 5 Squadron was based at Coningsby, and with LF363 in 56 Squadron markings, both of the Flight's Hurricanes were wearing markings of Tornado F.3 units then based at their home airfield.

PZ865's current scheme was applied after its six-yearly major service, an equalised maintenance programme and repaint conducted by the Aircraft Restoration Company (ARC) at Duxford, Cambridgeshire. This work was carried out between October 2004 and March 2005, and the aircraft underwent a deep-strip maintenance inspection and subsequent rectification work in ARC's dedicated hangar at the eastern edge of the Imperial War Museum airfield. As is the way of the world nowadays, the company won the contract from the Ministry of Defence under competitive contract rules.

ARC had previously serviced two of the Flight's Spitfires (AB910 and PS915), but this was the first RAF Hurricane to receive the company's attention. During the servicing programme, and as well as the scheduled maintenance, 'PZ' received new control cables and was fitted with a brand-new radiator.

The latest scheme represents Hurricane IIc BE581 JX-E *Night Reaper*, as it is believed to have appeared during 1 Squadron's night intruder operations when flown by Flight Lieutenant Karel Kuttelwascher DFC*. Squadron Leader Clive Rowley again tells the fascinating story behind the scheme (with historical information having been sourced with permission from the now out of print book *Night Hawk* by Roger Darlington):

Karel Miloslav Kuttelwascher, 'Kut' or 'Old Kuttel' as he was known to his wartime colleagues, was born in September 1916 in a town now called Havlickuv Brod in what is now the Czech Republic. He joined the Czechoslovakian Air Force when he was eighteen and had clocked up some 2200 flying hours before the

Germans occupied his homeland in 1939 and disbanded the armed forces. Three months after the invasion, 'Kut' made a daring escape from Czechoslovakia into Poland, hiding in a coal train.

Together with other Czechoslovak pilots, he was able to make his way from Poland to France where he was initially drafted into the Foreign Legion to await the imminent outbreak of war. When the war came he was re-drafted into the French Air Force and flew Morane-Sauliner MS.406 and Dewoitine D.520 fighters during the brief but fierce Battle of France, claiming a number of German aircraft.

*Coningsby Station Commander Group Captain Bob Judson carrying out his pre-flight walk-around checks prior to a sortie in PZ865. (Author)*

When France fell, 'Kut' managed to escape to Britain via Algeria and Morocco. He immediately joined the beleaguered RAF and was quickly posted to join 1 Squadron RAF, just in time to earn his place as one of 'The Few' during the Battle of Britain, thereby becoming one of the eighty-seven Czechoslovaks to fly with the RAF during the Battle.

'Kut' served a full two years with 1 Squadron. During the early 'Circus' operations in 1941, he shot down three Messerschmitt Bf 109s and was credited

*OC Ops at Coningsby, Wing Commander Russ Allchorne, is marshalled out for a sortie in 'PZ' by Junior Technician Rachel Warnes. (Author)*

*PZ865 is resplendent in its brand-new coat of paint en route from Duxford back to its Coningsby home on 5 April 2005, flown by then OC BBMF Squadron Leader Clive Rowley. PZ865 wears* Night Reaper *nose-art on its starboard side, as applied to BE581 of Flight Lieutenant Karel Kuttelwascher DFC. (Keith Brenchley/© Crown Copyright/MOD)*

*Group Captain Bob Judson looks to his ground crew for start-up clearance. (Author)*

with another as a 'probable', but his score would not remain at three.

In July 1941, 1 Squadron moved to Tangmere, three miles east of Chichester, and it was from here that they commenced night intruder operations on 1 April 1942. 'Kut's' experience and skill, plus his total professionalism and dedication to his craft, not to mention a burning determination and commitment to shoot down as many *Luftwaffe* aircraft as possible, then came to the fore.

Night intruder operations required a pilot with cunning, cool nerves and good eyesight, and the ability to capitalise on a chance that would last only seconds and turn it into a 'kill'. The single-seat Hurricanes were not radar-equipped, so targets could only be found visually. The pilots flew long sorties of 3 to $3^{1}/_{2}$ hours (with long-range drop tanks fitted), often in poor conditions and completely alone.

At 23:40 on 4 May 1942, Flight Lieutenant Karel Kuttelwascher DFC* lifted his fuel-laden Hurricane IIc BE581 into the night skies from Tangmere, Sussex, and headed south across the Channel. He crossed the French coast south of Fecamp at an altitude of 2000 ft.

Three searchlights sprang into life from the vicinity of the town and probed the night sky around his aircraft. But, much to his relief, when he flashed his navigation lights on and off twice, the searchlights were doused, those manning them clearly assuming that he was friendly. Nothing could have been further from the truth.

There was a slight haze and some cloud to the east, but otherwise the visibility over France was good that night. Below the canopy of stars, 'Kut' made for his chosen patrol area, the German airfield at Evreux, about 70 miles inland.

On reaching the area he orbited for ten minutes, but he could see neither lights nor any activity. Disappointed, he flew on a little further south to St Andre-de-l'Eure, where he had shot down a Dornier bomber less than three weeks earlier.

Reaching St Andre at 00:50, he circled the blacked-out base for ten minutes. Suddenly, the airfield lit up with a double flare path east to west and there, ready to land from a bombing mission over England, were no fewer than six enemy aircraft.

All were showing white tail lights and he was able to identify them by their silhouettes as Heinkel bombers, their crews no doubt relieved to be in sight of the sanctuary of their home base after a successful raid on Cowes on the Isle of Wight. They were circling at 1500 to 2000 ft, making ready to land. For two minutes 'Kut' circled outside their orbit like a lion stalking its prey, carefully positioning himself for a kill.

When the moment was right, he brought his Hurricane in behind one of the Germans, about 100 yards dead astern and slightly below; he took precise aim and fired a two-second burst of his cannon. The effect of such a well-aimed, close-range onslaught was devastating.

Four streams of 20-mm cannon shells converged in a cone of destruction on his aiming point, the starboard engine of the Heinkel, which immediately caught fire. The bomber twisted and dived into the ground north-east of the airfield, spreading flaming wreckage as it impacted.

Immediately, he was able to position behind another target and to repeat the tactic. A one-second burst of uncompromising accuracy caused that Heinkel also to plunge earthwards, flickering flames consuming it as it crashed into a wood east of the airfield.

Astonishingly, the remaining four German crews still seemed to be unaware of his presence so, quickly pressing home his advantage, 'Kut' lined up behind yet another Heinkel.

Ruthlessly, he fired a two-second burst from dead astern and saw his shells slam into the target. The enemy aircraft dived steeply down from 1500 ft, but then he lost sight of it, so was unsure whether he had secured a third 'kill'.

Thirty seconds later, as he swung round in a turn, he saw three separate fires burning on the ground, the lurid flames licking the black night. There could be no doubt about it; three German bombers had been destroyed in less than four minutes. He had used only 200 rounds of ammunition and he had certainly made them count.

At this point, the airfield lighting went out and anti-aircraft fire started. 'Kut' later told a BBC radio interviewer: 'They opened all the anti-aircraft fire on me and I had to fly through it. It was like going through hell.'

He had no choice but to depart this malevolent environment. The time was 01:05; he had been over the airfield for only fifteen minutes but had done enormous damage.

Despite this success, he did not head straight for home; he still had fuel and ammunition remaining with which to fight. 'Kut' headed for another enemy airfield at Dreux, but could find no activity there. So, at last, he turned north for home.

North of Dreux, four searchlights illuminated him. He tried to repeat his earlier technique and flashed his navigation lights, but this time it did not work. The searchlights remained on him, so he had to dive steeply and to one side before he managed to shake them off.

'Kut' then flew the long and lonely return crossing of the Channel at 3000 ft, listening to every beat of his Merlin engine, all that stood between him and an almost-certain watery death. At 02:05, almost three hours after leaving his base, he touched down on the Tangmere flare path, tired but elated, to report his astonishing achievement.

'Kut' flew all his night intruder sorties in Hurricane IIc BE581. For at least some of this period the aircraft retained its standard grey/green camouflage, while the underside was painted black. The squadron and aircraft code JX-E was painted in red as was the spinner and the aircraft wore an emblem on the starboard side of the engine cowling, depicting a scythe in yellow and across it a banner in red carrying the name *Night Reaper*.

A more appropriate name would be difficult to imagine as, in a brief three-month period, 'Kut' shot down fifteen enemy bombers over their own bases in France and damaged a further five, earning himself a Distinguished Flying Cross and bar in the process, and all this in only fifteen night missions. 'Kut' also shot up several German E-boats and steam locomotives on nights when he had ammunition to spare on the way home.

Quite remarkably, the rest of his war was relatively uneventful; while flying DH Mosquito night intruders he never even sighted another German aircraft. At the end of the war, 'Kut' returned briefly to Czechoslovakia. But, in 1946, on the day that the communists effectively took control of his homeland, he flew back to Britain where he became a Captain with British European Airways. His premature death occurred in August 1959 after a heart attack – he was only forty-two.

Since the beginning of the 2005 display season, PZ865 has been painted in the colour scheme believed to have been worn by 'Kut's BE581 JX-E, during the early stages of 1 Squadron's night intruder operations. The scheme includes the *Night Reaper* nose-art on its starboard engine cowling, reflecting his acute sense of vengeance, and has eleven swastika 'kill' symbols under the cockpit on the port side as it would have appeared on the day after his triple-kill sortie.

The camouflage is European grey/green on top with black undersides. The rudder and a panel on the port wing are painted black as these were replacement components from a 'Turbinlite' Flight Hurricane, BD770, fitted to replace flak-damaged parts.

The aircraft serves as a living and flying memorial, commemorating a dangerous and productive period in 1 Squadron's history (twenty-two enemy aircraft destroyed and thirteen damaged) and as a tribute to the remarkable courage and effectiveness of one of the many Czechoslovakian fighter pilots who served so valiantly with the RAF during World War Two.

# CHAPTER 7

# Spitfires

### Mk.IIa P7350

P7350 can perhaps be described as the pinnacle of the Flight's fighter fleet, having actually seen combat during the Battle of Britain. This wonderful aircraft is the oldest airworthy Spitfire in the world, and the only example of its type still flying to have fought in the Battle of Britain.

It is believed to be the fourteenth aircraft of the 11,989 built at Castle Bromwich, Warwickshire. On 18 August 1940 it was issued to 6 Maintenance Unit at Brize Norton, Oxfordshire, for its pre-service inspection. On 6 September 1940 it was issued to 266 'Rhodesia' Squadron at Wittering. On 17 October, when 266 'Rhodesia' Squadron reverted to Mk.Is, it was ferried with several other Mk.IIs to 603 (City of Edinburgh) Squadron at Hornchurch, Essex. On 25 October 1940, while being flown by Polish Pilot Officer Ludwig Martel, 'P7' was shot down.

Having been 'scrambled', the pilots received a warning that enemy aircraft were very

*Left: The distinctive air-sea rescue representation of 277 Squadron's* The Old Lady *is worn here as 'P7' comes in to land at Duxford during 1997. (Duncan Cubitt/FlyPast)*

*Below: P7350 as 41 Squadron's* Observer Corps *seen at the Great Warbirds Air Display at North Weald in 1985 along with PZ865* The Last of the Many!*(Duncan Cubitt/FlyPast)*

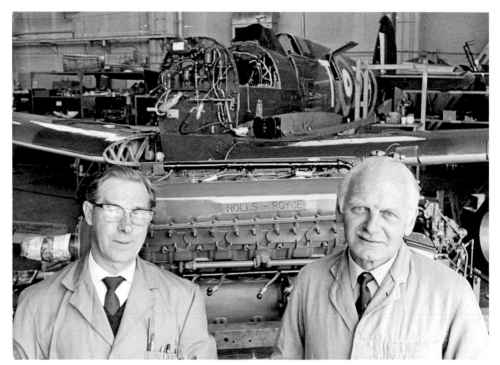

*In April 1969 'P7' was issued to 5 Maintenance Unit, Kemble, Gloucestershire, for overhaul and respray. Painted in 266 Squadron colours as ZH-T, it returned to Coltishall on 12 June. It is seen at Kemble behind two gentlemen who were working on it. (BBMF Archives)*

close. Moments later, a message was relayed letting the pilots know that their opposition was on top of them. As that message was received, Messerschmitt Bf 109s descended from above firing at the Spitfires. Four 'Spits' were immediately hit and shot down, P7350 being amongst them.

It had been hit on the port side, and there were holes in the port wing. Pilot Officer Martel had been injured too, and with his aircraft damaged it was difficult to control while he was in pain. Ludwig managed to nurse 'P7' back down to low altitude and found an open field near Hastings that was suitable for a wheels-up landing.

The Polish pilot was soon approached by some British soldiers, who were at first very suspicious of him because of his accent. However, once they saw the Polish insignia on his uniform all became clear.

P7350 was quickly repaired at 1 Civilian Repair Unit, Cowley, Oxfordshire, and flew again within weeks of being shot down. The repaired bullet holes can still be seen on the Spitfire's port wing. The fighter subsequently served operationally with 616 and 64 Squadrons. At the end of April 1942 it was relegated to support duties, including a period of service with the Central Gunnery School at Sutton Bridge, Lincolnshire. Its wartime duties over, on 24 July 1944 'P7' was issued to 39 Maintenance Unit, Colerne, Wiltshire, for storage.

Having survived the war, 'P7' was then sold for scrap to Messrs John Dale Ltd in 1948 for £25; fortunately the historical significance of the aircraft was recognised and she was generously presented to the RAF Colerne station museum collection. On 3 March 1967 the Spitfire was moved to Henlow, Bedfordshire, for use in the film *Battle of Britain* and was subsequently restored to flying condition. It was registered as G-AWIJ on 25 April 1968, to Spitfire Productions Ltd for flying during the film work. (Interestingly, its civilian registration was not cancelled until 29 February 1984, which was presumably an oversight as it became a military airframe again in November 1968!)

During the filming, P7350 wore a number of fictitious serial numbers and code letter combinations. These included N3310 AI-A and AI-E; N3312 CD-C and EI-C; N3316 CD-G; N3317 BO-H and N3321 DO-M. After filming was completed, 'P7' was presented to the Flight and flew to Coltishall on 8 November 1968.

Since 1999 P7350 has been painted to represent Spitfire Ia XT-D (L1067) *Blue Peter* of 603 Squadron, this being the personal aircraft of the Commanding Officer, Squadron Leader George Denholm DFC, who was affectionately known as 'Uncle George' by his pilots as, at thirty-two years old, he was considerably older than the rest of them. During the Battle of Britain, on 30 August 1940, whilst operating from Hornchurch, L1067 was badly damaged by return fire during a combat with Bf 110s over Deal in Kent. 'Uncle George' was forced to bale out, fortunately unharmed. The aircraft crashed at Hope Farm, Snargate, from where it was excavated in 1973, various parts being uncovered, including the fuel tank panel bearing the inscription *Blue Peter*. This was the name that George Denholm gave to his aircraft, naming it after a Derby-winning thoroughbred race horse. George Denholm survived the war, retiring as a Group Captain; he died in 1997 at the age of eighty-eight.

The latest identity taken on by 'P7' is XT-L, again of 603 Squadron, this time representing the aircraft of Pilot Officer Gerald 'Stapme' Stapleton during the Battle of Britain. 'Stapme' rose to the rank of Squadron Leader, was awarded the DFC and in recent years has become a good friend of the Flight, making the choice of the Spitfire's new identity again particularly appropriate.

Card I

Initial Issue
January 2006

Spitfire Mks II, V & IX
AP101B-7101-14

FLIGHT REFERENCE CARDS

Initial/
External
2

Internal
3

Starting
4

After Start/
Taxy/Test
of Engine/
Take-off
5

In Flight/
Range &
Endurance
6

Landing/
After Ldg/
Shutdown/
Limitations
Operating
Data
7

**SPITFIRE Mk II (P 7350)**
**Mk V (AB 910)**
**and Mk IX (MK 356)**

**NORMAL DRILLS**

Prepared by Handling Squadron

*P7350's cockpit in all
its glory. (Author)*

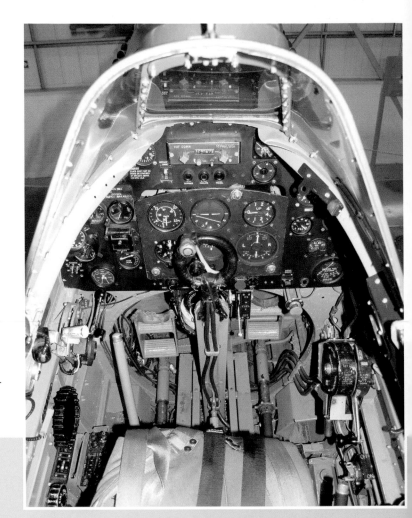

*Having already flown one
sortie earlier, the Spitfire II
has been primed before start-
up and hence as the Merlin
erupts into life the surplus fuel
ignites and causes a brief
plume of flames out of the
exhaust stubs. (Author)*

P7350's paint schemes with the Flight:

| | |
|---|---|
| 1969-71 | ZH-T of 266 Squadron (In September 1940, when P7350 served with 266 Squadron, the code letters were UO-ZH codes were only used from March 1942.) |
| 1972-6 | UO-T, the original 266 Squadron code it wore in September 1940 |
| 1977-81 | QV-B of 19 Squadron, circa 1940-41 |
| 1982-4 | 64 Squadron colours as SH-D, 1941 |
| 1985-8 | EB-Z of 41 Squadron (To celebrate the sixtieth anniversary of the Royal Observer Corps, painted as presentation aircraft *Observer Corps* circa 1940-41. The actual aircraft was P7666, handed over in November 1940.) |
| 1989-90 | Reverted to its genuine 266 (Rhodesia) Squadron code UO-T of 1940 ready for the fiftieth anniversary of the Battle of Britain commemorations in 1990 |
| 1991-3 | YT-F of 65 (East India) Squadron, 1941 |

*Left: A repaired bullet hole in the port wing of P7350, received courtesy of a Messerschmitt Bf 109 during the Battle of Britain on 25 October 1940. (Author)*

*Below: Quietly standing outside at Coningsby in 2006, 'P7' would once have been parked up like this awaiting a scramble call for combat during the Battle of Britain. (Author)*

1994-6    RN-S *Enniskillen* of 72 'Basutoland' Squadron, representing a presentation aircraft of 1941 (The actual aircraft was Mk.IIa P7832, handed over in January 1941 as a result of the Spitfire Fund run by the *Belfast Telegraph*.)

1997-8    BA-Y *The Old Lady* of air-sea rescue unit 277 Squadron, circa 1942-4. Again portraying another presentation aircraft, this time Mk.IIb P8509, which was financed in May 1941 by the Bank of England, hence *The Old Lady* (of Threadneedle Street)

1999-2006    XT-D *Blue Peter* of 603 Squadron, representing Mk.Ia L1067 as flown by Squadron Leader George 'Uncle' Denholm – CO of 603 June 1940 to April 1941.
(In May 2006 for a special air-to-air photo shoot, Plane Picture Company's John Dibbs wanted to portray P7350 wearing the codes it carried on 25 October 1940 – the day it was shot down – as a tribute to Ludwig Martel. After consultation with the pilot it was temporarily recoded as XT-W, which is believed to be the code it was wearing on that day.)

2007-    XT-L of 603 Squadron, the code worn on the aircraft of Pilot Officer 'Stapme' Stapleton during the Battle of Britain.

*AB910 seen soon after joining the Flight at a 'Battle of Britain at Home' day at North Weald in 1965. LF363 is visible at the right of the picture, and the tail of a Blackburn Beverley is evident in front of the Spitfire. (BBMF Archives)*

## Mk.Vb AB910

Spitfire Mk.Vb AB910 is a remarkable survivor with a history full of action, and not without mishaps. But this Spitfire has a fine pedigree as an operational fighter that is second to none, as it went through some three years of warfare.

AB910 was built at Castle Bromwich in 1941, another of the 11,989 Spitfires built at the 'shadow' factory. It was initially allocated to 222 (Natal) Squadron at North Weald on 22 August 1941, but its stay there was short, as by the end of the month it was damaged during a forced landing at Lympne. After repairs by Air Service Training at Hamble, it was moved to 37 Maintenance Unit at Burtonwood, and then allocated to 130 Squadron at Perranporth in Cornwall.

AB910 flew twelve operational missions with this unit, including several convoy patrols, and also escort patrols for the daylight bombing raids against the battle cruisers *Scharnhorst* and *Gneisenau* in December 1941. The pilot for the latter mission was a Pilot Officer Jones, and squadron records state that he was attacked by two Messerschmitt Bf 109s. Although the records do not mention any damage to the Spitfire, it flew no further ops with 130 Squadron and by 15 January 1942 was with the Westland Aircraft Company for repair. AB910's next unit was 133 'Eagle' Squadron at Biggin Hill, where it arrived in June 1942. It flew twenty-nine operational sorties with this unit, including four on 19 August 1942 during the fierce aerial battles in support of the Dieppe Raid.

At 12:25 on 19 August, Flight Sergeant 'Dixie' Alexander, an American volunteer pilot from Illinois, serving with the RAF's 133 'Eagle' Squadron, took off from Lympne in Kent flying AB910 for his second patrol of the day on Operation *Jubilee*, the now-infamous Dieppe Raid. During his first sortie that day, flying Spitfire BL773, 'Dixie' had claimed a kill against a Focke-Wulf Fw 190. On this second sortie he again found himself in combat as his formation became heavily engaged. In the mêlée 'Dixie' spotted a wave of Dornier Do 217s bombing the Allied convoy in the Channel below and dived to attack them. He lined one of the bombers up in his gun sight and, pressing the 'fire' button on the 'spade grip' of his control column to activate his fighter's 20-mm cannons and .303-in machine-guns simultaneously, fired a long burst into the German bomber. As he broke away he was rewarded with the sight of the Do 217 plummeting out of the sky on fire. There was no time to observe the final outcome of his target's apparently fatal plunge as the sky was full of danger, but he felt justified in claiming his second 'kill' of the day. This was also the second enemy aircraft that AB910's guns had scored hits against that day as, on an earlier sortie, in the hands of its regular pilot Flying Officer Doorly, the Spitfire had damaged another Do 217. AB910 flew a total of four operational sorties during the air battles of 19 August 1942.

When 133 Squadron upgraded to Spitfire Mk.IXs in September 1942, AB910 was transferred briefly to 242 Squadron, before that unit was posted to the Middle East. Following a spell at 12 Maintenance Unit at Kirkbride in Scotland, its next operational duties were with 416 Squadron, Royal Canadian Air Force (RCAF), between July 1943 and January 1944, when that unit too upgraded to Mk.IXs. AB910 was then put on the strength of 402 'Winnepeg Bear' Squadron RCAF, with which it finished its operational flying career, operating firstly from Digby, then Horne, Westhampnett and Merston, mainly in the fighter-bomber role.

In May 1944 AB910 became the personal aircraft of Canadian Flying Officer George

*For the 1986 season 'AB' emerged from a major servicing at the College of Aeronautics, Cranfield, Bedfordshire, wearing the markings BP-O of a 457 Squadron RAAF Spitfire. The inscription reads* In Memory of R J Mitchell, *as a tribute to the famous designer of the Spitfire who died in June 1937, and never saw what a great contribution the aircraft made to the defence of the country. (BBMF Archives)*

Lawson. Of particular note, AB910 played its part in the D-Day invasions of France in June 1944 that eventually brought the war in Europe to an end. George Lawson flew AB910 on beachhead cover patrol (Eastern Area) on D-Day, 6 June 1944, from 09:45 to 12:15, which was just about the maximum duration of a sortie in a Spitfire V without a drop tank. Later on that momentous day, from 22:00 to 23:59, AB910 was flown on a night beachhead cover patrol by Pilot Officer H C Nicholson.

On D-Day+1, 7 June, George Lawson again flew AB910, this time on a dawn beachhead cover patrol taking off at 04:30. Two and a half hours after landing the aircraft was airborne again as a spare for another beachhead patrol in the hands of Pilot Officer K E Heggie. AB910 continued to fly beachhead cover patrols and some convoy and shipping patrols in support of the invasion up to 13 July 1944, at which point its long and distinguished operational flying career came to an end. AB910 had amassed some 143 operational sorties during World War Two, with its operational career spanning almost three years from August 1941 to July 1944.

AB910 was then transferred to 53 Operational Training Unit (OTU) at Hibaldstow and it was here that one of the most bizarre incidents involving the aircraft occurred as, on 14 February 1945, it famously flew with an unauthorised 'passenger'. LACW Margaret Horton, a WAAF ground-crew fitter, had been sitting on the tail whilst the aircraft taxied out to the take-off point, as was common practice. She expected to be signalled as to when to dismount but the pilot, Flight Lieutenant Neil Cox DFC*, did not realise that she was there and took off with her still on the tail. Unable to get off safely, Margaret flung herself around the fin, with her lower body on one side of it and her torso on the other, and clung

*AB910 in its 402 Squadron AE-H paintwork, complete with Invasion stripes as it would have appeared when it took part in the D-Day operations of June 1944. (© Crown Copyright/MOD)*

on by gripping the elevator control surface. The combination of her weight on the tail and her grip on the elevator very nearly had disastrous results not least because, as the pilot struggled to control the aircraft around in a circuit to land, she apparently tried to alert him to her presence by waggling the elevator! As Neil Cox told Squadron Leader Clive

*At Nellis AFB in Nevada during April 1997, AB910 as XR-A makes the Flight's farthest flung ever appearance! Note the 'Eagle' Squadron badge on its forward fuselage. (Alan Warnes/AirForces Monthly)*

Rowley when they met in January 2005: 'Sometimes I had control and sometimes she did!' Fortunately for them both, he was able to maintain sufficient control, sometimes locking the stick in position with his knee, and he pulled off a remarkable landing, having to maintain a heavy push force on the control column and with a very frightened WAAF still wrapped around the tail! Once safely down and with the aircraft stopped, Margaret was able to dismount from the tail and, legend has it, she immediately and probably very shakily lit a cigarette!

AB910's final active service before being 'demobbed' was with 527 Squadron, a radar calibration unit based at Digby, with which it remained until 30 May 1946. In 1947 AB910 was purchased by Group Captain Alan Wheeler and was placed on the civil register as G-AISU for air racing. After a heavy landing during the King's Cup Air Race in 1953, it was returned to Vickers-Armstrong where it was refurbished and subsequently flown regularly by Jeffrey Quill, the famous Spitfire test pilot, until being donated to the Flight in 1965.

While in service with the Flight, AB910 has suffered three serious incidents. In June 1976 an undercarriage leg collapsed on landing at Duxford, though this resulted in only relatively minor damage. The most serious accident occurred in August 1978, when the aircraft was involved in a ground collision with a Harvard at Bex, Switzerland, at the start of the take-off run, resulting in severe damage. Fortunately, the decision was taken to repair the aircraft and this was completed at Abingdon using some parts from Spitfire IX MK372 (an aircraft now operated in flying condition by the RNLAF Historic Flight). Most recently, on its final planned flight of the 2004 season, AB910 suffered a deflated inner tube on the starboard wheel, which resulted in the aircraft tipping onto its nose at the end of the landing run, causing some damage. This was rectified in-house by the

*The Mk.Vb wearing its ZD-C* President Roosevelt *livery parked up at the Imperial War Museum Duxford, with the unmistakable curvature of the American Air Museum in the background. The date was September 2000, and the occasion was Duxford's Battle of Britain 60th Anniversary Air Show, which boasted the rare claim of getting all five of the Flight's Spitfires in attendance. (Author)*

*AB910 was photographed here undergoing repairs and deep maintenance at Coningsby following its accident at the end of the 2004 season. (Author)*

Flight in time for the 2005 display season.

In keeping with the Flight's policy of using its aircraft not only as display assets but also to commemorate various World War Two campaigns, units and, sometimes, specific individuals, AB910 has worn many colour schemes during its service with the Flight, including those it actually wore operationally on D-Day as 402 Squadron's AE-H.

The Mk.Vb also has the accolade of having made the Flight's furthest flung appearance, when in 1997 the Spitfire went to Nellis Air Force Base near Las Vegas in Nevada, USA, to participate in the celebrations of the fiftieth anniversary of the formation of the United States Air Force. For this, in early April 'AB' was flown to Brize Norton, Oxfordshire, where it was dismantled. It was then shipped out in the back of a Lockheed C-130 Hercules on 14 April, accompanied by a team of six BBMF engineers who would reassemble and care for the Spitfire once it had arrived in the USA. On 18 April AB910 was air-tested stateside by OC BBMF Squadron Leader Paul Day.

For its brief sojourn to the USA the Spitfire was painted up in the markings of 71 'Eagle' Squadron's XR-A, representing a fighter presented by the film company Warner Bros. It was also given an 'Eagle' Squadron badge, most appropriate as 'AB' was once on such a unit itself. There was also a reference to President Roosevelt, who was associated with it.

After reassembly it was air-tested on 18 April. Following two practice displays, on 23 and 24 April, the Spitfire carried out two flights each day on the 25th and 26th. One was a display and the other was to represent the type in flypasts of a variety of different aircraft types. After it had completed all its duties, AB910 was disassembled again and the Hercules returned it to Brize Norton during early May.

From 2003 to 2006 it flew in the desert camouflage scheme of Spitfire Vb AB502, which was the personal aircraft of Wing Commander Ian Richard Gleed DSO DFC when he became the Wing Leader of 244 Wing, Goubrine South, Tunisia, in 1943. 'Widge' Gleed was a Battle of France and Battle of Britain ace with fifteen confirmed kills to his credit; he had flown operationally from May 1940 through to May 1942 without a break. He flew AB502 on at least thirty-five missions before he was attacked by Bf 109s of JG77 during a patrol over the Cap Bon area on 16 April 1943; his aircraft was hit several times and badly damaged. He tried to get back to the safety of Tunisia but did not make it and was posted missing. The remains of his Spitfire were later discovered on sand dunes near the coast but his body was not found until much later. His remains were eventually reburied in the military cemetery at Enfidaville in 1944 – his final resting place. 'Widge' Gleed's aircraft carried his initials 'IR-G' in place of unit codes and 'Figaro the Cat' nose-art on the starboard side, which were replicated on AB910 as a tribute to a brave and successful fighter pilot who paid the ultimate price and to all those who contributed to the ultimately successful desert campaign in North Africa.

From the 2007 season AB910 has taken on another new identity, that of Spitfire Vb EN951 RF-D of 303 (Kosciuszko) Squadron. This was one of several Spitfires flown by Polish Squadron Leader Jan Zumbach, which had Donald Duck nose-art applied to them. The example chosen features the largest style of Donald artwork and will represent the Polish pilot's career as at September 1942. Having already fought in France, this pilot was a founding member of 303 Squadron and became an ace during the Battle of Britain, scoring eight aircraft destroyed and one probable during that period alone while flying Hurricane Is.

AB910's paint schemes with the Flight:

| | |
|---|---|
| 1965-8 | QJ-J (thin), 92 Squadron |
| 1969-72 | SO-T, 145 Squadron (initially coded PB-T by mistake, quickly changed). |
| 1973-8 | QJ-J (thick), 92 Squadron |
| 1981-5 | XT-M, 603 (City of Edinburgh) Squadron, Royal Auxiliary Air Force |
| 1986-9 | BP-O *In Memory of R J Mitchell*, 457 Squadron, Royal Australian Air Force |
| 1990 | EB-J *The Guinea Pig Club*, 41 Squadron |
| 1991-3 | MD-E *Eagle Squadron*, 133 (Eagle) Squadron |
| 1994-8 | AE-H, 402 Squadron, Royal Canadian Air Force (April 97-XR-A for visit to USA.) |
| 1999-2002 | ZD-C *President Roosevelt - Warner Bros*, 222 (Natal) Squadron |
| 2003-2006 | IR-G, 244 Wing |
| 2007- | RF-D, 303 Squadron. |

## LF.IXe MK356

MK356 is a relatively recent addition to the Flight, having arrived at Coningsby in November 1997. Of particular note, this Spitfire Mk.IX wears the same markings that it did during its participation in the D-Day invasion of France.

It was built at Castle Bromwich in early 1944 and delivered to Digby, Lincolnshire, that March fitted with a Merlin 66 engine, optimised for operations at low level below 25,000 ft. This Mk.IX was allocated to 443 'Hornet' Squadron, Royal Canadian Air Force, which became part of 144 Canadian Wing, commanded by Wing Commander J E 'Johnnie' Johnson.

It carried out its first operational mission from Westhampnett on 14 April 1944 as part of a 'Rodeo' fighter sweep over occupied France. In the weeks leading up to the D-Day invasion of France on 6 June 1944, MK356 was involved in various fighter and fighter-bomber missions. On D-Day +1, 7 June, Flying Officer Gordon E Ockenden flew two patrols over France on invasion duties – the second of which was in MK356. During this

*Here 'MK' is seen rolled out at Coningsby during a press call just before the D-Day sixtieth anniversary commemorations in June 2004. (Author)*

*MK356 is finished in the paint scheme of 443 'Hornet' Squadron RCAF, which it wore during the D-Day invasion of occupied France in June 1944. Note its clipped wings, which give the fighter better performance at low altitude. Since 2004 it has also sported a broad chord rudder, which has a more pointed tip than its previous one.*
*(JT Chris Elcock/© Crown Copyright/MOD)*

sortie he was involved in a low-level attack on four Messerschmitt Bf 109Gs. Flying Officer Ockenden gave chase to one of the Bf 109s in the Spitfire Mk.IX, and obtained a shared victory after hitting it with a number of strikes. His wingman, Flight Lieutenant Hugh Russell, finished it off, hence they were both credited with a 'shared kill'.

MK356 was damaged on a number of occasions, and a wheels-up landing ended its operational career on 13 June 1944. It had lost a wheel on take-off, but the pilot completed his mission then made a belly landing on his return. No. 443 Squadron moved to a forward operating base in France the next day, leaving MK356 behind to be collected and stored by a Maintenance Unit.

After repairs the Spitfire was relegated to instructional airframe status. In later years it was put on gate guard duties at Hawkinge and Locking. This Spitfire was another used during the making of *Battle of Britain*, though only as a representative static airframe at Duxford and North Weald. Post filming it was restored to Mk.IX status and was for many years displayed at the RAF Museum's reserve collection at RAF St Athan in Wales. A complete refurbishment to airworthy condition began in January 1992.

The restoration to flying condition was led by Chief Technician Chris Bunn. Major work was needed to return the aircraft to flying condition, and the wings of Spitfire Mk.XVI SL674 (this wasn't the first time this Spitfire had donated parts to the Flight – see page 47) were incorporated into the project. On completion of the rebuild and ground tests, the Flight's Commanding Officer, Squadron Leader Paul Day OBE AFC, air-tested the Mk.IX at St Athan on 7 November 1997 – the fighter had just made its first flight since World War Two. Some minor adjustments were completed by the following week, then the aircraft was flown to its new home at Coningsby where it arrived on 14 November. This added a fresh mark of R J Mitchell's famous design to the fleet, and was the first time in the Flight's history that a Spitfire Mk.IX had been on 'flying strength'.

The aircraft is a clipped-wing LF.IXe and carries the markings it wore operationally as

*The Flight's Spitfire Mk.IX awaits its pilot for the fighter's first pre-season air test of 2002. Under its wings and rear fuselage the D-Day veteran appropriately wears Invasion stripes. (Author)*

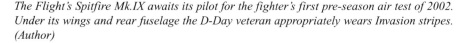

*MK356's clipped wings can be seen clearly in this view from the back of the Lancaster.
(RAF Coningsby/© Crown Copyright/MOD)*

2I-V of 443 Squadron RCAF, complete with black and white Invasion stripes on the underside of its wings and fuselage. This particular aircraft was believed to have less than 100 flying hours on the airframe when rebuilt, which at the time of its return to flight made it one of the lowest-houred 'original' Spitfires in the world.

MK356's paint schemes with the Flight:

> 1997-        2I-V, 443 Squadron, Royal Canadian Air Force.

## Mk.XVIe TE311

The latest addition to the Flight's inventory, TE311 has increased the Spitfire fleet to six. Although still under restoration in 'spare time' only, this aircraft is an incredibly exciting addition.

TE311 was built at Castle Bromwich in 1945. It was allocated to the Empire Central Flying School Handling Squadron at Hullavington, Wiltshire, on 5 October 1945. It served there until February 1946 whereupon it was placed into store.

On 31 May 1951 it was placed on charge to 1689 (Ferry Pilot Training) Flight, which was based at Aston Down, Gloucestershire. In July 1952 it was transferred to Flying Training Command and later allocated to the Ferry Training Unit at Benson, Oxfordshire, in April 1953. That September it was returned to store, before spending from January until February 1953 with 2 Civilian Anti-Aircraft Co-operation Unit at Langham, Norfolk.

In August 1955 TE311 was placed on gate guard duties at Tangmere, Sussex. It remained there until 1967, when it was loaned to Spitfire Productions Ltd for use in the classic aviation film *Battle of Britain*. For the film work the Mk.XVI was restored to taxiable condition and modified with a false rear fuselage to represent a Mk.I.

*Former RAF Exhibition Flight Spitfire Mk.XVIs TE311 (left) and TB382 were photographed in April 2001, a few months after their arrival inside the BBMF hangar and already stripped of their engines. (Author)*

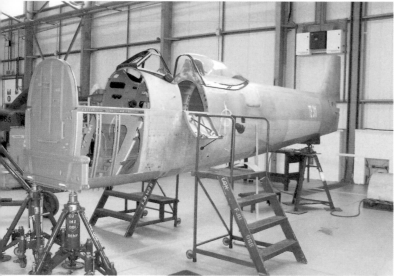

*Work was under way to turn TE311 into a spare fuselage when it was photographed in March 2004. (Author)*

*By April 2006 TE311 was undergoing a complete restoration to airworthy condition, though the engine fitted here was just in place to allow work to proceed to allow the cowlings to be fitted correctly. (Author)*

*TE311's cockpit is seen here in the process of being fitted out, revealing much that is not normally visible. (Author)*

In August 1968 the Spitfire was handed back to the RAF, returned to normal configuration and prepared for display at Benson, Oxfordshire. It arrived there in September and was exhibited at the Battle of Britain display later that month. TE311's stay at Benson was fairly short, as it was soon delivered to Abingdon, Berkshire, to join the RAF Exhibition Flight.

Along with fellow Mk.XVI TB382, which had also been part of the RAF's recruitment 'road show', in January 2001 TE311 was moved to the BBMF's hangar at Coningsby, Lincs. They had previously been stored in one of the air base's hardened aircraft shelters since October 1999, but the move ensured the pair would be cared for better after they became the property of the Flight.

Their Rolls-Royce Merlins were soon removed and one was refurbished for use in another Flight aircraft. This fitted ideally with the intention to use the two Mk.XVIs for spares reclamation where necessary to keep the Flight's other charges airworthy.

Facing fairly uncertain futures, TB382 and TE311 were structurally examined. While TB382's skin was in quite poor condition, TE311's bodywork was in remarkably good shape. It was also very original and many of its panels even carried the maker's 'TE311' stamps.

The poor condition of TB382 meant that it was dismantled for spares and struck off charge. Officially, TE311 was only retained as a spares recovery programme, but work to restore the fuselage as a 'spare' began in October 2001.

The work was, however, required to be carried out at no cost to the MOD. This resulted in the two technicians principally responsible for the project, Chief Technician Paul Blackah and Corporal Andy Bale, carrying out the work in their spare time. Generous help has also been given to the project by several companies and other BBMF engineers along the way. Because of the standard and extent of the work carried out, approval was subsequently granted to complete a full restoration to flying condition.

By late 2006 the four years plus spent restoring the 'Spit' resulted in an amazing turnaround. The skin was finished and very few new panels were required due to the reasons mentioned above. The wiring had been completed and by then electrical power had even been switched on.

The engine fitted to TE311 during 2006 was put in place in February that year. It was not serviceable and had only been installed so that the cowlings could be worked on and fitted correctly. TE311 will eventually be fitted with a Merlin 266. Progress was well under way on the main control cables and the fuel and air systems. Trim controls were at that time almost ready to be fitted.

As a result of all the hard work and good will given to TE311 by the BBMF personnel in their own time, the Flight should have another airworthy Spitfire, of a variant not currently represented, within an estimated two years. The paint scheme now applied is green/grey camouflage with the 74 Squadron code 4D-V. This addition to the Flight is incredibly appropriate to be able to include in this fiftieth anniversary book, as the BBMF will have an example of a low-back Spitfire Mk.XVI just as was used for the Flight's very first Battle of Britain flypast back in 1957.

## PR.XIX PM631

PM631 is the BBMF's longest-serving aircraft, and has in fact been in service with the Flight since its formation in July 1957. Therefore 2007 is its fiftieth year of continuous flying with the Flight.

PM631 was too late to see operational service in World War Two, having been built in November 1945 as a photo reconnaissance aircraft with a Rolls-Royce Griffon 66 engine and pressurised cockpit for operating at high altitude. It went to 6 Maintenance Unit at Brize Norton, Oxfordshire, on 6 November that year, and was delivered to 203 Advanced Flying School on 6 May 1949. In January 1950 it returned to 6 Maintenance Unit, and that June was transferred to 9 Maintenance Unit, Cosford. It is recorded as having spent two weeks at Bückeburg, Germany, in January 1951, returning to Cosford thereafter.

Modified for meteorological work, on 2 July 1951 PM631 then went under the care of Short Bros to be flown by civilian pilots with the Temperature and Humidity (THUM) Flight based at Hooton Park, and later Woodvale. After the last THUM Flight sortie

*Pictured in September 1957 is PM631, which had the interesting caption 'The last operational Spitfire still flying at R.A.F. Biggin Hill'. (BBMF Archives)*

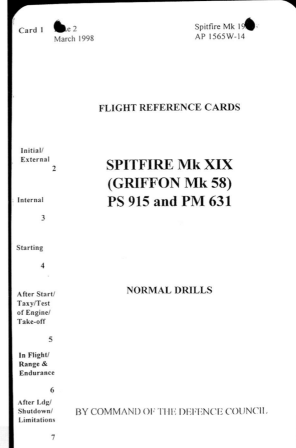

Card 1   Issue 2
March 1998

Spitfire Mk 19
AP 1565W-14

**FLIGHT REFERENCE CARDS**

Initial/ External   2

Internal   3

Starting   4

After Start/ Taxy/Test of Engine/ Take-off   5

In Flight/ Range & Endurance   6

After Ldg/ Shutdown/ Limitations   7

**SPITFIRE Mk XIX (GRIFFON Mk 58) PS 915 and PM 631**

**NORMAL DRILLS**

BY COMMAND OF THE DEFENCE COUNCIL

by PS853 on 10 June 1957, four days later its record card states that it was on the charge of RAF Biggin Hill. On 11 July 1957, in formation with fellow Spitfire PR.XIXs PS853 and PS915, the aircraft was flown to Biggin Hill to form the Historic Aircraft Flight, later becoming the BBMF.

PM631 is currently painted as an early PR.XIX of 541 Squadron, which performed high-altitude reconnaissance missions over the European theatre from early 1944 to the end of World War Two. Appropriately the 541 Squadron motto was 'Alone Above All'. In service, Spitfire PR.XIXs were unarmed but could fly at 370 mph at 40,000 ft (hence they needed pressurised cockpits) and had a range of 1500 miles.

*Left: To commemorate the fortieth anniversary of D-Day, PM631 emerged for the 1984 season wearing the DL-E code of 91 Squadron representing a Spitfire Mk.XIV with Invasion stripes. (Duncan Cubitt/FlyPast)*

*Right: A second 11 Squadron identity for PM631 was applied in 1990 when it was given SEAC paintwork as N Mary, pictured here en route to North Weald in 1994. (Duncan Cubitt/FlyPast)*

*Below: Seen in the company of a DH Tiger Moth at Duxford in September 2000 is 'PM' in another SEAC scheme, as S of 681 Squadron. (Author)*

PM631's paint schemes with the Flight:

| | |
|---|---|
| 1957-66 | Camouflaged, no unit markings |
| 1967-83 | AD-C, 11 Squadron |
| 1984-9 | DL-E, 91 Squadron (scheme of a Spitfire Mk.XIV at the time of D-Day complete with Invasion stripes, first applied to commemorate the fortieth anniversary). |
| 1990-95 | N *Mary*, 11 Squadron, South East Asia Command |
| 1996-2001 | S, 681 Squadron, South East Asia Command (though without standard SEAC wing stripes). |
| 2002- | 541 Squadron (no squadron code or identification letter, with Invasion stripes). |

*Right: Squadron Leader Ian 'Shiney' Simmons climbs out of PM631 after a sortie in April 2005. Owing to its pressurised cockpit the PR.XIX has no fold-out access door, making it more difficult to exit. (Author)*

*Below: With its Invasion stripes most evident, PM631's 541 Squadron paintwork features no squadron code or identification letter. (JT Chris Elcock/© Crown Copyright/MOD)*

## PR.XIX PS915

PS915 is another founder member of the Flight that is still on strength, though it hasn't been in continuous service. In fact, PS915 was not in the best shape when it arrived at Biggin Hill, and was quickly relegated to gate guard duties!

Like PM631, PS915 entered service just too late to see operations during World War Two. It went to 6 Maintenance Unit at Brize Norton on 17 April 1945, but quickly left there to go to Benson on the 26th. On 21 June that year it joined 541 Squadron at Benson. 'PS' next moved to 1 Pilot's Pool at the same base on 21 December 1945, before moving to the PR Development Unit also at Benson on 22 July 1946, where it took part in tests of new cameras.

On 8 July 1948 PS915 went on the strength of 2 (Army Co-operation) Squadron based at Wunsdorf in Germany as part of the British Air Forces of Occupation (BAFO). At that time this unit carried out high- and low-level strategic reconnaissance sorties in connection with the East/West divide of Europe. In March 1951 it went to the BAFO Communication Squadron, before being returned to the UK in May of the same year, going to 9 MU at Cosford. On 4 June 1954 it joined PM631 on the THUM Flight at Woodvale. Then in June 1957 PS915 became a founder member of the Historic Aircraft Flight, but its initial flight to Duxford on 12 June was delayed as it could not be started. Arriving at Biggin Hill with PM631 and PS853 on 11 July, owing to its poor condition 'PS' was quickly retired to gate guard duties at West Malling, being allocated this task as early as 2 August, and taking up residence by the 31st. It served in this capacity for nearly thirty years, later being moved to Leuchars, before a sojourn to Henlow for some involvement with the *Battle of Britain* film. Then it went back on the gate, though this time at Brawdy. After being modified to take an ex-Shackleton Griffon 58 engine and refurbished to flying condition by British Aerospace (Warton Division) as the result of a

*When PS915 returned to the Flight after thirty years in 1987, it wore an all-over PR blue scheme with no unit markings. (Duncan Cubitt/FlyPast)*

*Perhaps one of the most striking paint schemes ever worn by any of the Flight's aircraft was that applied to PS915 from 1992, when it received the colours of prototype Mk.XIV JF319, with camouflage topsides with a Prototype 'P' in a yellow circle on the fuselage – and bright yellow undersides! (Duncan Cubitt/FlyPast)*

project that began in June 1984, PS915 rejoined the Flight on 7 April 1987. By now it was in immaculate condition, unlike its first arrival thirty years previously!

Following a major servicing over the winter of 2003/4 carried out by the Aircraft Restoration Company at Duxford, Cambridgeshire, PS915 was painted in a scheme to replicate PS888, a PR.XIX of 81 Squadron based at Seletar, Singapore. This aircraft had the accolade of carrying out the last ever operational sortie flown by an RAF Spitfire

*Wearing the UM-G code of a 152 Squadron Mk.XIV, SEAC, and complete with a black panther motif on the port side of its fuselage, PS915 comes in to land at Duxford in May 1998. (Duncan Cubitt/FlyPast)*

*Left: PS888 of 81 Squadron had the honour of carrying out the last operational sortie by an RAF Spitfire on 1 April 1954, and to mark the event the Spitfire's ground crew painted a bold inscription reading 'The Last!' on the aircraft's port engine cowling. To commemorate the fiftieth anniversary of the occasion the Flight's PS915 was painted as such. (Author)*

*Below: After its winter servicing at Duxford over the winter of 2003/4, PS915 was successfully air-tested by OC BBMF Squadron Leader Clive Rowley MBE at the Cambridgeshire airfield on 16 March 2004. He returned to Duxford the following day to take the Spitfire, wearing a new coat of paint, back to the Flight's base at Coningsby. (RAF Coningsby/© Crown Copyright/MOD)*

*PS915's 'office'. (Author)*

*PS915 is seen here on its take-off roll at the Waddington International Air Show on 27 June 2006. With its powerful Rolls-Royce Griffon the Spitfire PR.XIX quickly gains speed and its tail wheel is soon in the air. (Author)*

*The five BBMF Spitfires are seen here in a neat stack* en route *to Duxford for the Battle of Britain Sixtieth Anniversary Air Show in September 2000. From bottom to top: PS915, P7350, MK356, AB910 and PM631. (Steve Fletcher/FlyPast)*

when, on 1 April 1954, Squadron Leader W P Swaby flew the final photographic reconnaissance mission over an area of jungle in Johore, where it was thought communist guerrillas were hiding out. To mark the occasion, ground crew painted a bold inscription on the port engine cowl that simply read 'The Last!'. As 2004 marked the fiftieth anniversary of this flight, the BBMF's careful research once again paid tribute to a most notable RAF aircraft and occasion.

The paint scheme is not the usual all-over PR blue. The Spitfire's lower sides and tail are finished in PR blue, though the top sides of the wings, fuselage and tailplanes are painted medium sea grey. As well as the inscription, PS915 also wears an 81 Squadron badge below the windshield on its port side. In keeping with BBMF practice, PS915 retains its own serial number, which in this case also appears on the undersides of the aircraft's wings.

PS915's paint schemes with the Flight:

| | |
|---|---|
| 1957 | Camouflage, no markings, soon retired |
| 1987-91 | PRU blue with no markings |
| 1992-7 | Livery of prototype Mk.XIV JF319, with camouflage topsides and yellow undersides. Prototype 'P' in a yellow circle on its fuselage sides |
| 1998-2003 | UM-G of 152 Squadron, SEAC, with black panther motif on port side of fuselage |
| 2004- | *The Last!*, 81 Squadron. |

*All five of the BBMF Spitfires were captured on camera off the end of the runway at Coningsby from the back of an RAF Hercules in September 1998. (Duncan Cubitt/FlyPast)*

*PA474 at Air Atlantique, Coventry, on 2 October 2006. It had arrived there ready for a major refurbishment over the winter, after which it would emerge wearing a new identity. This was its last sortie as QR-M Mickey the Moocher. (Author)*

# CHAPTER 8

# Lancaster I PA474

Due to its exclusivity and appeal, the Battle of Britain Memorial Flight's Avro Lancaster I PA474 has in many ways become the flagship of the fleet. The bomber's popularity in the UK is unsurpassed, its displays and flypasts generally being followed by a spontaneous round of applause from those on the ground as it pays its respects to the brave crews of Bomber Command in tremendous style.

The 'Lanc' has gained an incredibly high-profile status in the UK, having appeared several times on live national television broadcasts as it has carried out memorial, ceremonial and State duties.

PA474 was built as a B.I by Vickers-Armstrong at Hawarden, North Wales, in 1945. Initially it was planned that it would go on 'Tiger Force' operations and consequently serve in the Far East, though the war with Japan ended before the Lancaster could take part in any hostilities.

It then went into storage at 38 Maintenance Unit, Llandow, South Wales, on 18 August 1945. PA474 was next moved to 32 Maintenance Unit at St Athan, also in South Wales, on 26 November 1946. After this period in storage it was converted to PR.1 configuration by Armstrong Whitworth, with work beginning on 28 June 1947. It was ferried back to Llandow on 11 August and temporarily placed into store again.

On 23 September 1948, PA474 entered service with the RAF when it was assigned to B Flight of 82 Squadron for photographic reconnaissance duties in East and South Africa. After arrival with the squadron at Benson, Oxfordshire, it was given the identification letter M. PA474 spent the next four years carrying out survey work. It returned to Benson on 18 February 1952 to await a fairly uncertain future.

The Lancaster's long-term fate became even more doubtful when, from 26 May 1952, it was loaned to Flight Refuelling Ltd at Tarrant Rushton, Dorset, with the intention being to convert the 'Lanc' into a pilotless drone. Much design work followed while PA474 languished somewhat forgotten at Tarrant Rushton. However, before this proposed work began the Air Ministry made the decision to use an Avro Lincoln instead.

On 7 March 1954, PA474 was transferred to the College of Aeronautics at Cranfield, Bedfordshire, where it was to be used for trials with several experimental aerofoil sections, including the Handley Page Laminar Flow Wing. This new career effectively saved an airworthy Lancaster for the nation.

PA474 was used in this role until 1964, by which time the College of Aeronautics had completed the conversion of Lincoln B.2 G-36-3 (the former RF342). During October 1963 the RAF had talked to the College about taking PA474 back, with a view to putting it on display in the then planned RAF Museum.

On 22 April 1964, the 'Lanc' was ferried to 15 Maintenance Unit at Wroughton,

*On 18 August 1965, the departure of the Lancaster caused quite a stir around Henlow as it was believed to be just a museum relic, and most on site never expected it to fly. There was hardly an area on the base where disbelieving spectators didn't appear when the Merlins roared overhead. After take-off on that momentous day, PA474 is seen carrying out its low pass over the airfield before setting course for Waddington. From the flag on the front of the second car, it appears that even the Station Commander turned out to watch the 'Lanc'! (R S Fell/BBMF Archives)*

Wiltshire, and placed into storage. The RAF had regained PA474 and the first steps to it becoming a flying memorial to Bomber Command had been taken.

The aircraft was adopted by the Air Historical Branch with the intention of its inclusion in the new museum. It was soon painted with more appropriate wartime camouflage paintwork, though without any squadron markings. While at Wroughton, PA474 appeared in two films; *Operation Crossbow* and *The Guns of Navarone*. On 25 September 1964, the Lancaster moved to RAF Henlow, Bedfordshire, to be prepared for the RAF Museum.

In 1965 Wing Commander M A D'Arcy, the Commanding Officer of 44 (Rhodesia) Squadron, the first unit to be equipped with Lancasters, which was by then flying Avro Vulcans from RAF Waddington in Lincolnshire, asked permission for PA474 to be transferred into the care of the squadron. Part of the deal would see the aircraft stored inside a hangar at Waddington and it was also agreed that a start could be made on the restoration work required for its eventual display in the museum.

The account below, written by one of the Waddington team later involved with its pre-BBMF flying career, tells the story of the Lancaster's acquisition and subsequent transfer to the base in a way that has been little seen before. While I cannot say for definite who wrote this, it came from a file compiled by Chief Technician Dick Richardson who gathered a great deal of historical information on the Lancaster, and I feel this may be his account:

> Early in 1965, the Commanding Officer of No.44 Squadron, Wing Commander M. A. D'Arcy, suggested to three of his Officers that the Squadron should try and obtain an Historic aircraft to be held at RAF Waddington, one of the longest

*Just the No. 1 engine remains to be started as PA474 is readied for its first flight at Waddington on 7 November 1967. (BBMF Archives)*

*Leading light in getting the Lancaster returned to the air on a regular basis was Group Captain Arthur Griffiths AFC (left), Waddington's Station Commander at the time. On the right is his co-pilot, Squadron Leader Ken Hayward, and the pair are seen after the successful first flight on 7 November 1967. (BBMF Archives)*

established Bomber Stations in the United Kingdom.

A search was started and eventually a Lancaster was located at RAF Henlow. A Lancaster seemed the obvious choice as 44 Squadron at Waddington, was the first Squadron to operate Lancasters during the Second World War. As it had been standing outside at the mercy of all weathers, the Lancaster was rapidly deteriorating. The Commanding Officer contacted the Ministry of Defence requesting that PA474 be transferred to the care of No.44 Squadron at Waddington.

Eventually, approval was obtained for the transfer, and a party of ground crew, some of whom worked on Lancasters during the War, was gathered together and left for Henlow on May 12th 1965.

On close inspection, the aircraft appeared to be airworthy, so a further request

*This page from Group Captain Griffiths' logbook shows the entry for the Lancaster's first air test at Waddington on 7 November 1967, which lasted twenty minutes. He then flew PA474 on two more trips during December. The other entries for Vulcan B.2s include an interesting trip to Luqa, Malta, in XH557 on 19 October, returning on the 21st. (Courtesy Mrs N Griffiths)*

was sent to the Ministry of Defence that the Lanc be flown to Waddington. After due consideration, this request was granted, and a Recovery Servicing was drawn up. On July 26th 1965, a team of experienced technicians from Waddington started the Recovery Servicing. This consisted of a 25hr Servicing, undercarriage retraction tests, complete engine runs, Compass swing, flying control checks, electrical and instrument system checks and wheel brake checks.

Perhaps it should be recorded at this point, that after standing in the open for 12 months, the only servicing required on the Merlin engines was the clearing out of bird's nests from within the cowlings, spark plug cleaning, and fuel and oil checks! Apparently, the engines started as cleanly and as crisply as they would have done 20 years earlier!

Eventually, the aircraft was cleared as fully serviceable, and the aircrew arrived on August 18th for the memorable flight to Waddington. At 10.30 am the crew climbed aboard, and the pre-flight checks were carried out by the pilot, Flt. Lt. W. Niezreckie; the Flight Engineer, Mr H. Reid; and the Navigator, Flt. Lt. R. E. Leach.

After the usual fuel priming 'ritual' and the appropriate signals from the ground crew, one by one the Merlins crackled into life, chocks were drawn away, and PA 474 taxied across the rather rough grass field to the take-off point. A fair sized crowd had gathered to watch the proceedings, and they were rewarded by the sight

*A taste of things to come, as the Flight's Hurricane LF363 (right) and Spitfire Vb AB910 formate on the Lancaster for a practice sortie on 5 March 1968. The three-ship formation was to mark the stand-down of Fighter Command and Bomber Command, and the formation of Strike Command on 30 April that year. They are pictured flying over the RAF College Cranwell, in Lincolnshire. (BBMF Archives)*

of the Lancaster, with an All Up Weight of 42,186lb, slowly gathering speed and lifting off the field within 500 yards. Apparently, the departure of the Lanc caused quite a stir in and around Henlow as it was believed to be merely a Museum relic, and was never expected to fly. There was hardly an outside door on the Camp round which heads didn't appear when those Merlins went overhead! After a low pass over the airfield, the Lanc headed for Waddington in company with a Varsity which had been provided for the Press and Television personnel.

On arrival at Lincoln, the aircraft made several runs past the Cathedral to allow the photographers to film the Lanc with the Cathedral in the background. After this had been completed to the cameramen's satisfaction, the Varsity left to land at Waddington to enable the photographers to position themselves to film the Lanc's arrival. Meanwhile, the Lanc made two low, fast runs down Scampton's main runway. Finally, a rather heavy landing was made at Waddington at 1.30 pm.

As the aircraft was being stored in one of Waddington's hangars, it was decided to refurbish it in the markings of Squadron Leader J. D. Nettleton's Lancaster KM-B in which he earned his Victoria Cross whilst carrying out the famous low level daylight raid on the M.A.N. factory at Augsburg. [The markings were those of 44 Squadron Lancaster I R5508, and the Augsburg raid took place on 17 April 1942 - JC]

A restoration programme then began that would continue for many years. By 1966 work was progressing well and both the front and rear turrets were in place.

But the Lancaster was initially intended to only be a static exhibit, and its eventual return to the air was not straightforward as several hurdles presented themselves. Waddington's Station Commander at the time was Group Captain Arthur Griffiths AFC, and when the 'Lanc' was on static display outside the Officers' Mess he asked why it wasn't being flown. As the man principally responsible for getting the authority for it to fly again, and then to do so on a regular basis, his personal description of PA474's return to flight (he was its pilot on that occasion) written a few years later in March 1971, by which time he was an Air Commodore at Changi, Singapore, is particularly fascinating:

> Lancaster PA474 was brought to Waddington from Henlow under the sponsorship of the then Wing Commander D'Arcy, who was OC 44 Squadron and, of course, now commands Waddington. No. 44 was the first squadron to get Lancasters when they were stationed at Waddington in 1941. I believe that it was in 1965 that '474 was flown from Henlow for permanent static display at Waddington.
>
> I took over Waddington in April 1967 and noticed that PA474 had no permanent resting place. The aircraft was shunted from hangar to hangar, and from pan to pan, and few people seemed interested in it except for a Flight Lieutenant Leach of 44 Squadron who had done a great deal of work in researching the aircraft's history, and in begging and borrowing various items of equipment to bring the Lanc up to its former glory: eg turrets, astro-dome, tyres, interior fittings etc, etc. There are thick files at Waddington recording Leach's efforts.
>
> The other significant fellow at that time was Chief Technician Terry who, if I remember correctly, worked in MES and moved to Bournemouth when he retired. He did more than anyone to get the Lanc into flying shape.
>
> Like all flying men, I have always loved aeroplanes, and I could not bear to see PA474 looking forlorn and apparently unwanted. On one memorable day shortly

*PA474 is seen here nearing completion of major maintenance at Kemble in March 1975. Note that PA474 was by then wearing a large* City of Lincoln *name and Coat of Arms on its port side. Also of interest are the propeller tips, painted in the modern red and white style – on return to Waddington the yellow paint soon came out! (BBMF Archives)*

after my arrival at Waddington I crawled over the aircraft with the then OC Engineering Wing (Wing Commander Ferguson) and after a lengthy conversation with him and Terry, I decided that we must have a go at making the Lanc airworthy, and at gaining permission to fly it.

The project was supported by HQ 1 Group (Air Vice Marshal Le Bas) and HQBC (Air Chief Marshal Digger Kyle) but foundered initially in MOD, where financial approval was slow in forthcoming. What finally carried the day was the 50th Anniversary of Waddington in November 1967. The celebration culminated in a Guest Night in the Officers' Mess, to which Chief of Defence Staff (MRAF Sir Charles Elworthy – a former OC Waddington), ACM Kyle, ACM Broadhurst, ACM Dawson, ACM Fogarty, and numerous other distinguished guests were invited. I wanted to get the Lanc into the air before this great day.

*A salute to the Dam Busters as PA474 is joined by 617 Squadron Vulcan XL317 in 1978. (Derrick Warren/BBMF Archives)*

On November 6th, the long-awaited signal arrived giving permission for one air test. Since my flying experience over the past several years had been limited to jet aircraft, particularly the Vulcan, I borrowed a Hastings from Lindholme on November 7th for an hour's circuit work to refresh myself on things such as propellers, flaps and tail wheels.

I went straight over to the Lanc and in company with Squadron Leader Ken Hayward and Chief Technician

*View from the Lancaster's cockpit on Burma Star Air Day, on 4 September 1977. In the early days PA474's crew wore World War Two-style leather flying helmets, which were later replaced by the cloth type as seen here. (Lincolnshire Echo/BBMF Archives)*

Terry, started the four lovely Merlins and taxied out. After gulping a couple of times at the end of the runway (I hadn't flown a Lancaster for 19 years) I pushed the throttles open and away we went. In the event, there were no problems at all. The aircraft flew beautifully and was obviously delighted to be back in the air after so many years. For the first time for years (and, I might add, the last time) I made a perfect three-point landing and the three of us cheered with delight and relief as the aircraft rolled to a halt.

*Nowadays the Lancaster's crew wear modern-style flying helmets, typified here as the bomber makes its way back to Coningsby. (Dave Chadderton)*

The uneventful flight was well received in higher headquarters and we were subsequently allowed to fly on occasional test flights, but we were still to strike difficulties from time to time. Propeller oil leaks were a problem until we got some Gitts seals from Hong Kong. Feathering motors appeared unobtainable until MOD Harrogate bought a couple from a local scrap dealer. On one occasion, a double plug failure caused such vibration that I had to shut down the No.4 engine, and do my first three piston-engined landing for 20 years. But by and large, the aircraft

*This is a classic picture of PA474 over Lincoln Cathedral, which would have been a welcome sight to the crews returning home to 'Bomber County' often in severely shot-up aircraft. This picture was taken in May 1991 while the 'Lanc' was wearing the 103 Squadron PM-M² code of ED888, which completed 140 operations. (Crown Copyright)*

*From 1994 the markings of 9 Squadron's W4964 WS-J with its distinctive Johnnie Walker nose-art and Still Going Strong slogan were applied. This 'Lanc' became a veteran of 106 'ops', the hundreth of which saw it drop a 'Tallboy' bomb aimed at the mighty German battleship* Tirpitz *on 15 September 1944. (Duncan Cubitt/FlyPast)*

*Lancaster Captain Flight Lieutenant Ed Straw turns the bomber to port as it heads towards RAF Fairford in Gloucestershire for the 2005 Royal International Air Tattoo. (Dave Chadderton)*

*The view forward from the mid-upper turret as the 'Lanc' banks to port. (Neil Clegg/© Crown Copyright/MOD)*

*Flight Engineer Squadron Leader Ian Morton was photographed at work in the depths of the cockpit monitoring the Lancaster's system readouts. (Dave Chadderton)*

continued to fly beautifully, and the only real problem lay in gaining financial authority to fly it regularly. Gradually, as the aircraft continued to give little trouble, opposition decreased and we were invited increasingly to air shows throughout England, where the aircraft was always the star attraction.

In time, I checked out Ken Hayward and later, Squadron Leader John Stanley as pilots of the Lanc. For most of my flights the navigator was my Wing Commander Admin, Jack Wilson, who is now Group Captain SOA at HQ 11 Group, and the flight engineer was Warrant Officer Sparks.

Apart from the original flight on November 7th 1967, the most memorable trip was the visit to Northern France in June 1969, when we were invited to take part in the 25th Anniversary celebrations of the Normandy Landings.

I am delighted to have been fortunate enough to be in the right place at the right time to persuade (some people would call it bullying) authority that we could not possibly let the old aeroplane simply fade away. I am grateful for the efforts of so many Waddington men (particularly Leach and Terry, but lots of others helped) for their boundless enthusiasm and their remarkable ability to scavenge. And there is no doubt that many senior RAF Commanders and their staffs used their influence and persuasive powers to help get the aircraft into the air and to keep it flying. Long may it continue!

So from that description we learn of the reasons why there was a push to get PA474 back into the air and another personality whom we have much to thank for – and another little-known story behind what we see today.

While this period of the Lancaster's history is not part of the Flight's sphere of operations, I think it appropriate to include here as Group Captain Griffiths played a pivotal part in getting PA474 airborne on a regular basis and it is now so incredibly popular. Rising to the rank of Air Vice-Marshal, Arthur Griffiths was a former wartime fighter pilot. Flying a Spitfire V in a dogfight with over twenty Messerschmitt Bf 109s on 23 June 1944, he was shot down and was a prisoner-of-war until 1 May 1945. Post-war he went on to command

*From 2000 the Lancaster wore the nose-art of 61 Squadron Lancaster III EE176* Mickey the Moocher, *and is pictured here on 24 September 2006 shortly before it was to lose this identity complete with four poppy drop symbols added to the 'bomb tally'. (Author)*

101 Squadron on Vulcans. For this book I got in touch with his wife Mrs Nancy Griffiths, who gave the following recollections of the time and gives some hints as to why her husband may have been so keen to get PA474 airborne again:

On the day of the first flight I asked my husband if I could come and watch. He said 'I won't know whether you're there or not, I'm going to fly a Lancaster!' So I knew where I fitted in with the family of aeroplanes and things.

I went down and I stood by myself away from the group of chaps, the men who had worked on it and some of the officers. When it took off I expected some sort of

*Inside the Petwood Hotel after the Dam Busters sixtieth anniversary flypasts of 16 May 2003, the Lancaster's crew are seen with 617 Squadron Dams raid pilot Les Munro and star of* The Dam Busters *film Richard Todd. From left to right: Squadron Leader Stuart Reid, Les Munro CNZM DSO QSO DFC, Flight Lieutenant Ed Straw, Richard Todd and Flight Lieutenant Garry Simm. (Author)*

cheering or at least looks at each other as they were happy about it, but nobody made a movement. They just stood there and I wondered why they weren't happy about it. And then of course my husband flew around the airfield a couple of times and brought it in to land. It was then, when it landed, there was cheering and shouting and joy all over the place. I asked why they hadn't made any signs of happiness when the thing took off and they said they didn't know whether it would get down!

He loved his aeroplanes. We went to Canada and he was a lecturer at the RCAF Staff College. I think he flew every 'plane the Canadians had. He did the tour around all the stations in the far north when they opened up after the winter. He went on those every time, and he would go up and borrow an aeroplane and fly. My husband would have flown anything. Having been on Central Flying School where he was instructing and testing on Empire Training School he flew everything there was. One of the Canadian wives said: 'If he could get a bedstead up in the air he'd fly it.'

He told me once that the first time he flew a Dakota his Wing Commander told him to go and fly it and he said 'Well I've never flown one, sir.' He replied 'Well, you can read, can't you?' and threw the book at him! 'Go look at it.'

He felt the Lancaster was such a waste just sitting there. And then of course there was the awful business of not being able to get any money to help pay for it. But he was full of spirit and adventure.

With PA474 having gained permission to be flown regularly, this is another first-hand account about it a couple of years into its new lease of life, written again, I believe, by Dick Richardson:

During the Winter of 1969, a Primary Servicing was carried out which ensured that the aircraft was in good shape for the heavy flying commitment

*Looking aft as the Lancaster changes its course. (Dave Chadderton)*

*With the engines set at 3000 rpm and +7 boost, on the take-off roll PA474's tail wheel lifts after just twelve seconds. The 'Lanc' will normally rotate at 90 knots, which takes just over thirty seconds to reach. Here the bomber is seen soon into its take-off roll at Waddington on 27 June 2006. (Author)*

*As the Lancaster leads a BBMF three-ship formation over the countryside, its unmistakable shadow is cast on the ground below. (Dave Chadderton)*

during 1970. The first flight of 1970 was on April 14th which was of about an hour duration. This trip served as re-familiarisation for the crew, and a 'shake-down' for the aircraft. It so happened that the aircraft flew faultlessly and the crew were extremely happy with it, and, no doubt, were very happy to be airborne in the Lanc once again.

The next important flight came on May 7th when the aircraft flew to Jersey to take part in the 25th Anniversary of the Liberation of the Channel Isles. On arrival we were met by the Airport Commandant along with scores of onlookers. The Spitfire PR.19 from Coltishall was already tucked away in a hangar having arrived there earlier that day. Unfortunately, the weather wasn't very kind to us, and the numerous rain showers tended to seep into the Lanc's cockpit. It was unavoidable as there was insufficient hangar space for the Lanc, but the Airport Fire Chief was quick to loan us a boat cover which was secured over the cockpit and helped to stem the flow of water. No doubt it had been many years since the residents of Jersey had seen a Lancaster, consequently there was a steady flow of interested viewers, many of whom remarked how small the cockpit seemed.

The flypast, in company with the Spitfire, took place on Saturday May 9th, the pilot having a little difficulty finding in which village the commemorative service was taking place. On arrival back at Jersey Airport, the aircraft was locked, chocked and covered until our departure on Tuesday May 12th, the weather delaying our planned departure on Sunday.

It was with heavy hearts that we returned to the routine of Waddington and expensive cigarettes! From this time to October there were still 18 displays to do around the country on various air displays.

*Above: The view from below and aft of the Lancaster, with its mid-upper turret turned slightly to port. (Author)*

*Left: Flight Lieutenant Mike Leckey at the controls of the Lancaster, with PZ865 off its port wingtip. (Dave Chadderton)*

One of these was the official closure of RAF Stradishall on August 8th, at which the Lanc gave a 5 minute display, which was enjoyed by those attending the ceremony.

Only once during the numerous displays in 1970 did the Lancaster fail to get airborne. This was on May 25th when it was due to show its paces at the RAFA display at Hucknall. The crew had climbed aboard, completed pre-start checks, and the engine starting procedure was begun in the normal sequence of Nos 3-4-2-1. On attempting to start No.3 engine, all that was obtainable was rather alarming flames issuing from the exhaust stubs and enveloping the mainplane leading edge. To give this engine time to vent itself, the other three engines were started, and further

*The unmistakable shape of the bomber passes directly overhead in the skies of Lincolnshire. (Author)*

*Popular nowadays are Flying Proms events, where live orchestral music is played on a stage set up on an airfield. This is Duxford in July 2004, as Ed Straw puts the Lancaster through its paces to, what else, the* Dam Busters March. *The crowd went wild with patriotic fervour, waving flags and cheering to such a degree that the conductor, instead of getting his orchestra to play the next planned tune, gave an encore of the* Dam Busters! *(Author)*

attempts were made to start No.3 to no avail. It was decided at this point to shut down the serviceable engines, and to try and sort out No.3's problems. Off with the cowlings and all the usual checks were made, but we could find nothing in the time available. So, unfortunately, the crew left the aircraft and the next two days were spent searching for the elusive fault, which was eventually traced to a completely unserviceable right hand magneto. This was changed and all was well again. There was one other case of magneto trouble and that was due to a broken contact breaker spring – not an uncommon fault I'm told.

On July 6th, a visit to Waddington by five survivors of the crew of Lancaster PD 377 bought out PA 474 again. The five men climbed their way into the Lanc to their familiar crew stations, no doubt bringing back memories of that fateful day in April 1945 when WS-U crash landed in Holland. When all the photographs had been taken, we carried out a pre-flight inspection, and Sqn/Ldr John Stanley along with his willing ground crew boarded the aircraft for a quick 7 minute flypast for the benefit of Harry Denton's crew and the Press and Television cameras.

On September 19th came the annual Battle of Britain 'tour'… The crew arrived at the aircraft at 1.30 pm and we were airborne at 2.15 pm with the first display due at Finningley at 2.40 pm. On the way there it was arranged that we should meet the

*Looking out over the Nos 3 and 4 engines as the 'Lanc' arrives home after a two-hour sortie. (Author)*

*Right: PZ865 in formation with the bomber as they skirt the south coast of England along the white cliffs. (Dave Chadderton)*

*Below: The view from the bomb aimer's position of PA474 as the Lancaster approaches the Queen Elizabeth Bridge at Dartford in Kent, a well known landmark to the many motorists who regularly travel on the M25. (Author)*

*A wonderful view showing the topside of PA474 – note the white flying helmets of the four crew in the cockpit. The Captain is sat in the port pilot's seat, with the co-pilot immediately to his right. Behind the Captain is the navigator, and the flight engineer works with his panel behind the co-pilot. (Geoffrey Lee/Planefocus)*

Rolls-Royce Spitfire over Goole, but due to bad visibility the Spitfire was unable to be there to meet us. So the Lanc was put through its paces in the proper John Stanley tradition for 5 minutes, and we left for overhead Sywell where we were to meet Coltishall's Spitfire and Hurricane at 3.20 pm.

Right on time the two fighters hove into view and formated on our wingtips; the Hurricane to starboard and the Spitfire to port. The formation stayed that way through two more displays, one at Benson and one at Biggin Hill, where the other two aircraft left us to land. Our next port of call was Coltishall where another 5

*The Lancaster taxies towards the BBMF hangar after a sortie, with PZ865 and P7350 having already arrived and shut-down. (Dave Chadderton)*

minute display was performed, then the pilot set course for home and we droned on, reaching Waddington at 5.30 pm. A very pleasant 3$^1$/4 hours!

It was after this trip that the oil leaks from around the port propeller domes had become more apparent, as normally trips averaged out at about 1$^1$/2 hours with subsequent less build up of leaking oil. In 1971, the props should be leak-free as they were serviced during the winter of 1970/71.

The last flight in 1970 was the carriage of 617 Squadron's Commemorative covers from Waddington to Scampton, the covers having been brought to Waddington by road from Scampton for the trip. So with the display season ended, the Lancaster was moved into a hangar for its Minor Inspection.

PA474 joined the Flight in November 1973. In 1975 the 'Lanc' was adopted by the City of Lincoln; the name and Coat of Arms of which it still proudly wears over thirty years later. The Flight moved to its current home at RAF Coningsby in March 1976, and restoration work to put the Lancaster into wartime configuration was still ongoing. A mid-upper turret was finally fitted to the Lancaster the same year.

PA474 was marked up as KM-B until 1979. Following the 1979 display season, the bomber was flown to Lyneham, Wiltshire, where it was given the AJ-G code of 617 Squadron's ED932. This was the Lancaster famously flown by Wing Commander Guy Gibson VC DSO* DFC* during the 'Dam Busters' raid of 16/17 May 1943, probably the single most famous air raid in history.

A few years later, having undergone a major servicing at St Athan over the winter of 1983/4, PA474 was next painted as SR-D to represent an aircraft of 101 Squadron. PA474's next major service was contracted out to West Country Air Services at Exeter,

Devon. It returned to Coningsby in March 1988 wearing the PM-M² code of ED888 while it was with 103 Squadron. During its service life with 103 and 576 Squadrons this aircraft completed 140 operations – more than any other Lancaster. Due to the huge array of operations symbols, the Coat of Arms and *City of Lincoln* name was reduced in size and moved further forward.

With the frequency of the Lancaster's major servicing extended to six years, it was not until the winter of 1993/4 that PA474 received its next repaint. Carried out at St Athan, this saw the bomber applied with the markings of 9 Squadron's W4964 WS-J with its distinctive Johnnie Walker nose-art and 'Still Going Strong' slogan – and representing another Lancaster Centurion. This 'Lanc' became a veteran of 106 'ops', the hundreth of which saw it drop a 'Tallboy' bomb aimed at the mighty German battleship *Tirpitz* on 15 September 1944. The size and colourful nose-art of the aircraft represented meant that this time the Coat of Arms and *City of Lincoln* name had to be moved to the Lancaster's starboard side.

On 25 September 1995, having completed that year's display season, PA474 set off from Coningsby and flew to St Athan ready to undergo a major wing re-spar programme. A fatigue meter had been fitted on board PA474 when it joined the Flight. By the end of the 1983 flying season readings showed that the bomber had clocked up 3060 hours, leaving 1340 hours or about thirteen years remaining based on the usage at the time. In 1984 British Aerospace (BAe) determined the fatigue index to be 70.7, where an index of 100 indicates no fatigue life remaining. A decision that the spar booms would be replaced was made in 1990, and BAe was tasked to define the repair, which was originally planned to be carried out during the aircraft's 1993/4 major service.

The intention of the repair design was to replicate as much of the historic concept of the Lancaster as possible. This included the use of a unique method of attaching the skins to the boom on the outer wings, known as plug riveting. However, the repair would not in any way compromise modern-day design practices and fatigue enhancement measures.

There was a change of plan in October 1992, when a decision was made to keep the 'Lanc' flying for as long as there was sufficient fatigue life available, which by then had been calculated to expire in 1996. Flying restrictions were imposed on the aircraft to avoid any heavy manoeuvres, and fatigue meter readings were regularly sent to BAe for analysis.

It was agreed that the repair work would be performed by BAe at Chadderton, near Manchester. After its arrival at St Athan in 1995, PA474's engines and undercarriage were removed, then the airframe was separated and prepared for transportation. That November

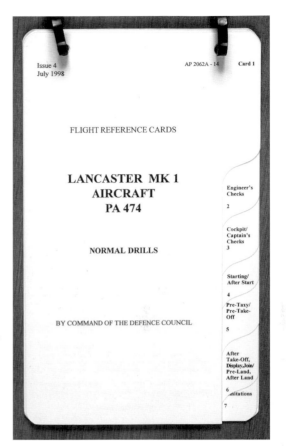

FLIGHT REFERENCE CARDS

**LANCASTER MK 1
AIRCRAFT
PA 474**

**NORMAL DRILLS**

BY COMMAND OF THE DEFENCE COUNCIL

Issue 4
July 1998

AP 2062A - 14     Card 1

Engineer's Checks
2

Cockpit/ Captain's Checks
3

Starting/ After Start
4

Pre-Taxy/ Pre-Take-Off
5

After Take-Off, Display,Join/ Pre-Land, After Land
6

Limitations
7

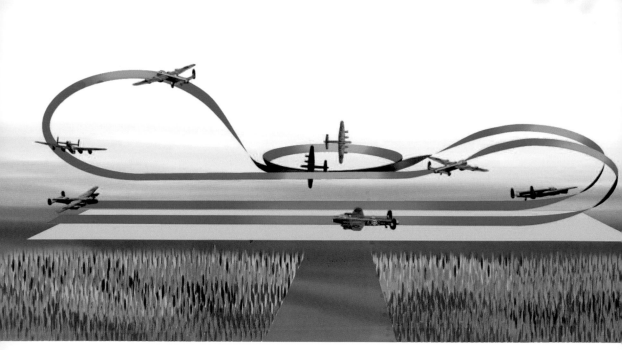

*Ribbon diagram of the Lancaster's display routine. Having arrived as a three-ship formation with a Hurricane and Spitfire, following the fighters' respective displays PA474 commences its solo with a flypast at 100 ft, with the engines set at 2400 rpm and zero boost, resulting in a speed of 180 knots. The 'nav' starts his stop watch as the bomber passes the datum point, and the crew count to eleven seconds for still air (but this may be adjusted depending on the length of the crowd line and the strength of the wind) before pulling up and away to reduce the speed to around 150 knots. The co-pilot then reduces the boost to -4, as the 'nav' opens the bomb bay doors. As the Lancaster approaches the display datum again, it commences a 360-degree turn at 300 ft to offer the crowd a good view of the bomb bay. The speed is now coming down to 130 knots, with the aircraft climbing to 400 ft during the far part of the turn. The bomb bay doors are then closed and the bomber continues the turn 'clean'. Having passed the datum again, with PA474 flying away from the crowd the Captain checks for speed below 150 knots and calls for flaps to 20 degrees. The undercarriage is lowered and as the aircraft returns to its audience the engines are increased to 2850 rpm. The navigator gives the fighters a 'one-minute rejoin' radio call and the Lancaster's gear-down pass is carried out at 110 knots, at a height of 100 ft. On passing the datum the brakes are briefly applied to stop the wheels turning in the wind, then released again. The Captain calls for gear up and as the wheels are retracted calls for +7 boost as the bomber turns away from the crowd. At 120 knots the flaps are retracted and the 'Lanc' accelerates towards 150 knots, with the power reset to 2000 rpm at +4 boost. As this happens the two fighters have caught up and are rejoining in formation. Because of its lower stalling speed, the Hurricane always rejoins on the inside of the turn. Once both fighters are in position on either side of the bomber, they call in and the three-ship formation will come around for one more three-ship pass. Turning at 140 to 150 knots, PA474 leads the formation along the display line at 300 ft to exit in the opposite direction from which the formation arrived. Dependent on wind strength and the venue, a typical BBMF Lancaster display will last for approximately five minutes. (Pete West)*

*The Lancaster comes in to land at Coningsby as a pair of Eurofighter Typhoons hold to await its clearance from the runway before they move on for take-off. (Author)*

various sections of the aircraft arrived at BAe. Completed sections were ready to be on their way back to St Athan during early February 1996.

At St Athan the bomber was reassembled and its first flight test was carried out on 13 May with Flt Lt Mike Chatterton as Captain. Two days later PA474 returned to Coningsby with its new spar in place – and this still has thousands of hours flying time remaining on it.

The Lancaster received its *Mickey the Moocher* paint scheme following another scheduled maintenance at St Athan, ready for the 2000 season. This identity represented 61 Squadron Lancaster III EE176 QR-M, another particularly notable example as it became one of the thirty-five known Lancaster Centurions after surviving in excess of 100 missions during World War Two (EE176 is thought to have flown between 115 and 128 operations).

Although aircraft lettered 'M' were usually known as 'Mike' or 'Mother', one of EE176's crews called it 'Mickey' and adorned the bomber's port forward fuselage with the artwork of Walt Disney's Mickey Mouse. Mickey was painted pulling a bomb trolley with a bomb sat on it, and the name *Mickey the Moocher* was applied too – this was a parody of the popular song of the time *Minnie the Moocher*. In front of the character is a signpost with two arms, the top of which reads '3 Reich' and the other 'Berlin',

*The Flight is always honoured and privileged to meet veterans. This is Warrant Officer Ron Clark DFC sat in PA474. Ron flew thirty operations in EE139* Phantom of the Ruhr, *the new paint scheme worn by the Lancaster from the 2007 season. (Author)*

presumably denoting where Mickey was heading with his 'bomb'. In fact, EE176's target was Berlin on some fifteen occasions.

PA474 is, of course, flown to the strictest of limitations and standards and always to visual flight rules (VFR). Being a military-owned and operated aircraft, it has to comply with current RAF regulations. It is also very important to state that the Lancaster is part of a Memorial Flight, *not* an entertainment display team – while the aircraft does carry out displays to show its performance and characteristics in the air, the primary aim is to keep it flying for as long as possible. During the course of a season the Flight's 'Lanc' will clock-up an average of between 85 to 100 hours flying time, but is limited to *no more* than 100. To further conserve the airframe's fatigue life, there is a maximum 'g' loading of 1.5 g and a 'never exceed' limit of 1.8 g.

The pilots also operate to strict crosswind limitations for take-offs and landings. This is limited to 10 knots initially, until the pilot has reached fifty hours on the aircraft, whereupon he may take off in crosswinds of up to 15 knots – which is PA474's permitted maximum.

Take-offs are timed quite precisely so that as many displays and flypasts as possible can be fitted into the retricted hours. Before a display or flypast the navigator will have carefully worked out a flight-plan that will see the 'Lanc' arrive at the relevant venue exactly on time.

No. 3 engine (starboard inner) is the first to be fired up in the sequence. This is because the aircraft's inboard engines each have a 1500-watt DC generator. Once all four engines have been started, the after starting checks have been carried out and the crew are ready, the pre-taxi checks will be carried out. With all this fulfilled, the engines are brought up to 1200 rpm and PA474 is taxied to the relevant active runway. There are then a total of eighteen pre-take-off checks, which must be carried out on the Lancaster. These include the engine run-ups and mag-drop checks, which necessitates the crew keeping the bomber sitting into the wind for some time before take-off.

If the display is a three-ship formation with one each of the Flight's Hurricanes and Spitfires, the take-off sequence will usually be Spitfire, Hurricane, then Lancaster. Once the Lancaster's crew see the Hurricane start to roll, boost will be set to zero. When the Hurricane is airborne the bomber's brakes will be released and the Captain will call for settings of 3000 rpm and +7 boost. The crew make a final check of the instruments and the Lancaster starts its take-off run. As PA474 rolls and gains speed, after around just 12 seconds the tail will be lifted. The 'Lanc' will normally rotate at 90 knots, which takes just over 30 seconds to reach. Once the undercarriage is up the aircraft maintains a shallow rate of climb until its speed builds. The 'Lanc' will be travelling at about 120 knots at a height of 150 ft when the Captain calls for flaps up. The fighters will soon join up in a loose formation and transit speed to a display venue is 150 knots, with the Lancaster's engines running at around 2000 rpm and zero boost.

On arrival at the display venue, the Flight will perform a three-ship formation flypast in front of the crowd at between 150 to 170 knots, at 300 ft. As they reach the end of the crowd line, the Lancaster's navigator will call 'Fighters, break, break, go!'

The two fighters will then peel off, and the 'Spit' will commence its solo display. Meanwhile the Hurricane will hold to the rear of the display site at 1500 ft, with the 'Lanc' doing likewise behind the crowd at 1000 ft. While in a holding pattern, the 'Lanc' crew will monitor the fighter displays in order that they are ready for their cue to begin the display. After the Spitfire comes the Hurricane's display, and its pilot will give a radio call one minute before the end of his routine, whereupon PA474 will be positioned ready for its first flypast.

As the Hurricane carries out the final manoeuvre in its sequence – a climbing victory roll at 600 ft – the 'Lanc' has commenced its first flypast at 100 ft and then carries out its solo display. If it is to land at an airfield where an air show is taking place, you'll note that PA474 will touch-down using a 'wheel it on' approach, rather than the 'three-pointer' type landing used during the war. The downwind leg is flown at 2400 rpm and zero boost, which gives a speed of around 140 knots.

By the end of the downwind leg the speed will have been reduced to 115 knots. Turning onto finals, the flaps will be lowered to 40 degrees and the engines will be brought up to 2850 rpm, with the boost remaining at zero. Power is reduced in increments of 2 in of boost, and the 'Lanc' approaches the threshold at 90 knots with a setting of -6 boost. Once safely down the engines are 'slow cut' and the flaps raised.

PA474 received a new identity for the 2007 flying season. It has now taken on the guise of *Phantom of the Ruhr*, representing Lancaster III EE139 of 100 and 550 Squadrons. Coded HW-R, EE139 flew thirty operations with 100 Squadron at Waltham (Grimsby), Lincolnshire, before moving to 550 Squadron. The latter unit was formed from 'C' Flight of 100 Squadron on 25 November 1943 at the same base. The Lancaster's code was changed to BQ-B and it went on to complete a total of 121 operations.

The new paint scheme is again particularly suitable. First, it represents a Lancaster 'Centurion' as has been common practice for aircraft represented by PA474 for its previous three paint schemes. Also, it represents a unit that was serving in Lincolnshire at the time portrayed – not only is the Flight based in Lincolnshire, but PA474 has close links with, and bears the name, *City of Lincoln* on its starboard side. Furthermore, the 'Lanc' wears the markings of a squadron that is still operational (100 Squadron is a target facilities unit operating BAe Hawk T.1As out of Leeming, Yorkshire).

It is also fitting that several members of the original crew of *Phantom of the Ruhr* are still alive and were contacted. These include WO Ron Clark DFC, the bomber's pilot, who flew twenty-five missions in EE139 while with 100 Squadron.

*Seen in front of PA474 wearing its new Phantom of the Ruhr artwork at RAF Coningsby on 27 April 2007 is Ron Clark (left), who flew EE139 on 25 of its 30 operations with 100 Squadron, and BBMF Lancaster Captain Flt Lt Ed Straw – who is wearing Ron's original wartime battledress which he presented to Ed before he flew a display sortie on this day. The event was the launch of the BBMF's 50th anniversary season and the Lancaster's new nose art was officially unveiled that day by Ron. The Rolls-Royce Phantom in the picture was the transport for Ron and family for the day! (Author)*

*With its 267 Squadron Pegasus emblems prominent, ZA947 is a wonderful tribute to the transport, supply and airborne forces operations that helped win the war. (John Dibbs/Plane Picture Company)*

# CHAPTER 9

# Dakota III ZA947

Since joining the Flight in March 1993, Dakota III ZA947 has become a year-round workhorse with many roles to play. It enables the Lancaster pilots to keep current on multi-engine piston taildraggers during the winter months when the bomber is out of action, it is a useful transport aircraft for personnel and spares, it is a fitting memorial to Airborne forces and transport operations – and it is of course a display aircraft in its own right.

It was built as a C-47A Skytrain, 42-24338, at Long Beach, California, and delivered to the United States Army Air Force on 7 September 1943. A little over a week later it was transferred to the Royal Canadian Air Force (RCAF) as 661, and served mainly in Canada but in 1965 was used in Europe. It was declared surplus to requirements in 1969.

The Royal Aircraft Establishment (RAE) then purchased the aircraft, which was allocated the British military serial number KG661, as it had carried the RCAF serial number 661. Firstly painted in an RAF Transport Command style white and grey scheme, it later received the RAE's red, white and blue 'raspberry ripple' paintwork. During the Dakota's service with the RAE at West Freugh in Scotland, it was used on a variety of

*When ZA947 was handed over to the Flight it was still wearing its RAE raspberry ripple livery, though it underwent a major overhaul and was soon to lose this colourful scheme in favour of authentic wartime paintwork. (Duncan Cubitt/FlyPast)*

*Wearing the identity of the aircraft in which Flight Lieutenant David Lord won the Victoria Cross, ZA947 touches down at Wroughton in 1994. (Steve Fletcher/FlyPast)*

tasks and trials, including dropping test sonabuoys off the Scottish coast.

For some time, however, there had been doubt about the aircraft's allotted serial number. It transpired that KG661 had been another Dakota III that had crashed on take-off from Crosby-on-Eden, Cumberland, on 13 December 1944. Therefore, in July 1979 the aircraft was allotted the new serial number ZA947. In 1992 the Defence Research Agency, successor to the RAE, declared the Dakota surplus to requirements and offered it up for disposal.

ZA947 was adopted by Strike Command and issued to the Flight in March 1993, after Air Atlantique at Coventry had completed engineering and structural work. It was repainted at RAF Marham into the 271 Squadron YS-DM paintwork of KG374, with

*The 'Dak', in its 77 Squadron Berlin Airlift scheme, is ready for a sortie out of Coningsby in April 2002. (Author)*

*Squadron Leader Stu Reid carries out his pre-flight walk-around checks prior to a sortie out of Duxford in April 2006. (Author)*

*The Dakota builds up speed down Coningsby's runway for take-off on a sortie to RAF Marham in June 2006. (Author)*

uniform olive green topsides, representing the aircraft of Flight Lieutenant David Lord VC DFC. This pilot was posthumously awarded the VC for his actions on 19 September 1944 in Operation *Market Garden* – the airborne assault on Arnhem. A report from *The London Gazette* of 13 November 1944 details his actions:

Flight Lieutenant David Samuel Anthony Lord, D.F.C. (49149), R.A.F., 271 Sqn. (deceased).

Flight Lieutenant Lord was pilot and captain of a Dakota aircraft detailed to drop supplies at Arnhem on the afternoon of 10th September 1944. Our airborne troops had been surrounded and were being pressed into a small area defended by a large number of anti-aircraft guns. Air crews were warned that intense opposition would be met over the dropping zone. To ensure accuracy they were ordered to fly at 900

*The Load Master's job in the back of the 'Dak' is often lonely, so when you see one waving during a flypast remember to wave back! Here Flight Lieutenant Scott Greig stands at the door as the Dakota turns for a flypast. (Author)*

feet when dropping their containers.

While flying at 1,500 feet near Arnhem the starboard wing of Flight Lieutenant Lord's aircraft was twice hit by anti-aircraft fire. The starboard engine was set on fire. He would have been justified in leaving the main stream of supply aircraft and continuing at the same height or even abandoning his aircraft. But on learning that his crew were uninjured and that the dropping zone would be reached in three minutes he said he would complete his mission, as the troops were in dire need of supplies.

By now the starboard engine was burning furiously. Flight Lieutenant Lord came down to 900 feet, where he was singled out for the concentrated fire of all the anti-aircraft guns. On reaching the dropping zone he kept the aircraft on a straight and level course while supplies were dropped. At the end of his run, he was told that two containers remained.

Although he must have known that the collapse of the starboard wing could not be long delayed, Flight Lieutenant Lord circled, rejoined the stream of aircraft and made a second run to drop the remaining supplies. These manoeuvres took eight minutes in all, the aircraft being continuously under heavy anti-aircraft fire.

*ZA947 was fitted with authentic seats in time for the D-Day sixtieth anniversary para-drop over Ranville on 5 June 2004. (Author)*

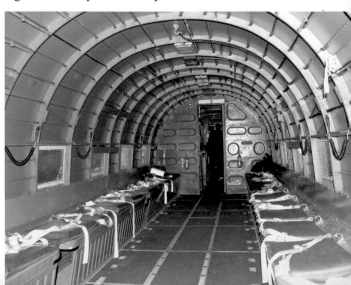

*ZA947 passes the village of Morton, just north of Bourne in Lincolnshire, while tracking back along the A15 heading home after an evening flypast. (Author)*

His task completed, Flight Lieutenant Lord ordered his crew to abandon the Dakota, making no attempt himself to leave the aircraft, which was down to 500 feet. A few seconds later, the starboard wing collapsed and the aircraft fell in flames. There was only one survivor, who was flung out while assisting other members of the crew to put on their parachutes.

By continuing his mission in a damaged and burning aircraft, descending to drop the supplies accurately, returning to the dropping zone a second time and, finally, remaining at the controls to give his crew a chance of escape, Flight Lieutenant Lord displayed supreme valour and sacrifice.

In 1994 the Dakota participated in the fiftieth anniversary of Operation *Overlord*. During these commemorations, ZA947 dropped the first paratroops of the day over Ranville DZ, near Pegasus Bridge. After this was the fiftieth anniversary of Operation *Market Garden*, which once more involved the Flight's 'Dak' dropping paratroops, this time onto Ginkel Heath near Arnhem. It returned to The Netherlands the following year and carried out various flypasts in the Arnhem area. Also in 1995 ZA947 took part in the VE Day flypast over London.

ZA947 went back to Air Atlantique for a winter servicing at the end of the 1997 season and emerged wearing new colours for 1998. This time it was given the markings of a 77 Squadron aircraft, YS-H, to represent an aircraft of that unit that participated in the Berlin Airlift of 1948/9 (No. 271 was renumbered as 77 Squadron on 1 December 1946). For the fiftieth anniversary commemorations of this, the 'Dak' made two trips to Berlin and one to Hamburg in 1998.

*ZA947 has become a display item in its own right, and is seen here at the renowned Flying Legends air show of 2006 at Duxford with LF363 waiting to accompany it out for take-off. (Author)*

*View out over the starboard wing as ZA947 makes a steep turn over RAF Marham in June 2006. The control tower is prominent on the ground below. (Author)*

ZA947 was next treated to a new look for the 2003 season, when it gained dark green/dark earth camouflage topsides with the markings of 267 Squadron, Italy, circa 1944. Most prominent are the squadron's Pegasus emblems on both sides of the forward fuselage. Red AI codes appear on the fuselage sides, and the undersides are now 'sky'. The repaint was carried out by Sprayavia, one of Europe's leading aircraft refinishing specialists based at Norwich Airport, Norfolk.

ZA947 was at Sprayavia's Norwich facility for nine days. The work undertaken began with chemically removing the existing paint, which in some places had up to fourteen layers. Once the 'Dak' had been taken back to bare metal, a thorough corrosion inspection was carried out – and ZA947 was found to be in very good condition. The new paint scheme was then applied and the Dakota left Norwich for its home at Coningsby on 17 February 2003.

No. 267 Squadron was re-formed in August 1940 for local transport duties in Egypt operating various smaller communications types. By August 1942 the unit had standardised with larger twin-engined transports, including the Dakota. Its area of operations extended throughout the Mediterranean region and its role included the movement of personnel and equipment, casualty evacuation and occasional supply drops

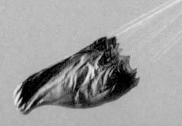

*Paratroops drop from the Flight's 'Dak' for the sixtieth anniversary of Operation Market Garden, paying a wonderful tribute to the vital role played by airborne forces during World War Two. (© Crown Copyright/MOD)*

to guerrilla groups in Italy and the Balkans.

No. 267 'Pegasus' Squadron flew in the transport, trooping and resupply roles in the Middle East and the Mediterranean Theatres during 1943/4. The squadron employed various colour schemes on its Dakotas, but always displayed its 'Pegasus' emblem prominently on an aircraft's nose. The squadron's role included the resupply of partisans and resistance fighters behind enemy lines, either by para-drops or by landing at clandestine airstrips.

In November 1943, the squadron moved to Bari, Italy. In February 1945 No. 267 Squadron was transferred to Burma where it carried supplies during the 14th Army's final offensive that cleared the Japanese.

During 2004, original and authentic para-seats were refitted to the Dakota, returning the cabin interior to the original, wartime specification. These were fitted in time for the D-Day sixtieth anniversary para-drop made over Ranville on 5 June 2004. On 10 July 2005 ZA947 had the honour of leading the 'Pegasus' formation, comprising three Dakotas, over Buckingham Palace on National Commemoration Day.

*The Dakota's Pegasus nose-art, which is worn on both sides of its forward fuselage. (Author)*

*WK518 wearing RAF College Cranwell paintwork at Waddington in October 1994. (FlyPast)*

# CHAPTER 10

# Chipmunks

The Flight's brace of de Havilland Canada Chipmunk T.10s are the last of the classic trainer still in RAF service. They are used year-round for the conversion and continuation training of BBMF pilots on taildragger aircraft.

The Chipmunk was de Havilland's successor to its Tiger Moth biplane trainer. The new low-wing monoplane type was designed by de Havilland Canada at its Toronto works. The prototype carried out its maiden flight on 22 May 1946.

After evaluations carried out using G-AKDN (equipped to RAF requirements) at Boscombe Down, Wiltshire, the type was adopted as an *ab initio* trainer for the RAF. Production of T.10s for the RAF began with WB549, and the first batch was delivered to Oxford University Air Squadron (UAS) at Kidlington to replace Tiger Moths in February 1950. Altogether some 740 Chipmunks were built for the RAF, the last being delivered on 1 October 1953.

'Chippies' quickly became the standard type on University Air Squadrons and Reserve Flying Schools of the RAF Volunteer Reserve. They were also later chosen for the

*Outside the BBMF hangar being readied for a local training sortie in June 2006. (Author)*

training of National Service pilots and replaced Percival Prentices at the RAF College Cranwell until the arrival of the Percival Provost in November 1954. Chipmunks remained on University Air Squadrons until the mid-1970s, at which time they were replaced by the Scottish Aviation Bulldog T.1.

Within the RAF, taildraggers are now unique to the BBMF and pilots new to the Flight commonly arrive with no previous tail wheel experience. Other uses of the 'Chippies' include the delivery or collection of pilots and also the reconnaissance of new venues. Both BBMF Chipmunks appear in the RAF's modern high-conspicuency black paint scheme with white bars, as applied to training types nowadays such as Hawks and Tucanos.

WK518 arrived with the Flight in April 1983. The aircraft was first delivered to the RAF in January 1952, going to the RAF College Cranwell. Other units that have operated WK518 include the University Air Squadrons for Liverpool, Manchester, Cambridge, Hull, Leeds and London Universities, the Cottesmore Station Flight and 1 Air Experience Flight at Manston.

WG486 was also delivered to the RAF in January 1952 and served with 5 Basic Flying Training School, 9 Refresher Flying School and 2 Flying Training School before being used by the Army with 651 and 657 Squadrons. It was subsequently operated by units that included the RAF College Cranwell, Initial Training School at South Cerney and Church Fenton, Bristol University Air Squadron and 3 Air Experience Flight.

WG486 served on operations with 114 Squadron in Nicosia, Cyprus, during Operation *Thwart* in 1958. The Chipmunks were used to carry out anti-terrorist operations from December 1958 to March 1959. No. 114 Squadron was especially re-formed for these operations and began duties as part of Operation *Thwart* on 12 December 1958. Their

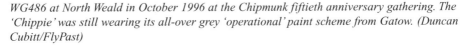

*WG486 at North Weald in October 1996 at the Chipmunk fiftieth anniversary gathering. The 'Chippie' was still wearing its all-over grey 'operational' paint scheme from Gatow. (Duncan Cubitt/FlyPast)*

tasks included observation and liaison, flying with Army officers in the rear seat.

In 1987 WG486 moved to Germany to operate as part of the Gatow Station Flight in Berlin, which was then surrounded by Soviet Bloc territory. From the 1950s Chipmunks were used to carry out air coverage of the 20-mile radius of territory around Berlin, where there were large concentrations of Soviet and East German forces. Operating at low level with hand-held cameras, the Chipmunk crews would often return to base with valuable photographs of the Warsaw Pact's equipment and personnel in operational and training roles. Sometimes hostile actions would occur – on at least one occasion a Chipmunk returned to Gatow with a bullet hole in its airframe.

Those who flew the aircraft were a mixture of aircrew on BRIXMIS strength and station executives, for whom the aircraft were based in Berlin, ostensibly 'to maintain their flying proficiency'.

When the Berlin Wall came down and the country was reunified, Gatow closed. The aircraft spent a year at Laarbruck before being delivered to the Flight in 1995.

The Flight's Chipmunks are therefore not only the sole examples of their type remaining in service with the RAF, but WG486 has the rare distinction for its type of having served operationally twice in its service life.

*Both Chipmunks carry the Flight's badge on their tails. WG486 has a G identification letter on its tail fin, while WK518 has a K. (Author)*

*WG486 and WK518 on a sortie out of Coningsby in 2006, wearing the RAF's modern high-conspicuency black paint scheme with white bars. (RAF Coningsby/© Crown Copyright/MOD)*

*Squadron Leader Clive Rowley climbs into 'P7' ready for a sortie. ZA947 can be seen in the distance, having just taken off from Coningsby. (Author)*

# CHAPTER 11

# BBMF Fighter Display Sequence

Squadron Leader Clive Rowley MBE flew with the BBMF for eleven seasons, including three as Officer Commanding. In this time he accrued over 500 hours on the fighters, and here he describes for us a typical fighter display routine. Clive goes on to discuss whether pilots prefer the Spitfire or Hurricane, and then outlines a typical fighter air test:

Many people have watched the BBMF Spitfires and Hurricanes at displays over the years and been delighted to see the shapes of these wonderful, charismatic and historic aircraft in the sky and to hear the sound of their powerful piston engines – the Rolls-Royce Merlin and Griffon V-12s. The knowledgeable amongst these audiences will know that the BBMF presents its aircraft in a gentle and graceful manner, as befits the vintage of these historic machines. BBMF pilots know that it is the aircraft that are the stars, not themselves, and that this is not a time to show the full extent of their flying skills but just another privileged opportunity to show the aircraft to the public in their natural environment – the air.

But what does a BBMF fighter display sequence consist of, and what is it like to fly a display in a Spitfire or a Hurricane? Here I'll take the reader through a typical BBMF display, which could perhaps be flown in Spitfire IIa P7350 ('P7' to BBMF personnel) – the oldest airworthy Spitfire in the world and the only one to have actually fought in the Battle of Britain still flying today. It is always an honour and a privilege to fly her and as some pilots have been heard to exclaim with some concern before doing so, 'No pressure there then!'

Before running in for the display I carry out the pre-display checks, checking the altimeter setting and the fuel, and caging the Direction Indicator (DI) so that its gyros are not damaged when 60° of bank or pitch are exceeded and the gyro topples. I loosen the seat harness shoulder straps slightly so that I can twist round to see over my shoulder, something I will need to do during the display to look back at the display line. I also set display power with the RPM lever and the throttle lever – 2650 RPM and +6 inches of boost, clamping the throttle setting tight with the throttle friction wheel so that when I take my left hand off the throttle it doesn't throttle back, as it otherwise would. The engine in this Spitfire is capable of producing up to +12 inches of boost so this setting is only half of what the engine is capable of – an example of how the aircraft are now operated to lower limits than those originally used during wartime. In a similar way, the G loading placed on the aircraft is now limited to a maximum of +4 G and the maximum speed to 270 knots.

Once the power is set, I trim the Spitfire out with the elevator and rudder trim wheels to fly hands and feet off at 180 knots. This is a good speed to set the rudder trim at, allowing for changes in the directional trim at speeds above or below this to be controlled with rudder inputs made with the feet on the rudder pedals. It is also a good starting point for the elevator trim, although I may well make changes to this during the display to keep the control column forces to reasonable levels. Whilst doing this I have positioned the aircraft at 1500 feet ready to run in for the display head-on to the crowd on the 90° axis and I have identified the display centre point, the 'datum', and the display line that must not be crossed so as to preserve the minimum laid-down separation between my aircraft and the crowd for safety reasons.

So, here goes, lowering the nose gently, I put my Spitfire into an accelerating dive,

*Squadron Leader Clive Rowley carries out his last victory roll with the BBMF while performing his final display on 24 September 2006, shortly before his retirement from the RAF. He was flying MK356 at the time, which shows off its Invasion stripes as the Spitfire Mk.IX gracefully rolls. (Author)*

*Squadron Leader Clive Rowley after his final Spitfire display, appropriately posed on the wing of PS915's - 'The Last!' (Author)*

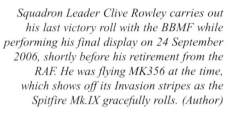

descending to the minimum display height of 100 feet and allowing the speed to build up to about 250 knots (over 300 mph) to ensure that there will be sufficient energy at the start of the display to fly all the manoeuvres without getting slow. It is worth pointing out here that Spitfire and Hurricane pilots have to judge the minimum display height entirely visually, as the altimeter is a rudimentary pressure instrument that suffers from significant pressure errors at speed and when turning hard. Its indications cannot be relied upon for height to within the required accuracy of 100 feet, so it is essential that BBMF pilots are able to judge their height accurately by visual references. With a wingspan of just under 37 feet this height is less than three wingspans if the Spitfire has 90° of bank applied, but if there is any doubt, pilots want to fly higher because 100 feet is the minimum cleared height for the BBMF.

*Clive has gone through his checks and fired up the Spitfire. The chocks will soon be pulled clear and he'll taxi out for take-off. (Author)*

As the speed builds up, I have to feed on some left rudder to keep the Spitfire from skidding to the right and to keep the nose pointing at the display datum. Levelling at 100 feet at 250 knots it is quite bumpy and it is as well that I am tightly strapped into the seat with the lap straps, even so the top of my flying helmet, the 'bonedome', contacts the canopy a couple of times in the bigger bumps. This isn't a comfortable ride. At an appropriate distance from the display line, taking into account the effects of the wind

*Spitfire IIa P7350 awaits its pilot for a display. (Author)*

blowing me towards or away from the line, I bank sharply to the left with a quick movement of the control column 'spade grip' to the left and some left rudder to make the Spitfire roll around its axis without 'dishing'. In less than a second I have 80° of left bank, so I stop the roll and pull +3 G, to 'break' through 110-120° to my left, or as the crowd sees it to their right, using the rudder pedals as required to ensure that this is a level break and that the aircraft's nose tracks around the horizon without climbing or descending. +3 G is not a lot to a fighter pilot (modern fairground rides expose the riders to this amount of G) but even so, as it is sustained for a few seconds during the break turn, it is best to 'G strain' – to tense up the muscles in the legs, arms and stomach so as to resist the insidious effects of the G causing the body's blood to pool in the lower half and extremities with resulting 'grey out' or, with higher G forces than this, even 'black out'.

I snap-roll the wings level as I reach a point where I will be tracking away from the crowd on a 20-30° cut. This has to be judged visually as the gyro-operated DI was caged before we commenced and so I have no heading reference in the cockpit whilst manoeuvring. I count for 3 seconds – '1001, 1002, 1003,' and then pitch the aircraft up into a steep climb, pulling +3 G and applying some pre-emptive left rudder as I pull so as to avoid the nose slicing to the right as a result of the gyroscopic forces on the propeller disc. I stop the pitch at approximately 30° climb angle, again judged visually as the artificial horizon toppled when I exceeded 60° bank angle on the initial break turn – it is roughly 'feet on the horizon'. I pause briefly and then roll left with full left aileron applied with the control column spade grip hard over to the left, to roll through 270°, finishing with 90° of bank to the right, using some left rudder to ensure that the Spitfire rolls around its axis but accepting that the roll will be slightly 'barrelled' and the nose will drop slightly during the roll, as these days we do not use less than +1 G for long-term preservation reasons. This manoeuvre is known as a 'Derry Wingover' named after the famous test and display pilot John Derry.

I 'top out' of the wingover at about 2000 feet with about 150 knots indicated and twist round in the cockpit to look back over my right shoulder and out of the top of the canopy to see the display line and ensure that as I pull back around the corner I will be back on the display line, whilst descending back down to 100 feet. There is a brief moment about halfway around the corner where I know that I have the turn radius and descent under control to achieve this, and I can afford to briefly look into the cockpit to scan the engine instruments for a 'health check' – I've only got one engine and I want to look after it!

The next pass along the line from the crowd's right to left is the so-called 'High Speed Pass', and the speed is again up at about 240 knots (just under 300 mph). This is bumpy again. At some venues this pass may be flown as a 'Topside Pass' with bank applied and following a gently curved path away from the line so that the crowd get a good view of the upper surfaces of the aircraft. I like doing this if I can to show a different aspect of the aircraft's shape. To fly a proper 'Topside Pass' it is important to ensure that the lower wingtip is not pointing at the crowd but that the aircraft has more bank than this, otherwise it is just a 'side-on pass'.

Just past the datum I pull up again into another 'Derry Wingover', rolling left through 270° until I have 90° of right bank and then slicing back round and down to the right to head back towards the datum from the crowd's left, coming in on the 45° axis.

As I reach the datum I already have about 60° of left bank applied and as soon as I am on the display line I just tighten slightly and pull up gently into a 360° orbit, flown obliquely as I have plenty of speed, climbing to about 1200 feet at the back of the circle and then descending back down to 100 feet as I return to the line and back to the datum. There normally has to be some allowance made for the effects of the wind during the '360', with some quarters of the circle flown tighter and some flown slacker than the others, to make the manoeuvre appear circular and symmetrical, so that the apex and halfway point are directly opposite the datum and to ensure that the completion of the '360' is at the datum.

Leaving the datum heading out to the crowd's right on the 20-30° axis, I count 5 seconds. Then I pull up at +3 G into another 30° climb, pause and roll right through 90° to top-out of a simple wingover manoeuvre, with another chance to check the engine instruments before pulling back round and descending back down to 100 feet onto the line.

Roaring along the line from the crowd's right at about 220 knots, I break right at the datum, through 90° and roll the wings level so that I am heading away from the crowd to the left of the 90° axis as they see it, into a manoeuvre the BBMF for some obtuse reason calls 'The Horseshoe', although it actually looks more like a trombone. After a few seconds' heading out on the 90, I pull up into a climb and bank to the right, climbing to the apex halfway round and then descending back down for the second half of the turn back towards the crowd, effectively another wingover, and then heading back head-on towards the crowd before breaking hard right back to the datum.

Continuing this hard turn out onto the 20-30° axis going away to the crowd's left, I count 3 seconds and pull up for the final wingover to the left to come back around and down onto the line from the crowd's left, positioning for the final 'Victory Roll'.

Running in from the crowd left to right at 100 feet, I ensure that I have at least 180 knots and then, just before the datum, pull up at +3 G to about 20° of pitch before rolling left through 360° for the climbing 'Victory Roll'. Looking out of the top of the canopy as I pass the inverted point I can see the display datum above me and can check whether I achieved the inverted position at the centre point as I aim to do. When the roll is completed I am back the right way up and at about 800 feet, flying away to the crowd's right.

A check of the engine instruments shows that both the oil temperature and the coolant temperature have increased during the display and so has my own body temperature – I am suddenly aware that I am breathing hard – that was actually quite physical. It's time to cool down both the engine and me. Another display completed – that was fun! Hopefully the crowd also enjoyed watching such a wonderful, historic aircraft still able to perform and enjoyed the spine-tingling sound of the engine at display power.

## Spitfire or Hurricane, which aircraft do BBMF fighter pilots prefer?

BBMF fighter pilots are often asked whether they prefer flying the Spitfire or the Hurricane – a perfectly reasonable question and one that I have always tried to answer in as few words as possible, as those asking it want. I have often asked the same question myself of veteran wartime pilots who have flown both types of aircraft and their answers are very varied and definitely do not fall in a majority on one side or the other. In truth the question is more complicated than can be answered in one sentence and, as with many questions, 'it depends' on what the circumstances are and what you are being asked to do

Briefly, the standard Flight fighter display sequence is as follows: Run in on the 90° axis, break turn left through 120°, 'Derry Wingover', 'high speed' pass (can be a topside pass),

'Derry Wingover', 360° orbit – in Spitfires this can be oblique – wingover, 'Horseshoe', wingover and climbing aileron/'victory' roll. A full fighter display sequence takes approximately 4¹/₂ minutes. There are variations though.

For the tailchase display, the same display is flown with the aircraft following each other in 100-150 yards trail. The Flight 'synchro' display routine is identical to the singleton fighter display, but is flown either by two Spitfires or by a Spitfire and Hurricane simultaneously, with the aircraft displaying synchronously. The No. 2 flies the display in 'mirror image' to the leader, with crossovers occurring at the display datum. (All Pete West)

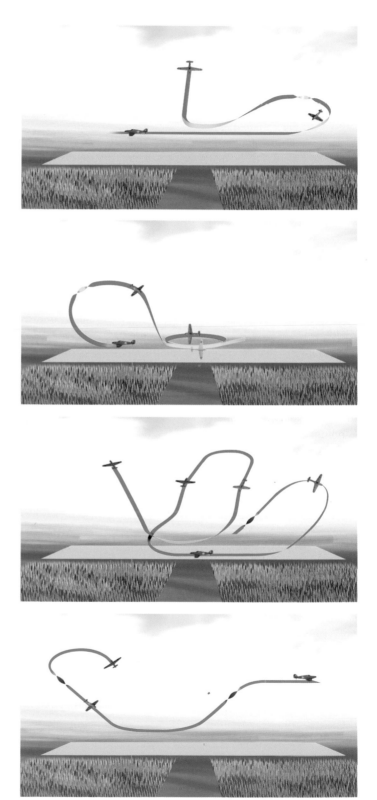

with the aircraft.

The veteran wartime pilots will tend to side with the aircraft that they flew most and many, perhaps surprisingly to today's public, tend to side with the less glamorous Hurricane. They certainly feel that the Hurricane is the unsung hero and its exploits and achievements deserve greater credit than it has tended to receive. When the BBMF was unable to include a Hurricane in the flypast along The Mall in London over HRH the Queen Mother's funeral cortège in April 2002, due simply to the event occurring so early in the BBMF flying season, the Flight came in for all sorts of criticism from Hurricane veterans for not having 'their' aircraft represented. Those that state a preference for the Hurricane generally do not have much flying time on the Spitfire and will often stress the Hurricane's sturdiness and the robustness of its undercarriage in comparison with the dainty Spitfire. When I recently asked a 90-year-old veteran pilot what his preference was, as he was ensconced in the cockpit of one of the BBMF Hurricanes reliving old memories, he said without hesitation, 'This – this has got an undercarriage. You can't call that an undercarriage!' pointing to the Spitfire alongside. Another actually confided in me that he preferred the Hurricane to the Spitfire because he thought he was rather too 'ham fisted' to handle the Spitfire well and therein lies the nub of the matter.

Of course when you ask these veteran fighter pilots what their views are they will, naturally, answer the question with war fighting in mind, not just pure flying thrills. They, after all, used these aircraft as machines of war in very dangerous circumstances and were more interested, quite rightly, in the capability of the machines they flew to keep them alive in all the various environments in which they found themselves and in the likelihood of achieving operational success in those conditions. Today the BBMF fighter pilots fly these aircraft not as machines of war but purely to display them to the public, so we are more inclined to consider their merits in terms of pure flying, landing and ground handling characteristics alone. That said, as modern fighter pilots, we are not blind to the characteristics that would make the aircraft good operational fighting platforms.

All the BBMF fighter pilots feel truly privileged to be able to fly the Flight's Hurricanes. These aircraft have a superb pedigree and today airworthy Hurricanes are considerably rarer than Spitfires. There are twelve airworthy Hurricanes in the world, only six in the UK, compared with around fifty Spitfires world-wide. The BBMF fighter pilots start their 'warbird' flying on the Hurricanes, prior to graduating to the Spitfires. This is principally because the Hurricane's broad and 'spongy' undercarriage, coupled with the substantial fin and rudder, which provide quite good directional stability when the tail is down, mean that the aircraft is considerably more forgiving of minor pilot errors on landing than the 'skittish' Spitfire. In truth the Hurricane has more complicated cockpit controls and systems than the Spitfire and it is slightly more difficult to fly, once off the ground. The Hurricane is slightly heavier on the controls than the Spitfire and does not react to control inputs in the same immediate and controllable manner. The roll rate of the Hurricane is noticeably slower once the full roll control of the Spitfire has been sampled. It does rather need hauling around the skies and takes some muscle on occasions to overcome the control forces involved. 'Hauling' the Hurricane about needs care though to conserve speed and energy because it is considerably more 'sluggish' in performance terms than the Spitfire for the same use of power, even though the engine power output for the BBMF Hurricanes and Merlin-engine 'Baby' Spitfires is the same. This is due to the extra weight of the Hurricane over the Spitfire and the drag from its thick wing section. The visibility from the Hurricane is generally better than from the Spitfire, especially over the sloping nose. However, when it comes to landing, all the BBMF fighter pilots would rather be in a Hurricane than a Spitfire when there is a 'limits' crosswind on the modern limited-direction runways that most airfields offer today.

BBMF fighter pilots warm to the Hurricane during their first year on the Flight, whilst building their flying hours ready for their conversion to the Spitfire. Most have no intention of becoming 'Spitfire snobs', but after that first flight in a Spitfire the world is a different place. After his first Spitfire flight in 2005, Group Captain Bob Judson simply said, 'I see what you mean'. Squadron Leader Ian Smith's comment as we met him in the cockpit after he had shut down from his first Spitfire flight in the summer of 2006 was, 'Wow!' followed by, 'That's it, I'm a Spitfire snob!'

The thing about the Spitfire from a pilot's point of view, quite apart from its beauty and charisma, is that it is the finest-handling aircraft that it is possible to imagine. It does take skill and finesse to handle it well, but once 'hooked up' the result is ultimately satisfying to a good pilot. Everything that has been written about it by very many wartime pilots is true – you really can become one with the machine, you just have to think about what it is you want it to do, bank, roll, pitch and, with the slightest touch on the controls you're doing it. It's almost as if you are just the machine's brain and that you are built into it, as if your arms were extending up the wings, as if the interconnection between your hands and feet and the controls was almost superfluous. It is wonderfully satisfying to fly and, as it is so agile and pitches and rolls so rapidly, it sometimes feels like a rapier in your hands, which you are swishing about the sky.

The Spitfire is virtually viceless in the air, it tells the pilot when he is doing something wrong and has no unpleasant handling characteristics at all. For the same engine power from its 27-litre Merlin V-12 engine as the Hurricane, the Spitfire is considerably lighter and less 'draggy' so the performance is markedly more sports car-like. Here I am really referring to the Merlin-engine 'Baby' Spitfires, the later Griffon-engine Mk.XIX Spitfires are heavier aircraft but possessed of even greater power output from their 37-litre engine. To stick with the sports car analogy, these Spitfires are great straight-line power machines rather like a TVR versus the light-weight agility of a Lotus.

Of course, throughout the joyful experience of flying a Spitfire is that nagging worry that it is going to have to be landed at the end of the sortie and it is here that the aircraft's vices show up and will bite the unwary or any pilot who gives it insufficient respect. The narrow-track undercarriage does not assist the Spitfire to 'tramline' and the relatively small fin and rudder do not endow it with great directional control, especially once the tail wheel is down on the ground and the nose and fuselage are blanking the tail. In fact, the Spitfire possesses all the directional stability of a typical supermarket shopping trolley! As soon as the wheels touch the ground on landing, it can be totally unpredictable and can quite unexpectedly wag off in any direction it cares to take rather than continuing to go where it appeared to be pointing. When this happens it requires instant and positive correction to keep it under control or a ground loop is the likely outcome. If you had to operate from rough desert or jungle strips in wartime you can imagine why the Hurricane might be the preferred option over the Spitfire.

As I have said, the BBMF fighter pilot will tend to look at the comparison of Hurricane versus Spitfire from a pure flying point of view, but these machines were built for war and perhaps the last word should go to Bob Stanford-Tuck DSO DFC**, my personal hero and a great wartime fighter pilot who flew the Spitfire first, with 65 and 92 Squadrons, achieving more than 1000 hours on Spits, and was then posted to command 257 Squadron – flying Hurricanes. Stanford-Tuck scored twenty-nine aerial victories and eight probables; fifteen of his kills were achieved whilst flying the Hurricane. He was the RAF's eighth highest scoring fighter ace of World War Two. This was his view of the Hurricane after his first flight in the type:

My first reaction wasn't good. After the Spit, she was like a brick – a great, lumbering farmyard stallion compared with a dainty, gentle thoroughbred. The Spit was so much smaller, sleeker, smoother – and a bit faster too. It nearly broke my heart, because things seemed tough enough without having to take on 109s in a heavy great kite like this. But after the first few minutes I began to realise the Hurri had virtues of its own. She was solid, obviously able to stand up to an awful lot of punishment... steady as a rock – a wonderful gun platform... just as well powered as any other fighter in the world, with the same Merlin I knew and trusted so well... The pilot's visibility was considerably better than in the Spit, because the nose sloped downwards more steeply from the cockpit to the spinner. This, of course, gave much better shooting conditions. The undercart was wider and, I think, stronger than the Spit's. This made landing a lot less tricky, particularly on rough ground. The controls were much heavier and it took a lot of muscle to haul her around the sky – and yet, you know, after that first hop, after I'd got the feel of her, I never seemed to notice this or any of the other differences any more.

There you have it. Bob Stanford-Tuck was undoubtedly better qualified than any of us to compare the two aircraft comprehensively – how can you be a 'Spitfire snob' after that?

## Air Tests

Each of the BBMF aircraft has to be air-tested by a qualified air test pilot when they emerge from winter servicing at the start of each flying/display season and on other occasions when major work, such as an engine change, has been carried out. The Lancaster and Dakota are air-tested with the Bomber Leader or his deputy as the aircraft captain, and the BBMF fighters are air-tested by the Fighter Leader. In this role I have air-tested each of the Flight's fighter aircraft over three years and with this experience I will attempt to give the reader an insight into what is involved.

Pre-season/post-winter-servicing air tests, particularly, focus the pilot's mind as he knows that the aircraft will not have flown for some six months. Major work will have been carried out on the airframe and possibly on the engine and, just to compound the circumstances, it is quite likely that the pilot himself has not flown that type of aircraft for six months as all the Flight's display aircraft have been out of service during the winter servicing period. Without wishing to over-dramatise the issue, there is more likelihood of something going wrong with the aircraft on an air test than at other times, due to the lack of any previous 'shakedown', and the pilot needs to be prepared for those eventualities, relying on his experience, despite his own possible lack of currency on type. I know for my own part that I approached each pre-season (or indeed subsequent) air test with a very focused attitude and with considerable personal mental preparation to ensure that I would be ready for any eventuality.

During the many air tests that I conducted I experienced a number of failures. I suffered an air-speed-indicator failure on the Spitfire IX, which required a 'chase plane' in the shape of the BBMF Chipmunk to lead me back to earth safely. I experienced a failure of an undercarriage micro-switch on the Spitfire IIa, meaning that I had no definite indication of undercarriage lock-down and had to fly past the air traffic control tower several times for a visual inspection and then 'blow' the undercarriage down using the emergency 'blow down' system to ensure the best possible chance of the undercarriage not collapsing on landing – which fortunately it didn't! I had an interesting time getting the Spitfire Vb to stall normally one year, over several air test sorties, after work had been carried out on the undercarriage legs and doors and I sometimes had to cut air test flights short and recover to the airfield via a precautionary forced landing due to abnormal engine indications. Of course, there were many more faultless air test flights, which throw great credit on the marvellous work done by the BBMF engineers and which culminated in the usual low, fast pass over the BBMF hangar to inform those waiting expectantly below that the aircraft had passed the test and that all their work had reached a successful conclusion.

The BBMF air tests are conducted in accordance with a flight test schedule, which is based on the original test profiles flown on the aircraft as they emerged from the factory after being built during World War Two, but updated to accord with modern RAF requirements, in common with all the other engineering documentation used by the BBMF. The aircraft is presented to the pilot for the air test with a signed statement by the engineering officer on the flight test schedule, which includes any special requirements. The pilot takes the flight test schedule into the air with him and records the results of the air test on it.

Although the BBMF pilots have the utmost confidence in the Flight's engineers, when the pilot first arrives at the aircraft for an air test flight, he will conduct an extremely thorough set of external checks before strapping into the aircraft; he is, after all, the 'last

*Hurricane displays are very popular with the public as they are less common than those by Spitfires. LF363 is seen transitting back to Coningsby here. (Author)*

link in the chain' to prevent anything untoward happening. He will, as well as conducting his normal 'walk round' checks, ensure that all the panels are securely fastened as many will have been removed for servicing and then refitted. He will also conduct other extra checks such as setting the rudder and elevator trim fully in one direction in the cockpit before his 'walk round' so that he can confirm that the trim systems have been set up in the correct sense. Once confident that the exterior of the aircraft is 100%, he will strap in and conduct an equally thorough check of the cockpit before starting.

During the start-up sequence the pilot must note the oil pressure, that the fuel low pressure warning light and the generator warning light extinguish at specified engine RPMs and also record the voltmeter reading. The engine temperatures and pressures are recorded before take-off and then it is time to earn his flying pay and get the aircraft airborne again.

During the take-off roll, which lasts only a few seconds, whilst concentrating on keeping the aircraft straight, monitoring the engine instruments as the engine strains to provide take-off power and flying the aircraft safely off the ground, the pilot must also note the 'unstick' speed when the aircraft is happy to lift off. Once the aircraft is 'cleaned up' (undercarriage raised) and the climb power and parameters are set, the stopwatch is started and the aircraft is timed for its climb to 7000 feet ($3^{1}/2$ minutes for a Spitfire, $4^{1}/2$ minutes for a Hurricane). Level at 7000 feet after settling the aircraft down and cooling the engine, the aircraft is put through a 'clean' (flaps and undercarriage up) stall and a stall with the flaps and undercarriage down, to confirm normal handling and to note the stalling speeds. This is also an opportunity to confirm normal operation of the flaps and undercarriage. After this there are a series of engine checks to conduct, flying for 5 minutes at 'representative cruise' power and recording the maximum speed attained and the engine temperatures and pressures and then doing the same at maximum RPM and the maximum permitted engine boost (considerably less than the original limits). If these checks are satisfactory, the aircraft is then dived at the maximum BBMF air speed limit (270 knots) from 7000 feet down to 1000 feet, checking for normal handling on the speed limit and observing the engine behaviour. Finally, a number of display manoeuvres, such as rolls, are flown to ensure normal airframe and engine handling during display manoeuvres and under display G forces. It is then time to return to base, with a low, fast flypast over the BBMF hangar if the air test was successful. Throughout the flight and the taxi out and back, all systems and instruments are checked for normal operation and, at the end of the sortie, when the test pilot climbs out, he needs to be confident that the aircraft is ready for the other pilots on the Flight or he needs to 'snag' any areas where further work is required.

The air test is the final check that work done by the engineers has produced an aircraft that is fully airworthy and ready to be used by all the Flight's pilots day-to-day. As such it is an important, indeed vital, step in the airworthiness chain. From a pilot's point of view it is one of those sorties that has an extra 'buzz' about it!

*Having flown over Buckingham Palace on 17 June 2006, the BBMF formation turns to starboard as it clears the line of the flypast. (Author)*

# CHAPTER 12

# Over the Palace

As the Flight was formed with a primary aim to provide aircraft for the annual Battle of Britain flypast over London, which had been carried out each September since the end of World War Two, it is most appropriate that it is still such events that keep the Flight in the headline news and broadcast on live television during major occasions. Therefore this chapter concentrates on relatively recent flypasts that have been become very prominent events in the Flight's history.

## Battle of Britain Fiftieth

One such major event took place on 15 September 1990 to commemorate the fiftieth anniversary of the Battle of Britain. The event included a display of various static aircraft, historic and modern, on Horse Guards Parade. There was also a parade of RAF personnel on Horse Guards, who then marched to Buckingham Palace behind the RAF band. Then came the highlight, a flypast by 168 aircraft over The Mall led by the five Spitfires and two Hurricanes of the Battle of Britain Memorial Flight. The sight of seven single piston-engined fighters over London is incredibly rare in modern times, and the permission needed to carry this out highlights the importance that the occasion was given.

Leading the BBMF formation in P7350 was Air Vice-Marshal W J Wratten, who at the time was AOC 11 Group. In line astern behind him in PM631 was Squadron Leader Paul Day (Deputy Leader), with Wing Commander Dave Moss at the rear of the formation in AB910. In the two Hurricanes were Group Captain Martin Widdowson (LF363) and Squadron Leader Allan Martin (PZ865). The other two Spitfire XIXs were flown by Squadron Leader Chris Stevens (PS915) and Flight Lieutenant Jim Wild (PS853).

The formation that followed was made up of masses of operational RAF aircraft, such as a wave of sixteen BAe Harriers for example. At the rear of the formation was Lancaster PA474 on its own, with Squadron Leader Colin Paterson (Captain) and Flight Lieutenant Mike Chatterton (co-pilot) at the controls, and Flight Lieutenant Doug Eke as navigator and Flight Lieutenant Ian Leddra the flight engineer.

After making their first pass over the Palace, P7350 and LF363 went to the rear of the formation. Once the Lancaster was clear they came in towards the RAF parade and carried out a break in front of Buckingham Palace to conclude the Battle of Britain fiftieth anniversary commemorations with a most fitting finale. The Flight aircraft had launched from Wattisham, the Lancaster at 11:20 and the fighters at 11:25. PA474's time over the Buckingham Palace was 12:05.10 and it landed at Lyneham at 12:40. The fighters recovered back home to Coningsby.

*Michael Turner's wonderful painting of the BBMF leading the Battle of Britain fiftieth anniversary flypast over Buckingham Palace on 15 September 1990. Behind the Flight fighters the mass RAF flypast is depicted steadily making its way up The Mall, with the parade of RAF personnel formed up in front of the Palace accurately painted on the ground below. (Michael Turner PFGAvA )*

*After the mass flypast for the fiftieth anniversary of the Battle of Britain, P7350 and LF363 had made their way back around to fly towards Buckingham Palace then break away as a fitting final salute for the occasion. They are seen during the break here, 'LF' on the left of the picture and 'P7' on the right. (© Crown Copyright/MOD)*

## VE and VJ Day Fiftieths

There were two flights over Buckingham Palace in 1995 to commemorate the fiftieth anniversaries of Victory in Europe Day and later Victory in Japan Day. The VE Day celebration ran over the holiday weekend of 6 to 8 May, and within the massive exhibition in London's Hyde Park the huge crowds were awash with 'VE Day fever'.

The 40-acre area had many pavilions and displays dedicated to every aspect of World War Two, complemented by a variety of arena events. The park was dominated by the largest open air concert stage that had to date been put up in Europe, and it was flanked with a replica Spitfire and Hurricane, each suspended from large cranes. Real aircraft, both historic and modern, were put on display too. These included the RAF Exhibition Flight's Spitfire XVI TB382, at the time painted up as MK673 SK-E of 165 Squadron, and which years later would temporarily join the assets of the Flight.

As well-known nostalgic wartime tunes were played on the stage during the Saturday evening (6 May), the 100,000-strong audience rose to their feet clapping and waving Union Flags as the BBMF's three-ship formation came into view. PA474 was flanked by Hurricane PZ865 and Spitfire V AB910, and the trio carried out two flypasts at 750 ft.

*PA474 carries out one of its incredibly poignant and popular high-profile poppy drops along The Mall to commemorate the fiftieth anniversary of VJ Day on 19 August 1995. (© Crown Copyright/MOD)*

On Monday 8 May a huge crowd gathered in front of Buckingham Palace, evoking memories of the masses of people gathered there on the original VE Day in 1945. The Flight again participated in the VE Day flypast that took place for the fiftieth anniversary and flew overhead the Palace.

In commemoration of the fiftieth anniversary of VJ Day in 1995, PA474 carried out one of its incredibly poignant and popular high-profile poppy drops along The Mall and over Buckingham Palace on 19 August. Towards the end of a two-minute silence, the rumble of the Lancaster's four Rolls-Royce Merlins could be heard approaching as it passed over Admiralty Arch at the top of The Mall with Flight Lieutenant Mike Chatterton at the controls. As the Lancaster approached the designated drop point at just 500 ft, the bomb doors were opened and out poured one million poppies, fluttering through the air and each one symbolising a lost life.

As well as the Lancaster, a Spitfire and Hurricane flew over The Mall that afternoon, and in the evening a Spitfire flew along the River Thames from Kew Bridge to Tower Bridge, where HMRY *Britannia* was anchored with the Royal Family on board. Flown by Squadron Leader Allan Martin, the Spitfire then reversed its track. For these sorties over London, the Flight aircraft had been operated out of Northolt.

## Queen Mother's Funeral

The funeral of Her Majesty Queen Elizabeth The Queen Mother in London on 9 April 2002 stirred the emotions of the whole nation. The Queen Mother personified the wartime spirit that helped Britain through World War Two, and thus a flypast of her funeral cortège by the Flight was totally appropriate on a day so rich with symbolism.

As patron of the Battle of Britain Fighter Association, The Queen Mother had also written the Foreword in the BBMF's 2002 brochure. Some words quoted from Her Majesty's message in the brochure are tremendously relevant for mention at this point:

> It remains as true today as it was in 1940 that the price of peace is eternal vigilance and to that end the Royal Air Force is deployed and engaged in theatres throughout the world in defence of peace and security. The aircraft of the Memorial Flight provide a tangible link between 'The Few', the crews of Bomber Command who paid such a heavy price, and their counterparts of today.

So it was wholly fitting that part of the 'Tay Bridge' Operation Order, which outlined the details of The Queen Mother's funeral, included the provision for a flypast of BBMF aircraft. However, were it not for a fortunate spell of good springtime weather that year this may not have been possible, as the Flight's principal operating season is from May until September – and therefore the aircraft could easily have been excluded from the proceedings.

At the time the Flight was in its pre-season work-up period and the then OC, Squadron Leader Paul Day OBE AFC, was fortunately in a position to be able to offer PA474 and two Spitfires when approached by 1 Group on 4 April. This was due to the fact that the Lancaster had performed a completely successful air test that very day and needed no rectification work, and also by virtue of the fact that the fair weather had allowed the fighter pilots to carry out a number of Spitfire currency sorties.

Taking part in the flypast with the Lancaster would be the BBMF's two PR.XIXs, PM631 and PS915 – both founder members of the Flight. The former would be making its public debut in a new 541 Squadron paint scheme. The reason that a Hurricane was not part of the flypast, which would of course have been a more representative BBMF formation, was simply that Mk.IIc LF363 – the only one of the Flight's two examples airworthy at that point – was considered by Squadron Leader Day to not be cosmetically acceptable for a public display, let alone a State occasion such as this.

Leading the formation in PM631 was Squadron Leader Day, with PS915 flown by Squadron Leader Clive Rowley MBE. Crewing the Lancaster were Squadron Leader Stuart Reid (Captain), Flight Lieutenant Andy Sell (co-pilot), Squadron Leader Brian Clark (navigator) and Flight Sergeant Ian Woolley (air engineer).

The original order asked for a flypast of Parliament Square at 11:21, though when the Assistant Chief of the Air Staff (ACAS) went to see the Royal Family on 6 April it was requested that the flypast coincide with the funeral cortège being halfway down The Mall.

It should also be pointed out that ACAS has the authority to allow single-engined aircraft to fly over London for an occasion such as this. The new plan required a different holding point (with provision for flexibility in the timing) and run-in route.

Once the cortège left Westminster Abbey following the funeral service, it should have taken precisely $7\frac{1}{2}$ minutes to be halfway down The Mall where the flypast was to coincide with it. With no guarantee as to precisely what time The Queen Mother's hearse would leave Westminster Abbey though, a 1 Group Staff Officer on the ground was in radio communication with the formation to give them their cue.

As it happened the procession ran slower than anticipated and when the Flight aircraft reached their position, with precise timing to the second, the cortège had only reached

*The Flight's Lancaster and two Spitfire PR.XIXs overfly The Queen Mother's funeral cortège as it proceeds down The Mall on 9 April 2002. (© Crown Copyright/MOD)*

Admiralty Arch. A snap decision was therefore taken to make a second pass in order to ensure the flypast coincided with the procession being halfway down The Mall on the approach to Buckingham Palace. The formation turned 180 degrees, flew downwind for one minute then turned to position themselves for the second run – and as they flew over Admiralty Arch saw that the cortège was now in the correct position. As the Flight overflew the hearse at 1000 ft, the Spitfires dipped their wings as a salute to The Queen Mother – whilst the huge crowds who had made the trip to London to pay their respects gazed in admiration.

Due to the importance of this occasion, it was entirely appropriate that the decision to go round again was taken. Her Majesty Queen Elizabeth II was seen looking up emotionally at the flypast as the historic aircraft passed overhead to pay the RAF's tribute to our sovereign's mother.

The aircraft were waved off and greeted on their return to Coningsby by large crowds along the outside of the perimeter fence, many of whom were waving Union Flags due to the occasion. It was a most considerate gesture by the crews to take the time to go over to the fence and talk to the spectators on their return following the flypast. Touches such as this make these occasions even more memorable for the enthusiastic spectators, as to have the crews tell them personally about such a significant sortie will remain a talking point for them for many years to come.

All the Flight's personnel were quite rightly very proud of the part they had played in such a historic occasion. The aircraft are synonymous with a time when The Queen Mother refused to leave London and instead offered her support to victims of the Blitz, and their appearance added a very special tribute to her.

## National Commemoration Day

They called it the 'Last Parade', because it was thought likely that this would be the last time so many World War Two veterans would gather for an event of this kind. And there simply couldn't have been a more appropriate occasion for this to happen. National Commemoration Day on 10 July 2005 was the culmination of an impressive week-long programme of events and commemorations to mark the sixtieth anniversary of the end of World War Two.

Mid-way between VE Day and VJ Day, 10 July was designated as a symbolic date, rather than historically significant. The occasion attracted all sorts – smartly dressed veterans, young families, students and tourists all massed along The Mall and in St James's Park to watch the proceedings. It is estimated that around 250,000 people came together in the glorious summer sunshine to honour those who had fought in the conflict.

At 11:00 the official proceedings began with a Service of Thanksgiving attended by Her Majesty Queen Elizabeth II at Westminster Abbey. Afterwards 2000 veterans enjoyed lunch in the grounds of Buckingham Palace hosted by The Queen.

At 14:30 there was a Reflections of World War Two Commemorative Show on Horse Guards Parade, again attended by The Queen. This featured celebrities from film and television, with Robert Hardy taking the role of Churchill, Jane Horrocks portraying Gracie Fields, and Simon Callow hosting the proceedings. Other well-known names included Petula Clark, Bruce Forsyth, Penelope Keith and modern-day 'forces sweetheart' Claire Sweeney.

*Above: Her Majesty The Queen and The Duke of Edinburgh at the head of the procession down The Mall on National Commemoration Day on 10 July 2005. A tri-service band and over 700 standard bearers are seen following the Royal car. (Author)*

*Left: 'Pegasus Formation', comprising three Dakotas led by ZA947, is cheered by the mass of spectators along the entire length of The Mall on National Commemoration Day. (Author)*

During the commemoration section of the show, buglers of the Royal Marines played *The Last Post*, just before RAF Jaguars flew overhead in a 'missing man' formation. There then followed a two-minute silence.

The show concluded with the famous wartime song *We'll Meet Again* sung by all the cast, but joined unexpectedly by Dame Vera Lynn herself. Dame Vera stole the show as she kept the promise of the song's title to many of those present.

After the show Her Majesty addressed the nation. At the same time as honouring the veterans, her thoughtful and succinct speech reflected the horrific bombing of London just three days earlier. Extracts include:

*Fascinating view inside the Lancaster's bomb bay, filled with one million poppies, each of which has to be loaded by hand! Note the protective sleeving that is fitted to protect the mechanical workings. (Author)*

Today we commemorate all those who lived, worked and fought through six long years of unremitting hardship and sacrifice. We remember also the unswerving support of the people of the Commonwealth, the United States and of all our Allies. It was the triumph of this great alliance that saved the world from tyranny.

I am sure that this commemoration will encourage those who have lived through these post-war years of peace and prosperity to reflect on the debt they owe to our wartime generation. It does not surprise me, that during the present difficult days for London, people turn to the example set by that generation – of resilience, humour, sustained courage, often under conditions of great deprivation. That example, and those memories, should be kept alive by younger generations as they

*The Flight's three-ship formation approaches Buckingham Palace on 10 July 2005 ready to drop the one million poppies. (SAC Scott Robertson/© Crown Copyright/MOD)*

*There they go! A million poppies fall into a neat stream behind PA474 on National Commemoration Day. Favourable weather conditions meant that the poppies weren't blown off course after being dropped. (Author)*

in turn strive to keep the peace in our troubled world.

But there is another reason why we must never forget. An act of remembrance is an act of honour – to those who sacrificed all, who bore the sufferings of war, who had the wisdom to build the peace. It is a tribute to you, the veterans, and your loved ones.

At this special occasion I wish to express on behalf of the nation our admiration, our respect and our thanks to you for what you gave all those years ago in the cause of freedom and our way of life – which we shall continue to defend as you did.

Her Majesty and HRH The Duke of Edinburgh, followed by a tri-service band, then led a procession of more than 700 banners and standards of military and home front veterans' organisations down The Mall and into the forecourt of Buckingham Palace. Despite the heightened security in place, Her Majesty chose to travel in an open-top Range Rover.

As the parade progressed, a police cordon slowly allowed the massed ranks of spectators to fill the length of The Mall and surround the Queen Victoria Monument in front of Buckingham Palace.

Just before 5 pm the Royal Family gathered on the Palace balcony to watch the grand finale of National Commemoration Day – a flypast of historic aircraft. It was a scene that was reminiscent of the Victory Parade flypast of 1946.

The flypast was planned by the RAF's 2 Group Headquarters at High Wycombe, Buckinghamshire. Approval came from Air Marshal Clive Loader, Deputy Commander-in-Chief Strike Command.

It comprised a total of nineteen aircraft, in five waves. Taking off from Duxford, Cambridgeshire, during the Flying Legends air show, they were to overfly Buckingham

*Above: The view from the rear gun turret of PA474 as the poppies stream behind the Lancaster over The Mall on 10 July 2005. (Corporal Norman Pringle/© Crown Copyright/MOD)*

*This is the view from the top of the Palace as the symbolic poppies flutter to earth. (© Crown Copyright/MOD)*

Palace at 1000 ft with the first wave of aircraft scheduled to be in place at 17:00.

That first formation consisted of five DH Dragon Rapides, led by Lee Proudfoot in G-AGJG. The others were G-AEML, G-AGSH, G-AGTM and G-AIDL.

Second up was a wave of four aircraft, led by Bernard Chabbert's Lockheed 12A Electra Junior F-AZLL. Then came Air Atlantique's Avro Anson C.21 WD413 (G-VROE) and BAE Systems' Avro XIX G-AHKX, with the Plane Sailing Consolidated PBY-5A Catalina '433915' (G-PBYA) at the back.

Three Douglas Dakotas in 'vic' formation made up the third wave, led by Flight Lieutenant Ed Straw in the Flight's ZA947. Air Atlantique's KK116 (G-AMPY) and G-AMRA completed the trio.

A strong US bomber theme influenced the fourth wave, as two Boeing B-17G Flying

Fortresses and two North American B-25J Mitchells rumbled over the capital. Led by B-17 Preservation's *Sally B* (G-BEDF), the B-25 wingmen comprised the Duke of Brabant Air Force's 'N5-149' *Sarinah* (N320SQ) and Jet Alpine Fighter's 458811 (HB-RDE). Following them was Association Fortresse Toujours Volant en France's *Pink Lady* (F-AZDX).

As each of the waves flew over the crowds, those on the ground cheered and proudly brandished Union Flags. The whole atmosphere was electric, and greatly contributed to by the band in the Palace forecourt playing familiar themes from such aviation film classics as *633 Squadron*,

*Right: Poppies settled all over the ground in front of Buckingham Palace on National Commemoration Day in salute of all who lost their lives during World War Two. (Author)*

*Above: View from the Queen Victoria Monument as the poppies rain down over Buckingham Palace and The Mall. The Flight's three-ship formation can be seen to the right of the Royal Standard, just below the three larger poppies. (Author)*

*Battle of Britain* and *The Dam Busters*. But eager anticipation was building for the flypast finale when a million poppy petals would be dropped by the BBMF's Lancaster.

Bang on cue PA474 appeared, flanked by Spitfire IIa P7350 to port and Hurricane IIc LF363 to starboard – the only two single-engined aircraft permitted to take part in the flypast. With the then OC BBMF Squadron Leader Clive Rowley MBE flying the Spitfire and Squadron Leader Al Pinner MBE in the Hurricane, the Lancaster's aircrew consisted of captain Squadron Leader Stu Reid, co-pilot Flight Lieutenant Mike Leckey, navigator Squadron Leader Dick George and air engineer Squadron Leader Ian Morton.

Also on board the 'Lanc' was Marshal of the Royal Air Force Sir Michael Beetham. Sir Michael, by then eighty-two, had flown a Lancaster over London as part of the 1946 Victory Parade.

As the three iconic wartime aircraft flew over The Mall and the sound of their six Rolls-Royce Merlins resonated around the city, the patriotic fervour below went into overdrive. Then all went momentarily quiet as hundreds of thousands of faces gazed upwards, and everyone waited for the poppies to be released.

As the formation reached the monument, a cloud of bright red burst into the blue sky behind the Lancaster and the crowds cheered with excitement. As the aircraft made their way over the Palace, the poppies fell into a neat stream along the Lancaster's flight path – the warm still air could not have been more perfect; for once with such things, the weather was co-operating completely.

Soon after, the symbolic poppies of remembrance began to flutter down on the crowd. This was an experience that will live on in the memories of everyone there.

National Commemoration Day was a resounding success. Not only did it honour the veterans who had survived to see it and their fallen comrades, it also served to teach subsequent generations about the sacrifices made to secure the freedom we all enjoy today.

## Queen's Eightieth Birthday

To celebrate Her Majesty Queen Elizabeth II's official eightieth birthday on 17 June 2006, the largest RAF flypast over Buckingham Palace for many years was staged. Led by the Battle of Britain Memorial Flight, the flypast comprised almost fifty aircraft.

Celebrations began with the annual Trooping the Colour parade at 11:00 am, consisting of the high-profile grand military parade and march-past by Household Troops on Horse Guards Parade, Whitehall, which marks the Queen's official birthday. But as this was Her Majesty's eightieth birthday, a number of additional tributes were added to that year's celebrations. Following the parade, The Queen and other members of the Royal Family gathered on the balcony of Buckingham Palace to view the amazing flypast courtesy of the RAF.

The first wave was given the call sign 'Memorial Flight', and comprised the Flight's Avro Lancaster I PA474 in the No. 1 position flanked by two Spitfires and two Hurricanes in 'vic' formation. The 'Lanc' was flown by Squadron Leader Stu Reid (captain) and Flight Lieutenant Jim Baddeley (co-pilot), with Squadron Leader Jeff Hesketh as navigator and Wing Commander Colin Reeves as flight engineer.

Flying the Spitfires were OC BBMF Squadron Leader Al Pinner MBE (AB910) and Wing Commander Russ Allchorne (P7350). In the Hurricanes were Squadron Leader

Clive Rowley MBE (LF363) and Squadron Leader Ian Smith (PZ865).

'Memorial Flight' arrived overhead the Palace precisely on schedule at 13:00. The aircraft were flying at 1500 ft, and it must be mentioned that four single piston-engined fighters being granted permission to fly over London is unprecedented in recent years.

Following a minute behind the BBMF was 'Windsor Formation', comprising eight separate elements that overflew the Palace at forty-second intervals. At the rear were the nine BAe Hawk T.1s of the 'Red Arrows' aerobatic team from RAF Scampton, Lincolnshire, joined by an EE Canberra PR.9 from 39(1PRU) Squadron based at Marham, Norfolk. The Canberra's participation in the flypast was most appropriate, as the type was being retired at the end of July after fifty-five years of RAF service.

In total there were forty-nine aircraft, of fifteen different types. They ranged from the Spitfires, Hurricanes and Lancaster from the World War Two era, to the state-of-the-art Eurofighter Typhoon multi-role fighter, which had only just entered front-line operational RAF service in April that year.

Flying one of the Typhoons was Group Captain Bob Judson, Station Commander of Coningsby. Group Captain Judson was also a BBMF pilot, meaning that all five of the Flight's fighter pilots participated in the formation.

The flypast was followed by a 'Feu de Joie' (Fire of Joy), which consisted of a cascade of blank rounds fired by the Old Guard, the New Guard and six Half-Companies of Street-Liners situated in the Palace forecourt. The gunfire was interspersed with bars of the National Anthem, and this was the first time that a 'Feu de Joie' has been fired for Her Majesty during her reign. Afterwards the troops on the forecourt laid down their weapons, removed their bearskins and chanted 'Three cheers for Her Majesty The Queen'.

*A large Royal Family gathering on the balcony of Buckingham Palace on 17 June 2006, waiting for the RAF flypast, led by the BBMF, in tribute of the Queen's eightieth birthday. (Author)*

*At the head of the forty-nine-aircraft flypast for the Queen's eightieth birthday were five aircraft of the BBMF, comprising the Lancaster flanked by two Spitfires and two Hurricanes. (Author)*

# Officers Commanding BBMF

| | |
|---|---|
| Sqn Ldr Ken Jackson AFC | 1977-1981 |
| Sqn Ldr C S M Anderson | 1981-1984 |
| Sqn Ldr Tony Banfield | 1984-1987 |
| Sqn Ldr Colin Paterson | 1987-1991 |
| Sqn Ldr Andy Tomalin | 1991-1994 |
| Sqn Ldr Rick Groombridge | 1994-1996 |
| Sqn Ldr Paul Day OBE AFC RAF | 1996-2003 |
| Sqn Ldr Clive Rowley MBE RAF | 2003-2006 |
| Sqn Ldr Al Pinner MBE RAF | 2006- |

**Author's note:** At first glance this list may look somewhat amiss – the Flight having been formed in 1957! However, when researching the list of OCs I found I had a huge gap that seemed impossible to fill – certainly within the time constraints I had facing me. On talking to two of the Flight's former OCs, Squadron Leaders Ken Jackson and Scott Anderson, the reason for the missing information came to light. 'Jacko' was the first established OC BBMF. Prior to this, the post had been a secondary duty taken on by many

of the relevant bases' officers in posts such as OC Ops, or earlier OC Flying. Therefore, while I did find some names of those who had taken on the post in the earlier years, I decided to just list the officers who had been OC BBMF since it has been formally established.

*Squadron Leader 'Jacko' Jackson AFC is seen here at the helm of PA474 in June 1977. 'Jacko' can still be seen at the controls of a moving Lancaster, as he pilots ground taxi runs of NX611 at the Lincolnshire Aviation Heritage Centre at East Kirkby. (BBMF Archives)*

*A historic milestone in British military aviation occurred on 21 July 1999, when Squadron Leader Paul Day OBE AFC clocked up 1000 hours flying Spitfires. Paul, known throughout the aviation fraternity as 'The Major', had been flying with the RAF's Battle of Britain Memorial Flight since 1980, the year in which he is pictured. At the time he reached 1000 hours, 'The Major' was at the controls of PR.XIX PM631 in transit to a flypast at Mountbatten, near Plymouth, Devon. He gained his nickname 'The Major' during an exchange tour in the USA with the 311th and 550th Tactical Fighter Squadrons in Arizona, as the USAF had no equivalent rank to the RAF's Squadron Leader! Joining the BBMF in 1980, Paul Day was the first non-piston-trained pilot with the Flight. He was converted onto the fighters via the Chipmunk, and then flew his first two seasons on the Hurricanes. Paul's first flight in a Spitfire took place on 5 May 1982, in Mk.Vb AB910. He took over command of the BBMF from Squadron Leader Rick Groombridge in April 1996, and retired from the RAF at the end of the 2003 season. Not only had he amassed an incredible twenty-three years with the Flight, but eight of them had been as Officer Commanding! (© Crown Copyright/MOD)*

# APPENDIX II

# Visitor Centre

Members of the public have been able to view the Flight's aircraft inside their Coningsby home since 1986. This is part of a special arrangement between Lincolnshire County Council and the RAF, and since opening, the BBMF Visitor Centre has welcomed around 400,000 people.

Visitors are led on a guided tour around the BBMF hangar by knowledgeable volunteer guides, and are given the opportunity to see the aircraft at close quarters and to observe them being pulled out for a sortie or undergoing maintenance depending on the time of their visit.

Entry to the car park, recently refurbished exhibition centre and well-stocked souvenir shop is free. There is a small charge for guided tours of the hangar, with special rates for groups (including school parties). Please note that entry to the BBMF hangar is by guided tour only, and the tours last approximately one hour.

The site offers facilities for the disabled, including toilets and manual wheelchair access (please note that due to Health and Safety Regulations electric wheelchairs are prohibited in the BBMF hangar).

With the exception of Public Holidays and two weeks over Christmas, the aircraft can

*A large group on arrival at the BBMF Visitor Centre – as in evidence here the site offers a fascinating experience for all ages. (Author)*

be viewed every weekday from 10 am until 5 pm. The last guided tour begins at 3.30 pm. If you are going especially to see any particular aircraft, remember that during the flying season some are occasionally away and during the winter some may be at other sites undergoing maintenance.

Call the Visitor Centre on 01526 344041 for further information, details of any special events or occasional weekend openings. Coningsby is located on the A153 south of Horncastle, then follow the brown signs for the Battle of Britain Memorial Flight. The website address is www.bbmf.co.uk/visitorcentre.

*The well-stocked shop offers a wide range of gifts and souvenirs, including clothing, books, models, ceramics, key rings, pens, badges and much more. (Author)*

*A group of visitors inside the BBMF hangar behind Spitfire PR.XIX PS915, being given an informative guided tour of the facility. (Author)*

---

# APPENDIX III

# BBMF Association

To coincide with the fiftieth anniversary of the Flight, a BBMF Association has been formed. Its aim is to provide a focal point for past and present BBMF members, enabling them to remain in contact with ex-colleagues and keep up to date with the Flight's activities. Members benefit from access to the Association website, copies of the latest BBMF publicity packs and an annual social function. The website includes news and announcements, in addition to being a forum for comments by Association members.

The Association is open to members of the BBMF, past and present, including all ground and aircrew as well as civilian staff. A registration form is available online at www.bbmf.co.uk/assoc/. Alternatively, prospective members can telephone Mrs Jeanette O'Connell on 01526 347992.

*BBMF ground crew with LF363 at Coltishall in January 1972. Any former member of the Flight can join the recently formed BBMF Association. (BBMF Archives)*

# APPENDIX IV

# Royal Air Force Benevolent Fund

A proportion of the Author's Royalties from the sales of this book are being donated to the Royal Air Force Benevolent Fund. The Author was based at RAF Brüggen in West Germany at the time that the first Gulf War began. He had worked with Brüggen-based aircrew who were lost during the Tornado operations in the Gulf, and with all the RAF families who lost loved ones as a result of this conflict it especially brought home to him the invaluable work that the RAFBF does to support those left behind.

The RAFBF was founded in 1919, the year after the formation of the RAF. Since then the aim of the Fund, the relief of distress among the RAF family, has remained constant. This family is widespread and includes all those who are serving or have served in the RAF, their partners and dependants. Essentially the Fund is a financial welfare organisation and relies on many other organisations; including the Sailors', Soldiers' and Airmen's Families Association, the Royal Air Forces Association and the Royal British Legion to act as its agents in the field. The RAFBF welcomes and seeks support from as many as possible for other areas. In one year over £19 million was granted to help some 29,000 people. To maintain this level of expenditure and, sadly, it is still very much required, there is a need to fundraise and the RAFBF welcomes interest from people who might take a collection box or perhaps act as a collector. The Fund attends a number of events throughout the year to raise the much-needed money.

An example of its work can be typified by the following case study:

At the time he got assistance from the RAFBF, Tony Rogers was eighty-two years old. Originating from Poland, Tony flew twenty-nine different types of aircraft during World War Two. His life had been dedicated to the RAF and his love of flying and abilities made him a fine pilot.

As a young man Tony was interned in a concentration camp in Siberia because he fought in the Polish Campaign. After surviving freezing temperatures and barbaric conditions, he was freed. At just twenty years of age, showing an incredible strength of character, he enrolled in the Polish Armed Forces before making his way to Britain to join the RAF.

Determined to fly, he progressed from air gunner to pilot and flew Wellington bombers on thirty operational missions, although his great love was the Lancaster. Tony recounted a tale where on one night-time raid to Hamburg ninety-two RAF crews were lost – but he survived: 'It was an incredibly difficult time to be a pilot, I lost many friends'.

His bravery during the war earned him several medals including the Polish Cross for

Valour. He remained in the Service after the war where he met and married a member of the WRAF. Tony finally retired from the RAF in 1962.

At eighty-two Tony was able to recount tales from every mission he had flown, but even with all his fight and enthusiasm, he found getting older difficult. His difficulties became worse when he had a stroke that left him with limited mobility and unable to walk more than a few yards. This loss of independence for someone so active was a tremendous blow to Tony; and was compounded when, sadly, his loving wife and principal carer died suddenly. Without the resources to help himself and feeling that he had nowhere else to turn, Tony applied for assistance to the RAFBF, which was able to provide him with an electric scooter.

This has given him a whole new lease of life and untold newfound freedom. It may not seem like a lot for such a brave veteran, but it has improved the quality of Tony's life. With his new-found mobility, Tony soon visited the Royal International Air Tattoo (RIAT) where he exchanged stories with BBMF Lancaster pilot Flight Lieutenant Ed Straw.

Tony is an amazing man who has faced challenges few of us could comprehend. He considers himself lucky that he has been part of the RAF and even luckier that he had a charity that he could turn to when he needed it. He commented: 'I am really grateful to the Fund for giving me a new toy to test-drive, it is not quite a Eurofighter but it has given me back my life.'

More information can be found on the RAFBF website at: www.rafbf.org.
The Fund Supportline is 0800 169 2942.

Above: World War Two pilot Tony Rogers recounts a
story from his operational flying days to Flight
Lieutenant Ed Straw and other BBMF personnel at
RIAT 2004. (RAFBF)

Left: Tony Rogers pictured in 1943 while serving as an
RAF bomber pilot. (Via Tony Rogers)

# APPENDIX V

# Where Are They Now?

Over the years the Flight has lost a number of key aircraft that have fortunately all gone on in various ways to secure futures. Here's a look at four of the more prominent examples.

*Spitfire Mk.XVI TE330 carried out the Flight's first Battle of Britain flypast over London on 15 September 1957. Donated to the United States Air Force Academy at Colorado Springs on 2 July the following year, this Spitfire later moved to the USAF Museum at Dayton, Ohio. After further moves, it is currently undergoing restoration back to airworthy condition by owner Don Subritzky at North Shore, Auckland, New Zealand. It is seen in November 2006. (David Atchinson)*

*For its handover to the USAF, TE330 was given the inscription 'This Spitfire is representative of the aircraft flown by the pilots of Fighter Command during the Second World War' on both sides of its forward fuselage. Its current owner Don Subritzky has painstakingly worked to preserve the original artwork on the newly repainted Spitfire XVI. (David Atchinson)*

*Following its landing accident at Martlesham Heath on 10 September 1959, TE476 was retired from the Flight and later went on the gate at Neatishead, Norfolk, in January 1960. TE476 now forms part of the collection at Kermit Weeks' Fantasy of Flight aviation complex at Polk City, Florida, where it was airworthy for several years named* Winston Churchill. *It is seen here just after take-off from Polk City in April 1997. (Duncan Cubitt/FlyPast)*

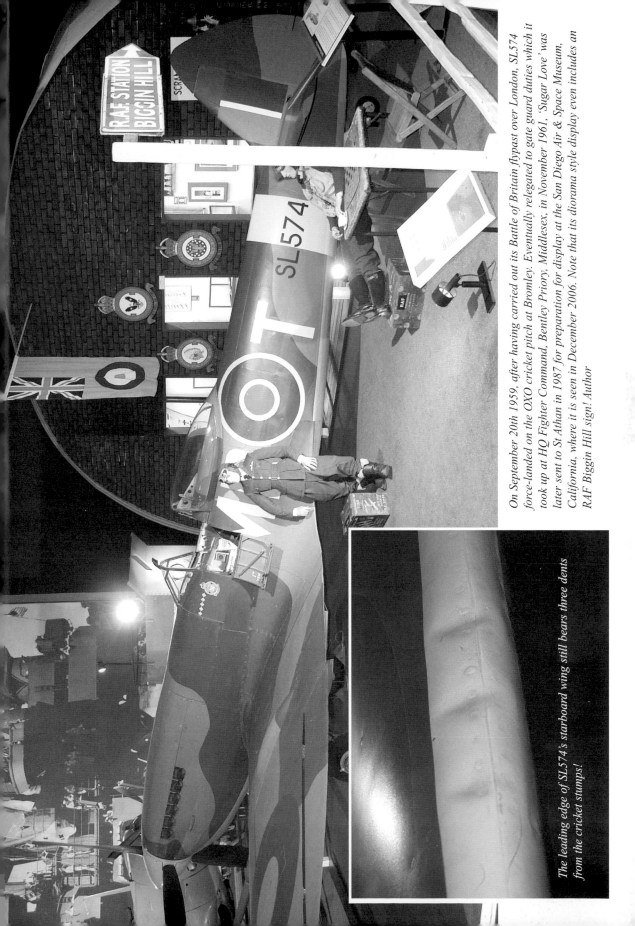

On September 20th 1959, after having carried out its Battle of Britain flypast over London, SL574 force-landed on the OXO cricket pitch at Bromley. Eventually relegated to gate guard duties which it took up at HQ Fighter Command, Bentley Priory, Middlesex, in November 1961, 'Sugar Love' was later sent to St Athan in 1987 for preparation for display at the San Diego Air & Space Museum, California, where it is seen in December 2006. Note that its diorama style display even includes an RAF Biggin Hill sign! Author

The leading edge of SL574's starboard wing still bears three dents from the cricket stumps!

*One of the founder members of the Flight, Spitfire XIX PS853 was sold in 1994 to pay for the rebuild of fellow founder-member Hurricane LF363. After an uncertain start in civilian life, nowadays it is appropriately operated by Rolls-Royce and makes regular air show appearances. It is seen here reunited with its former BBMF stablemates at Coningsby in September 2006. (Author)*

# Bibliography

In addition to research taken from individual interviews, e-mail contact and looking through pilots' logbooks, other resources referred to for information or verification have included the following:

**Documents and Letters**

AF/CX1403/68 Battle of Britain Memorial Flight Engineering Policy Directive

AF/CT2430/64/BF1/DDOG(RAF), The BBMF and the Waddington Lancaster, 10 April 1969

Air Ministry Form 78 – Hurricane IIb LF363

Air Ministry Form 78 – Hurricane IIb PZ865

Air Ministry Form 78 – Lancaster I PA474

Air Ministry Form 78 – Spitfire IIa P7350

Air Ministry Form 78 – Spitfire Vb AB910

Air Ministry Form 78 – Spitfire PR.XIX PM631

Air Ministry Form 78 – Spitfire PR.XIX PS853

Air Ministry Form 78 – Spitfire PR.XIX PS915

Air Ministry Form 78 – Spitfire LF.XVI SL574

Air Ministry Form 78 – Spitfire LF.XVIe SL674

Air Ministry Form 78 – Spitfire LF.XVIe TE330

Air Ministry Form 78 – Spitfire LF.XVIe TE476

Battle of Britain Memorial Flight, 8 September 1957, Family Records, Sqn Ldr E H Sowden

Letter AMSO/517, BBMF and the Waddington Lancaster, 01 April 1969

Letter AMSO 1/21, The Battle of Britain Memorial Flight, 23 June 1977

Letter STC/30100/3839/EST, 8 October 1975

Letter AF/CX23/73, 18 June 1975

Letter D/S of S 118/76, 15 May 1976

Letter STC/C11301/56925/Ops BBMF and the Waddington Lancaster, 09 April 1969

Letter STC/18892/5959/MECH ENG, 19 February 1969

Annex A to STC/18892/5959/MECH ENG, 19 February 1969

Letter USofS(RAF)/5/27/1, 19 August 1975

Loose Minute AF/50/00/924, 2 October 1975

Loose Minute AF/4464/Pt VI/S9b(Air), 30 September 1975

Loose Minute AF/CX23/73/S9b(Air), 2 October 1975

Loose Minute AF/268/S 4d(Air), 6 October 1975

Loose Minute AF/CX761/75, 25 March 1977

MoD Press Release 71/75, Battle of Britain Memorial Flight to Move, 17 June 1975

Move of BBMF from RAF Coltishall to RAF Coningsby, 21 October 1975

Note AG/CX23/73, 1977

RAF Form 4801 – Spitfire PR.XIX PM631

RAF Form 4801 – Spitfire PR.XIX PS853

RAF Form 4801 – Spitfire PR.XIX PS915

**Books, magazines and other publications**

*Air Clues*, November 1958

*All together again!, FlyPast*, November 1997

Battle of Britain Memorial Flight Brochures:
1986/7/8/9/90/1/2/3/4/5/6/7/8/9/2000/1/2/3/4/5/6/7

*BBMF's new Spitfire, FlyPast* January 1998

Cotter, Jarrod, *BBMF in good shape for new season, FlyPast*, June 2001

Cotter, Jarrod, *Operation 'Tay Bridge', FlyPast*, June 2002

Cotter, Jarrod, *Memorial Flight Spitfire becomes 'The Last!', FlyPast*, May 2004

Cotter, Jarrod, *BBMF Dakota gets 'Pegasus' makeover, FlyPast*, May 2003

Cotter, Jarrod, *Occupying Barkston Heath, FlyPast*, August 2003

Cotter, Jarrod, *'Dam Busters' 60th tribute, FlyPast*, August 2003

Cotter, Jarrod, *A million thanks, FlyPast*, September 2005

Cotter, Jarrod, *Queen's Birthday flypast, FlyPast*, August 2006

Darlington, Roger, *Night Hawk*, William Kimber, 1985

Flintham, Vic, and Thomas, Andrew, *Combat Codes*, Airlife Publishing Ltd, 2003

Gunston, Bill, *Jane's Aerospace Dictionary*, Jane's, 1988

*Hurricane back in action!, FlyPast*, December 1998

Lake, Alan, *Flying Units of the RAF*, Airlife Publishing Ltd, 1999

*New BBMF Centre Opens up at Coningsby, FlyPast*, June 1999

*New and Old Fly in Formation, The Times*, 17 August 1959

Pearcy, Arthur, *Douglas DC-3 Survivors – Volume Two*, Aston Publications, 1988

Riley, Gordon, and Trant, Graham, *Spitfire Survivors Round The World*, Aston Publications, 1986

*The Last Spitfire Prangs, Daily Express*, 21 September 1959

# Index

*Page references in italics refer to illustration captions.*